Financial Planning for the Utterly Confused

Sixth Edition

Financial Planning for the Utterly Confused

Sixth Edition

Joel Lerner

McGraw-Hill

New York   Chicago   San Francisco   Lisbon   London
Madrid   Mexico City   Milan   New Delhi   San Juan
Seoul   Singapore   Sydney   Toronto

1 2 3 4 5 6 7 8 9 0   FGR/FGR   0 9 8 7

ISBN-13: 978-0-07-147783-3
ISBN-10:   0-07-147783-7

This publication is designed to provide accurate and authoritative information in regard to the subject matter covered. It is sold with the understanding that the publisher is not engaged in rendering legal, accounting, or other professional service. If legal advice or other expert assistance is required, the services of a competent professional person should be sought.

—*From a declaration of principles jointly adopted by a committee of the American Bar Association and a committee of publishers.*

McGraw-Hill books are available at special quantity discounts to use as premiums and sales promotions, or for use in corporate training programs. For more information, please write to the Director of Special Sales, Professional Publishing, McGraw-Hill, Two Penn Plaza, New York, NY 10121-2298. Or contact your local bookstore.

This book is printed on acid-free paper.

No birth certificate is issued when a friendship is born. There is nothing tangible. There is just a feeling that your life is different and that your capacity to love and care has miraculously been enlarged without any effort on your part. It's like having a tiny apartment and somebody moves in with you, but instead of becoming cramped and crowded, the space expands, and you discover rooms you never knew you had until your friend moved in with you.

Contents

◆◆

Preface

◆◆◆◆◆◆◆◆◆◆◆◆◆◆◆◆◆◆◆◆◆◆◆◆◆◆◆◆◆◆◆◆◆◆◆◆◆

I am a retired professor, not a stockbroker, bank executive, or insurance salesperson. My specialty isn't fancy jargon, hucksterism, or statistics. Rather, it's explaining financial and economic matters to ordinary people in plain English. That's what *Financial Planning for the Utterly Confused* is all about, now in this new, sixth edition.

There used to be a time when most of us thought that investing was something only for the rich and that very few people could afford to take on any apparent risk. But of course, times have changed as we have become a nation of investors who realize that we cannot achieve financial freedom from social security (whether privatized or not) and company-based pension plans that are slowly being reduced in size and employer contributions. And just as we, as potential investors, have increased in number, so too have the various types of investment choices. At one time, the only choices were stocks or bonds, but now the possibilities are vast, including annuities, CDs, Ginnie Maes, index funds, money markets, mutual funds, Treasury obligations, zero coupons—the list goes on and on. As you are aware, everyone wants choice, but too many alternatives can be confusing. This book attempts not only to narrow down those choices and explain each financial instrument for the layperson, but also to show you how each instrument can be adapted to today's ever-changing economic environment. You won't find tips on high-flying stocks that promise to help you double your money overnight. As you already know, no one can make such promises with any certainly. What you will find here is an honest appraisal of the advantages, disadvantages, costs, and benefits of each type of financial instrument—an appraisal based on current tax laws and their effects upon you, the investor.

A glossary of common financial terms is provided (at the end of the book) to serve as a handy reference tool as you read the money-managing columns in your daily newspaper or your favorite magazine. It should help you penetrate some of the verbal fog generated by brokers, bankers, salespeople, and especially government agencies that enforce the many financial policies of the current administration.

My hope is that *Financial Planning for the Utterly Confused* will be a valuable tool for the millions of Americans who need help in managing their small to medium-sized investment plans. The information in this book can be the first building block in the creation of a secure and comfortable financial future that only you can initiate. There is a saying that sums up financial planning in 10 two-letter words:

If it is to be,
It is up to me.

Introduction

◆▬▬◆◆◆◆◆◆◆◆◆◆◆◆◆◆◆◆◆◆◆◆◆◆◆◆◆◆◆◆◆◆◆◆◆◆◆◆◆▬▬◆

"Though no one can go back and make a brand new start, anyone can start from now and make a brand new end."

Do I Need to Read This Chapter?

- Do I know something about my finances—but not enough?

- Am I making the mistake of expecting others to do my work for me?

- Have I identified and prioritized my financial goals?

- Am I where I should be, given my age and family situation?

- Does risk scare me?

- Do I know the "hidden" factors that might be eating away at my nest egg right now?

- Am I keeping the right records?

The best investment you can make is in yourself. Financially you must have some knowledge about your own affairs because you cannot hand over everything to a financial adviser (see Chapter 27) or broker and expect that person to do it all. Each month you know doubt receive a monthly statement of your financial position, but do you really have any idea what those figures mean? If you will take the time to learn about money matters, you will receive a rich reward—dividends in understanding that in the long run will improve your financial position.

How Do You Begin a Financial Plan?

The first step in creating a financially secure plan is to identify your personal and family financial goals. Goals are based on what is most important to you. Short-term goals (up to a year) are what things you desire soon (say, household appliances), while long-term goals are items you want later on in life (a home, education for your children, sufficient retirement income). Take these short- and long-term goals and establish priorities, making sure you have an emergency fund as the first item. Then estimate the cost of each goal, and set a target date to reach it. See Table I.1.

Although every financial plan will be different, each should be meet certain criteria:

1. An emergency fund equal to 3 months of net income (after taxes)
2. Adequate insurance
3. Specific amounts for investments set aside on a regular basis

A rule of thumb states that you should have a retirement fund that is 20 times the amount of money you need to supplement social security and a pension. For example, if you want $30,000 a year beyond your pension and social security, you will need to save $600,000.

Interested in calculating your investment strategy? Here's the first step the experts advise. Apply the simple formula called the *rule of 72*. It will help you figure out how long it will take, or what interest rate you will need, to double your money.

For example, if you invested $10,000 at 6 percent, it would take you 12 years to have $20,000 (72 ÷ 6). You simply divide the number 72 by the interest. On the other hand, suppose you knew the length of time your money would be invested, but you wanted to know the rate of interest you would need to "double" at the end of time period. You would divide 72 by the number of years, which would result in the required interest. For example, if you were 56 years old and you wanted to retire at 65, 9 years from now, you would need 8 percent interest each year to double your money (72 ÷ 9). As a sidelight, if you were interested in tripling your money, use the number 115 instead of 72 and then continue with your calculation.

You are all aware of the changing life cycle. Your goals must be updated as your needs and circumstances change. In your young adult years, short-term

Table I.1 Interest Tables to Meet Your Goals

1. $10,000 Lump Sum

Rate of Earnings	5 Years	10 Years	15 Years	20 Years	25 Years	30 Years
5%	$12,763	$16,289	$20,789	$26,533	$33,864	$43,219
6%	13,382	17,908	23,966	32,071	42,919	57,435
7%	14,026	19,672	27,590	38,697	54,274	76,123
8%	14,693	21,589	31,722	46,610	68,485	100,627
9%	15,386	23,674	36,425	56,044	86,231	132,677
10%	16,105	25,937	41,772	67,275	108,347	174,494
11%	16,851	28,394	47,846	80,623	135,855	228,923
12%	17,623	31,058	54,736	96,463	170,001	299,599

2. $100-per-Month Investment

Rate of Earnings	5 Years	10 Years	15 Years	20 Years	25 Years	30 Years
5%	$6,801	$15,528	$26,729	$41,103	$59,551	$83,226
6%	6,977	16,388	29,082	46,204	69,299	100,452
7%	7,159	17,308	31,696	52,093	81,007	121,997
8%	7,348	18,295	34,604	58,902	95,103	149,035
9%	7,542	19,351	37,841	66,789	112,112	183,074
10%	7,744	20,484	41,447	75,937	132,683	226,049
11%	7,952	21,700	45,469	86,564	157,613	280,452
12%	8,167	23,004	49,958	98,926	187,885	349,496

3. Annual Investment Required to Reach $100,000

Rate of Earnings	5 Years	10 Years	15 Years	20 Years	25 Years	30 Years
5%	$17,236	$7,572	$4,414	$2,880	$1,966	$1,433
6%	16,736	7,157	4,053	2,565	1,720	1,193
7%	16,254	6,764	3,719	2,280	1,478	989
8%	15,783	6,392	3,410	2,024	1,267	817
9%	15,332	6,039	3,124	1,793	1,083	673
10%	14,890	5,704	2,861	1,587	924	552
11%	14,467	5,388	2,618	1,403	787	452
12%	14,005	5,088	2,395	1,239	669	369

Notes: Amounts are to nearest dollar.
    Rates are compounded annually.
    These are year-end values.

goals may include obtaining adequate insurance, establishing good credit, and generally just getting your adult life under way. During your middle years, the goals shift from immediate personal spending to education for children and retirement planning. In your later years, travel may become a primary goal. Also when planning for your future, age is a vital factor.

How Does Age Enter into Financial Planning

Here are some guidelines to use, depending on your present age:

Ages 20 to 40. When you are young, growth of financial resources should be a primary goal; a relatively high degree of risk is tolerable. *Suggestion:* Invest in a diversified portfolio of common stocks or in a mutual fund managed for growth of assets, not income. Speculation (real estate, coins, metals, etc.) is acceptable.

Ages 40 to 50. This is the period of time when the 20/20 rule goes into effect, working now for about 20 years and having 20 years more to go before retirement. Stocks are still an attractive choice, but now you need a more balanced approach. Begin to invest in fixed-rate instruments (bonds), and look into ones that are tax free (municipals) only if your present or near-future income is high enough to warrant it.

Ages 50 to 60. At this point, growth is less important and risk less acceptable. Move a portion of your investments out of stocks and into bonds in order to minimize risk and increase your current flow of income.

Age 60 and Over. By now, the majority of your funds should be in income-producing investments to provide safety and maximum current interest.

There is a rule of thumb that may be appropriate here. It is based on the concept that the percentage of your portfolio in bonds should approximate your age, the balance going into equalities or slight-risk vehicles. For example, at age 40 you would keep 40 percent in bonds and 60 percent in equities. At age 60 the reverse would be appropriate—60 percent bonds and 40 percent equities. Of course, this is a very general idea and may not be appropriate for everyone.

When planning investments for your age bracket, consider the following:

1. *Security of principal.* This refers to the preservation of your original capital. Treasury securities are guaranteed by the government, while stocks fluctuate greatly.

2. *Return*. This means the money you earn on your investment (interest, dividends, profit).

3. *Liquidity*. This pertains to the ease of converting your investment into cash.

4. *Convenience*. This refers to the time and energy you are willing to expend on your investment.

5. *Tax status*. Depending on your tax bracket, each investment will bear heavily on your personal situation. Municipal bonds are tax free while certificates of deposit (CDs) are fully taxable.

6. *Your personal circumstances*. Included under this category would be your income, your health, your individual circumstances, and your ability to tolerate risk.

How Should You Deal with Financial Risk in Planning for the Future?

The single most important factor in deciding on the best investments for you is the level of risk you can afford to take. Thus, the first step in formulating your investment plan is a careful self-examination. How much money do you have to invest? How great will your financial needs be for the foreseeable future? How much of your capital can you realistically afford to risk losing, and how great a degree of risk can you and your family handle psychologically? Each of these factors will have a bearing on the degree of risk you can tolerate in investment decisions. The trade-off is simple: to get larger rewards, you have to take greater risks.

You can achieve a balance by investing in a pyramid fashion. Begin with conservative (safe) investments at the foundation (Treasury obligations, insured money markets, CDs), and then gradually build up, accepting a bit more risk at each step. Stocks are a very common method of investing, but how much of a percentage should you invest? A rule of thumb you might use as a guide is to subtract your age from 100. However, this is only one estimate of many. At the very top, you may have high-risk investments (coins, gold, real estate), but because of the pyramid, the investments will be small compared with the rest of your holdings. Also, to minimize loss, you should have at least two different types of investments that perform differently during a specific period of time. For example, when interest rates are low, your portfolio of stocks usually gains while bonds do poorly. Diversify!

How Can You Overcome Obstacles to Your Financial Plan?

Regardless of how well you plan financially, certain obstacles will always arise. Four factors that could have a major impact on your investment objectives are as follows:

1. *Inflation.* When it comes to investing and inflation, what matters most isn't what you make, but what you keep. It is obvious that if you are to plan financially for your future, you must receive a return that is high enough to outpace any long-term effects of inflation. If, for example, you kept retirement money in a savings account paying 3.5 percent per year and over the same period of time the inflation rate averaged 5 percent per year, your investment world have less purchasing power at retirement than it did when it was started. Table I.2 is designed to illustrate the effect of the inflation rate on the cost of living for future years. Look down the "Years to Retirement" column to the number of years until you retire, and read across the rows to find the estimated inflation rates. Multiply your plan or budget by the inflation rate to adjust for future costs. For example, if you are planning to retire in 10 years and the inflation rate is 4 percent, multiply your cost of investment or budget by 1.480 in order to reflect inflation-adjusted costs. Ten years from now, it would cost you $59,200 to buy the same items you could have bought today for $40,000 ($40,000 × 1.480 = $59,200).

2. *Interest rate risk.* A change in interest rates will cause the value and price of fixed-rate instruments (bonds) to move in the opposite direction of interest rates. If interest rates go down, the value of bonds goes up; and, conversely, if interest rates go up, the value of bonds goes down. You have interest rate risk with all types of bonds. The longer the maturity of the bond, the greater the interest rate risk; so if you are concerned about this risk, stay short term.

   Here's a series of guidelines for handling risk. They should make you more "comfortable"—in both senses of the word.

   - Don't invest in any instrument in which you can lose more than you can potentially gain. This factor is sometimes referred to as *risk-reward balance*.

   - Diversify your holdings. Spread your investment dollars among a variety of instruments, thereby minimizing the risk potential.

   - When investments fail to perform up to your expectations (the period to hold them is based upon your objectives), sell them. "Cutting your losses"

Table I.2 Effect of Inflation Rate on Cost of Living in Future Years

Years to Retirement	3%	4%	5%	6%	7%	8%	9%	10%
1	1.030	1.040	1.050	1.060	1.070	1.080	1.090	1.100
2	1.061	1.082	1.103	1.124	1.145	1.166	1.188	1.210
3	1.093	1.125	1.158	1.191	1.225	1.260	1.285	1.331
4	1.126	1.170	1.216	1.262	1.311	1.360	1.412	1.464
5	1.159	1.217	1.276	1.338	1.403	1.469	1.539	1.611
6	1.194	1.265	1.340	1.419	1.501	1.587	1.677	1.772
7	1.230	1.316	1.407	1.504	1.606	1.714	1.828	1.949
8	1.267	1.369	1.477	1.594	1.718	1.851	1.993	2.144
9	1.305	1.423	1.551	1.689	1.838	1.999	2.172	2.358
10	1.344	1.480	1.629	1.791	1.967	2.159	2.367	2.594
11	1.384	1.539	1.710	1.898	2.105	2.332	2.580	2.853
12	1.426	1.601	1.796	2.012	2.252	2.518	2.813	3.138
13	1.469	1.665	1.886	2.133	2.410	2.720	3.066	3.452
14	1.513	1.732	1.980	2.261	2.579	3.937	3.342	3.797
15	1.558	1.801	2.079	2.397	2.759	3.172	3.642	4.177
16	1.605	1.873	2.183	2.540	2.952	3.426	3.970	4.595
17	1.653	1.948	2.292	2.693	3.159	3.700	4.328	5.054
18	1.702	2.026	2.407	2.854	3.380	3.996	4.717	5.560
19	1.754	2.107	2.527	3.026	3.617	4.316	5.142	6.116
20	1.806	2.191	2.653	3.207	3.870	4.661	5.604	6.727
25	2.094	2.666	3.386	4.292	5.427	6.848	8.623	10.835
30	2.427	3.243	4.322	5.743	7.612	10.063	13.268	17.449

is the only sure way to prevent minor setbacks from turning into financial nightmares. A rule of thumb is to sell an investment when its value declines by 10 percent of your original cost.

- Did you ever hear of a "stop order"? Most small market investors have not, and yet it can cut your losses automatically. When you purchase a stock, you give your broker instructions to sell that stock if it should decline by, say, 10 percent of its original purchase price. The moment the predetermined level is reached, your stock will be sold.

- Don't discount risk altogether. The rewards may justify taking a chance. Remember the turtle. It makes progress only when it sticks its neck out.

3. *Taxation.* Determining to what extent any tax-advantaged investment would help you is a serious consideration. You must therefore take into account your tax bracket, present income, future income, and investment holdings before you do financial planning. Also consider the value of assets that will be exempt from estate tax for future income, and investment holdings before you do financial planning. Also consider the value of assets that will be exempt from estate tax for future years. Presently assets that are exempt from estate tax will increase until 2010 when the estate tax will be 0, but all exempted amounts will return in 2011 at $1 million.

Year	Estate Tax Exemption	Top Estate Tax Rate
2007	$2 million	45%
2008	$2 million	45%
2009	$3.5 million	45%

Remember that there is no tax on a surviving spouse who receives any amount of inheritance.

4. *Procrastination.* This is an obstacle that depends solely on you. Don't imitate the person who says, "Someday I'm going to stop procrastinating." Regardless of how well a financial plan is structured, if you don't follow it through, it will be doomed before it begins.

Now that your goals have been defined and the areas of risks and rewards examined, the next step is getting all the "paper" together.

What Financial Records Should You Keep?

Start by developing a "road map" so that you or your heirs (in case of disability or death) will know where documents are. Records that should be kept available are:

1. Professional numbers: Telephone numbers of your lawyer, doctor, accountant, insurance company, business associates, and financial advisor or broker

2. Account numbers: Brokerage, bank, credit cards, insurance policies (and beneficiaries), and safe deposit box (keys and authorized deputies)

3. Business records: Tax returns, company books, payroll data, etc.

4. Personal records: An updated will and trust agreements

5. Health records: Living will, health care proxy, etc.

6. Retirement benefits: Social security, IRAs, 401(k)s, and the like

7. Burial arrangements: Cemetery plots, deeds

8. Any outstanding liabilities

This introduction to financial planning lays the foundation for all the topics in the forthcoming pages of this new edition. You owe it to yourself to read business periodicals (newspapers, magazines, annual reports), learn (seminars, courses), ask (brokers, financial planners), and make certain that you can apply the knowledge gained from the following chapters so that when opportunity does knock, you are not in the backyard looking for four-leaf clovers.

"The difficulty is not buying on time—it's paying on time."

Financial Planning for the Utterly Confused

CHAPTER 1

Annuities for Today's Living

"Forever is a long time, but not as long as it was yesterday."

Do I Need to Read This Chapter?

- Am I worried about retirement?

- Do I run the risk of outliving my money?

- Have I considered annuities?

- Am I choosing the right type of annuity?

- Do I realize that insurers that sell annuities can go bankrupt?

- How can I make sure my annuity investment is safe?

- What do all those safety rankings, like "Aa2," really mean?

- I'm middle class. Will annuities have special tax benefits for me?

- Do annuities compare favorably with mutual funds?

Today, either tax-free municipal bonds (see Chapters 12 and 13) or tax-deferred annuities seem to be at the center of many investment portfolios. The insurance industry's offering of the annuity has become a serious alternative for investors who wish to look for deferred income, possible tax deduction, and safety of investment.

How Does an Annuity Work?

When you retire, you will want to be able to live comfortably for life on the income from your investments. However, because of modern medicine, many people run the risk of outliving their investment income. With this increasing longevity, a person's retirement can span 20 to 30 years.

To avoid this problem, the purchasing of an annuity could be a possible solution. An annuity may be considered the opposite of a traditional life insurance policy. When you buy insurance, you agree to pay annual premiums to an insurance company. In return, the company will pay, according to your instructions, the face value of the policy in a lump sum to your beneficiaries when you die. By contrast, when you buy an annuity, you pay the company a sum of money and, in return, receive a monthly income for as long as you live. Naturally, the longer you survive, the more money you'll receive. Therefore, you can never outlive your return regardless of how old you become. It thus can be stated that life insurance protects against financial loss as a result of *dying too soon*, while an annuity protects you against financial loss as a result of *living too long*.

What Are the Different Characteristics of Annuities?

There are several different types of annuities. They can be categorized according to three main characteristics: premiums, payment return, and return on investment.

Premiums

The cost of the annuity will depend on many factors:

1. How much you will contribute to your account
2. The rate of return earned by the fund
3. The length of time the money is left in the fund
4. The procedure for distribution of the funds to beneficiaries (note that options can raise or lower your monthly annuity return)

An annuity may be purchased either through a single lump-sum premium or through annual premium payments. If you happen to have a large sum of money to invest at one time—for example, from an inheritance or from a pension fund—you may want to purchase an annuity with a lump-sum payment. This is known as a single-premium deferred annuity (SPDA). Once you have made the initial investment, no further contribution is required. An SPDA is a base annuity that works in the following way: You buy a contract and pay a lump sum up front, which guarantees future payments. If you die before you begin to receive withdrawals, the policy will pay the estate the contract's face value plus interest. If you live past age 59½, you may begin your withdrawal program or you may cash in the policy and receive your principal plus all interest earned on it tax deferred. This is similar to a nondeductible IRA since the income earned stays tax deferred in the annuity until it is withdrawn; yet it is better because you are not limited to a maximum deposit.

Annuity income depends on life expectancy and is thus classified as life insurance. This is important for you to understand, because the classification allows the annuity's investment earnings to be treated as tax deferred, with no tax on its accumulation until the money is withdrawn. This is surprising since well over 95 percent of the annuity is investment while only a very small balance is for insurance.

But watch out if you withdraw before age 59½. Except in certain cases (see Chapter 22), a premature withdrawal will cost you an IRS penalty of 10 percent. There is also an insurance company surrender penalty (in some cases) of 7 percent of your investment if you withdraw it during the first year, 6 percent during the second year, 5 percent during the third year, and so on. From the eighth year on, no penalty is charged. Make sure you find out about surrender charges before deciding on where to invest in an annuity, and be sure to ask your agent or broker about sales charges (if there are any) before you buy. These charges could affect your total yield and future income. Find out the amount of the fee before you invest, and compare the rates charged by several companies. These fees are important in determining the annuity to be chosen because they directly affect the yield. The Securities and Exchange Commission requires the annuity companies to show their charges in a standardized table located near the beginning of the information booklet known as a prospectus.

These charges could include:

- Front-end sales commissions
- Annual maintenance costs
- Annual mortality and expense charges
- Annual investment advisory fees
- Surrender charges

Payment Return

An annuity may provide for either *immediate* return to the investor or *deferred* return. An *immediate* annuity is purchased at the time you want to start receiving income, and requires a single lump-sum premium. The insurance company begins sending you monthly checks right away. One of the most important advantages of a fixed-rate immediate annuity is that it allows you to lock in an interest rate for the rest of your life when rates are high. You always know exactly how much you will receive. However, bear in mind that once the rate is set, it can never change. If current rates drop, you know you did the right thing; but if they should rise, there isn't a thing you can do about it but feel bad. Also, that fixed amount today may seem high but diminishes as time goes by because of inflation. Table 1.1 shows spendable income needed.

A *deferred* annuity, on the other hand, is purchased prior to the time when the income is needed (deferred period). During this period, which may be very short or may last as long as 40 years, your investment earns interest tax free. If you should decide to cancel your annuity before withdrawal time, you may have to pay a surrender charge, which will vary from company to company.

Table 1.1 Spendable Income Needed During Retirement to Buy What $10,000 Buys at the Start of Retirement

Number of years after the Start of Retirement	Inflation Rate			
	3%	4%	5%	6%
5 years	$11,041	$12,167	$13,382	$14,693
10 years	12,190	14,802	17,908	21,589
15 years	13,459	18,009	23,966	31,722
20 years	14,859	21,911	32,071	46,610
25 years	16,406	26,658	42,919	68,485

Return on Investment

Annuities may be classified as either *fixed dollar* or *variable. Fixed-dollar* annuities guarantee you a certain minimum interest rate. The actual rate you'll receive is fixed for only a few months or years, but there is a minimum rate below which your return cannot drop. Insurance companies usually invest fixed-dollar annuity funds in highly secure investments, such as government bonds. With a fixed-dollar annuity, you'll know that your principal is secure and that you'll receive at least a specified minimum income. Some companies will offer what is known as a "bailout" provision in their annuity contract, which states that if the annuity fails to earn a specified interest rate, the holder can withdraw his or her money without penalty. *Variable annuities*, on the other hand, are usually invested in more risky, but potentially more lucrative, instruments. The amount of interest your money earns, and therefore the size of the payment you'll receive, will vary according to the success of the insurance company's investments. However, your principal is not untouchable, as a market disaster could wipe out a good part of your investment. Thus you may earn more with a variable annuity, but the risk you take is greater. Variable annuities are best for those individuals who start their retirement programs late in life, as it is a fast (though risky) way to "catch up."

Whichever type of annuity you choose, your ability to tolerate risk should be the deciding factor. Younger people may move toward the variable annuity because they may feel that there will be enough time to recoup any possible losses, whereas older people may choose fixed-rate annuities because of the guaranteed yield. Regardless of which type you choose, insurance products are still among the safest savings plans around.

What Are the Different Repayment Options That Annuities Offer?

As I've explained earlier, with an annuity, the longer you live, the greater the return you can expect to earn. This means, of course, that if you die early, you may never recoup the amount you originally paid for the annuity. Because of the different needs of investors, there are several repayment options from which to choose:

1. *Individual life annuity.* Here, payments (which are the highest of any option) are continued throughout your life, with no further payment made after you

die (even if you should die only a year or two after payments begin). This plan is designed only for a person who wants the highest amount of regular income and has no spouse or other dependents who might need financial support after the annuitant dies. If you are married, federal law requires you to obtain a notarized waiver of benefits from your spouse.

2. *Joint-survivor annuity.* This plan provides monthly payments for as long as either you or your spouse lives. In other words, at your demise, your spouse would continue receiving payments until he or she died. It is obvious that the payments each month would be smaller than the individual life annuity because the payments extend to two lives and therefore will have to stretch over a longer period.

3. *Guaranteed-minimum annuity.* Under the terms of this annuity, there is an established minimum payout period. In the event that the annuity holder dies shortly after the payouts begin, continued payments will be made to the beneficiaries for a specified period of time. For example, an investor might buy this type of policy in order to receive payments for the rest of his or her life but wants to make certain that the insurance company will make payments for, say, at least 10 years. This is known as a 10-year certain contract. If the investor dies after receiving 2 years of payouts, he or she will be assured that whoever is designated as the beneficiary will receive money for the next 8 years. For this privilege, the investor will receive a smaller payback (about 6 percent less than from the other previously mentioned options). Also, if the investor should die before distribution begins, the named beneficiaries can receive the full value of the annuity, which will bypass probate and its time and cost procedures.

What Are the Advantages, Risks, and Tax Consequences Associated with Annuities?

Regardless of where you purchase an annuity, even at a bank, the insurance company—and not the bank—stands behind the policy. Although banks are federally insured, insurance companies are not. If the insurance company should fail, your deposits can be frozen for years.

A large portion of what you receive in each payment will be a tax-free return on the money you invest as long as the annuity you bought was not funded from an IRA or a company retirement plan. Only the amount that represents earnings is taxed. If, however, the money comes from an IRA or tax-deferred plan, most likely it will be fully taxable because the money used to buy the annuity was untaxed originally. If you are fortunate to outlive your life expectancy, all the payments you receive from that point are taxable because you have recovered your initial immediate investment. If, however, you should die before recovering all your investment, your estate can claim a deduction on your final tax return of the balance you did not receive.

Annuities have certain other distinct advantages. The most important benefit lies in the fact that annuity income is guaranteed for life, no matter how long you live. It's pretty comforting to retire with an income that you know will always be there. Also, when death does occur, regardless of the payout plan you choose, the annuity is free from probate because an annuity is an insurance product having a named beneficiary with the proceeds going directly to the designated heirs, bypassing court costs, legal fees, and long delays.

In the middle class? Feeling squeezed? It's a pretty rare investment that offers special tax benefits, but I believe that annuities qualify. With annuities, you'll find that your assets accumulate more quickly than occurs with some other investments because the interest you earn is not subject to income tax until you begin to withdraw it.

As stated before, you can save in three ways:

1. Your principal earns interest.
2. That interest earns interest.
3. You earn interest on the money you save in current taxes.

And on the topic of interest, remember that "old bankers never die; they just lose their interest."

It's a Wrap

- Annuities are a form of insurance in which the policyholder pays a specified premium and, in return, receives regular payments for the rest of his or her life.
- The several different types of annuities are classified according to premiums (lump sum or annual), payment return (immediate or deferred), and return on investment (fixed dollar or variable).

- Annuities offer several different repayment options: individual life, joint survivor, and guaranteed minimum.

- You must carefully evaluate the credit rating of any insurer that sells annuities. That's because insurers, unlike banks, are not federally insured—and if they default, your funds may be frozen for years.

- Annuities provide certain income tax benefits that are of special advantage to middle-class investors.

- When evaluating annuities, pay attention to four details: minimum initial investments, maximum age for starting to receive payouts, terms for switching among funds, and rules for partial withdrawals. These details can be found in each contract's prospectus.

"The truth is that you can spend your life anyway you want, but you can spend it only once."

CHAPTER 2

Certificates of Deposit— Old Faithful

◆◆

"It may not seem as exciting as trading in pork bellies, but it always brings home the bacon."

Do I Need to Read This Chapter?

- How much of my certificate of deposit (CD) investments is federally insured?

- How can I get around the $100,000 insurance limit?

- Are CDs too safe?

- When do CDs make sense?

- What are the different ways my interest can be compounded?

- How can I shop for the best deal on a CD?

At one time, you needed $100,000 or more to invest in a bank certificate of deposit. This restriction had been established by the Federal Reserve Board in order to protect savings banks, savings and loan institutions, and credit unions from competition with commercial banks. The fear was that if commercial banks could issue high-yielding certificates of deposit in small denominations, small savers would withdraw their funds from low-yielding passbook savings accounts in order to buy the certificates. This, in turn, would adversely affect the savings banks, most of whose holdings were tied up in low-yielding, long-term mortgages. In effect, the Federal Reserve sought to protect the banks at the expense of small savers.

All this changed about 35 years ago when the first money market mutual fund offered its shares for sale for as little as $1,000. Money market funds, which paid rates comparable to those offered on bank certificates, quickly became a favorite investment for small savers. The savings banks began to lose customers. As a result, the banks themselves demanded that the rules be changed so as to allow them to compete with the money market funds. Thus was born the certificate of deposit for the small investor.

Today, most federal restrictions governing insured time deposits in banks have been lifted since banks are free to compete with one another in setting terms for their own CDs. You can now buy a CD from a savings and loan institution, a savings bank, a credit union, a commercial bank, or a broker.

How Does the Certificate of Deposit Work?

The concept of the CD is simple. It is a time-based, fixed-income instrument issued by a financial institution that pays you interest at a guaranteed rate for a specified term. When the CD reaches maturity, you will receive your principal and all interest earned. Unlike bond interest (paid periodically), the interest from a CD usually compounds, which means you will be earning interest on your interest. The amount you invest in a CD is insured by the federal government for up to $100,000. However, it is not wise to put the entire $100,000 in one account since the federal insurance ceiling applies to both principal and interest. I suggest that you have no more than $85,000 to $90,000 in any single certificate, because any interest you earn on the CD could increase your balance, surpassing the maximum insured sum and thereby not being automatically protected if the bank should fail.

Who Should Purchase CDs?

Generally, I do not believe in certificates of deposit in an investment portfolio because there are so many better alternatives. Many millions of people own them because of their safety, convenience, and general familiarity with their bank; yet investors lose because they deny themselves the chance for higher yields which come about with accepting more risk. However, there are certain times when CDs do make sense:

1. *Emergency savings.* As stated, you need an emergency fund (after taxes) equal to at least three months of your salary. Short-term CDs are excellent for this as they can be very liquid.

2. *Short-term goals.* Savings for a house in two or three years make a good justification for CDs.

3. *Completion of a long-term goal.* For sixteen years, since the birth of your child, you have invested in stocks in a mutual fund. Now, as college looms in two years, you want to safeguard those funds. In steps the CD.

4. *The parking lot theory.* An inheritance, switching jobs, any windfall may give you a large sum of money. However, you may need a little time to decide where to invest. CDs make a fine short-term parking lot for those funds.

What Plans Should You Make When Purchasing a CD?

There are two primary considerations in planning for your investment in a CD: term and rate of return.

Term

The most popular type of CD is the 6-month certificate, but CDs are available with maturities ranging from 7 days to 10 years. During the term of your CD, the money you've invested is relatively costly to liquidate (illiquid). If an emergency arises which requires you to withdraw your money before maturity, you'll be penalized for it. This penalty is known as *EWP (early withdrawal penalty)* and will vary from bank to bank. Thus, before you invest in a CD, you'll want to consider carefully when you're likely to need the money. If a college tuition bill is due to be paid in 1 year and 3 months, you know that you'll want a certificate that matures at that time. It may pay for you to buy CDs in smaller denominations instead of purchasing one large certificate. Remember, you never know what the future holds, and at some time you may need to withdraw a portion of the funds. For example, if you were to buy a $50,000 1-year CD and 8 months later you needed $10,000, some banks would charge you a penalty on the entire $50,000 since you would have to cash in the full CD. You would have been wiser to have purchased five $10,000 CDs, thus having to break only one of them, leaving the other four intact. And the interest rate may be the same on five smaller certificates ($10,000 each) as it is on one larger one ($50,000).

Rate of Return

The interest paid on a CD will vary not only according to the term of the certificate but also from time to time (as interest rates fluctuate) as well as from bank to bank. Don't buy your CD at the first bank you visit; the competing bank across the street may well be offering half a point more. Shop around! In these times of low interest yields, you have no other choice. Ask about how the bank credits the interest earned to your account. The more frequently interest is credited, the better for you, since each time your account grows through an interest payment, the amount of money you have working for you grows as well.

For example, a $10,000, 6 percent, 10-year certificate would pay at maturity the following various amounts:

- *Simple interest, no compounding:* The money grows only to $16,000 because interest is paid only on the original principal.
- *Interest compounded quarterly:* The money grows to $18,140.
- *Interest compounded daily:* The original $10,000 grows to $18,220.

Thus, it pays to investigate these various bank policies. If you find a bank that compounds your interest on a daily basis, you may want to make a switch and do your investing there.

How many times have you seen two rates offered by banks in their advertisements? Banks will sometimes reflect their compounding policies by listing a true rate of return (known as the *effective annual yield*) along with the no-compounding nominal rate (known as the *interest rate*) for a given CD. Thus a CD with an interest rate of 6.05 percent may pay an effective annual yield of 6.32 percent. Use the effective rate, if available, for comparison.

Also, for comparison purposes, look at this scenario. An investment company proudly states that its instrument has had an average annual return of 20 percent a year for the last 10 years. Sounds great? Not necessarily. The investment increased 200 percent (20 percent × 10 years) over a decade, based upon simple interest. But this 20 percent earns only 11.6 percent compounded interest.

If you want to compare simple and compound rates of return on CDs, but don't have a compound interest table, try this formula (it's easier than it looks!):

$$A = P(1 + R)^T$$

where A = amount of money you'll have at the end of a specific period of time
P = principal
R = rate of interest
T = time period

For example, a $1,000 investment that yields 5 percent in 3 years compounded annually would produce $1,160:

$$A = 1,000 \ (1 + .05)^3$$
$$A = 1,000 \ (1.05)^3$$
$$A = 1,000 \ (1.05 \times 1.05 \times 1.05)$$
$$A = 1,160$$

What Else Should You Know about Certificates of Deposit?

1. *Laddering.* Stagger your maturity dates. In this way, as you receive your principal back, you will be able to reinvest it in higher-yielding CDs if rates have gone up or in another investment if rates have fallen.

2. *Bulleting.* The bullet concept involves purchasing CDs at different times—but having them all mature on the same date. By staggering them you reduce risk when buying rates are at their shortest point.

3. *Changing.* Ask whether you can increase the size of your investment after the original purchase of your CD has been made. This can be advantageous if you expect more funds to be available shortly (and if you expect interest rates to decline in the future).

4. *Taxes.* Although CD interest is subject to all three taxes—federal, state, and local—the lower your state and local taxes are, the better it is to look at the CD as an investment in your portfolio. If you want to compare state and local taxes on a CD with the rate on exempt state and local tax instruments, such as Treasuries, combine your state and local tax rate, subtract it from 100, and then multiply your CD rate. If the result is higher than a Treasury, pick the CD.

For example, assume a state and local combined tax rate of 7 percent and a CD rate of 6 percent.

Subtract combined tax rate from 100: $100 - 7 = 93$
Multiply by CD rate: $93 \times .06 = 5.58$

If the Treasury rate is 5 percent, it would pay to invest in a CD, as you would be receiving at least ½ percent more from your certificate.

5. *Other points.* Bear in mind the following when determining how to spread around your CD investments:

- When a bank has several branches, the main office and all branch offices are considered one bank.
- Individual retirement accounts (IRAs), 401(k)s, and Keogh plan funds held in trust, or in a custodial capacity by a bank, are insured separately from any other deposits owned by the same investor—to a maximum of $250,000.
- Actual title to each insured account must be in the name of the account holder designated.
- Each co-owner of a joint account must have equal withdrawal rights and must personally sign a signature card.

Before buying any CD, ask your banker or broker these questions:

1. I am not concerned about yield or rate, but how much money will I receive at maturity?
2. What, if any, is the early withdrawal penalty, and how is it applied?
3. Do I get a better rate if I am a current bank customer?
4. Are there higher rates offered for larger deposits that will still be covered by federal insurance?
5. And to add some humor, ask bankers why are there eight windows at the bank and only two tellers?

Types of Certificates

Different types of CDs are available:

1. *Traditional.* A fixed amount is deposited for a fixed period at a fixed interest rate.

2. *Bump-up.* Rising interest allows you to take advantage of advancing rates by increasing your original CD rate.

3. *Liquid.* This type of certificate allows you to withdraw, in certain cases, without penalty.

4. *Jumbo.* These certificates are usually of $100,000 or more with higher rates of return.

Although CDs generate low yields, and the general investing public is "crying" about the returns, CDs are still being bought in huge amounts. Thus it seems safe to say that the bank certificate—with its high degree of safety and flexibility as to maturity—will remain a popular investment choice for people.

And on the topic of choice, it may be true that there are two sides to every question, but it is also true that there are two sides to a sheet of flypaper, and it makes a big difference to the fly which side it chooses.

It's a Wrap

- Certificates of deposit are savings instruments issued by banks that pay interest at a guaranteed rate for a specified term.
- CDs are federally insured to a maximum of $100,000 *per certificate.*
- You can circumvent the insurance limit by having certificates from different issuers—which is to say, putting your eggs in more than one corporate basket.
- There may be severe penalties for early withdrawal.
- The upside of CDs is safety, liquidity, and convenience. The downside is lower yields.
- CDs make sense as emergency funds, savings for short-term goals, a way to complete a long-term goal, and a place to "park" money while you study more lucrative investments.
- CDs should be evaluated by length until maturity (term) and rate of return.
- In CDs your money is safe, so do not fret. It is insured by a government trillions in debt.

"Never be afraid to try something new. Remember an amateur built the ark; professionals built the **Titanic.** *"*

CHAPTER 3

Corporate Bond Market—For the Future

◆◆◆◆◆◆◆◆◆◆◆◆◆◆◆◆◆◆◆◆◆◆◆◆◆◆◆◆◆◆◆◆

"If a company can't pay as it goes, it may be going too fast."

Do I Need to Read This Chapter?

- I've heard that corporate bonds are a good investment, but I don't really understand what they are or how they work.

- What's the difference between a primary and a secondary bond market, and how does it affect me?

- What happens to corporate bonds when interest rates rise or fall?

- Can corporate bonds be recalled?

- What are the various types of yields I can expect?

- How can I identify and assess the risks involved in buying corporate bonds?

- How do I decipher those fine-print bond listings in the financial pages of the newspaper?

Although stocks are more known to most investors, the bond market is far larger but widely misunderstood. There are many kinds of bonds, and investing in them wisely can be a complex, challenging task. However, the rewards are often great, and bonds are an option well worth investigating for the middle-income investor.

How Do Corporate Bonds Work?

A bond is a form of debt issued by a corporation. In exchange for a sum of money lent by the buyer of the bond, the issuer of the bond promises to pay a specific amount of interest at stated intervals for a specific period of time. At the end of the repayment period (known as *maturity*), the issuing corporation repays the amount of money borrowed. You can read about the bonds issued by governments (local, state, and federal) elsewhere in this book. However, in this section we'll limit our discussion to the special characteristics of corporate bonds.

Newly issued corporate bonds are usually sold by a brokerage firm, which acts as underwriter of the issue. The underwriter receives the bonds from the issuing corporation and guarantees the corporation a specified level of sales, and then the underwriter sells the bonds to the public. This is known as the *primary* bond market.

There is also a *secondary* bond market operated through brokerage firms. The secondary market deals in previously issued bonds, which, as you'll see, may have either increased or decreased in value since their initial offering.

What Are the Characteristics of Bonds?

Some bonds are issued with property (such as land, buildings, machinery, or other equipment) as collateral against the loan, just as you might offer collateral to a bank in exchange for a personal loan. These bonds are known as *secured* bonds. Bonds not secured by collateral are called *debentures*. The value of a debenture is guaranteed by the good faith of the corporation, and if issued by a strong corporation, the debenture can be a highly secure investment.

All bonds bear both a face value and a maturity date. The *face value* is the amount you will receive when the bond reaches its maturity date. The *maturity date* is when the face value of the bond must be repaid. Thus a 20-year bond issued in 2008 must be repaid in full by the year 2028.

Interest on corporate bonds is usually paid in one of two ways. *Coupon bonds*, also called *bearer bonds*, have interest coupons attached to them.

You clip the coupons as they become due and present them for payment of interest. Your name usually doesn't appear on a coupon bond; it is a negotiable instrument, and anyone who clips the coupons can claim the interest due. However, this type of bond is no longer issued, but was described here because it may still be available in the secondary marketplace.

All bonds issued today are registered. This means that the issuer of the bonds records the purchase and sends out the interest checks. If the bonds are registered in your name, the issuer must notify you of a call. A bond may be called back by the issuing corporation and the principal repaid to the bondholder at any time according to the terms of the bond. (For a full explanation, see the section on "Callability.") If the bonds are registered in the street-name account held by your broker, the broker will be notified of the call and in turn will notify you. For bonds issued before July 1983 that were not registered (coupon bonds), it is the bondholder's responsibility to find out about the call.

Corporate bonds are usually issued in denominations of $1,000, known as *par value*. After issue, however, their prices vary and the bond's value at any given time is quoted as a percentage of par. Thus a bond quoted at 100 is selling at 100 percent of par, or $1,000. If the price is quoted at 95, it is selling at 95 percent of par; you could buy such a bond for $950. This is known as a *discounted bond*. A *premium bond* is one that sells at a price higher than par. A bond with a quoted price of 102, for example, will cost $1,020, which is 102 percent of par.

It's important to understand the differences between corporate bondholders and corporate stockholders. Here's a brief explanation. The holder of a corporate bond is a creditor of the corporation that issues the bond, not part owner like a stockholder. Therefore, if the corporation's profits increase during the term of the bond, the bondholder will not benefit; the amount of interest he or she receives is fixed at the time the bond is purchased. On the other hand, the bondholder's investment is safer than that of the stockholder, as interest on bonds is paid out before dividends are distributed to stockholders. Furthermore, if the corporation goes bankrupt, the claims of bondholders take precedence over those of stockholders.

What Are the Different Types of Bonds?

There are many variations in the types of bonds issued by corporations.

A bond may be issued with a *callability* clause. A callable bond may be redeemed by the issuing corporation prior to the maturity date; that is, the corporation may, at its option, call in the bonds early and repay them at that time (though usually at a premium over the face value). The corporation is likely to exercise this option when market interest rates have fallen below those in effect at the time the bond was issued. If new market conditions call for interest rates of 7 percent, why should a corporation continue to pay 9 percent on its previously issued bonds? As you can see, callability is a drawback for investors since it prevents them from locking in the high interest rates until maturity. For this reason, callable bonds usually pay higher interest rates than comparable noncallable bonds. Most bonds issued today are callable.

Today most corporations have begun to offer protection for a specified period against the possibility of a bond being called. The "call protection" usually runs 5 to 10 years and guarantees the bondholders a specific interest rate for at least a minimum number of years. Always check the call provision in any bond contract you are considering.

Corporations may also issue bonds with a *convertibility* feature. These bonds may be exchanged for shares of the corporation's common stock at the option of the bondholder and can allow you to participate in a greater-than-expected growth in the profits and value of the corporation. Convertible bonds thus combine the stability and safety of bonds with the growth opportunity of common stock. If you believe a company will move upward but you are concerned about the ups and downs over the short term, the convertible bond would be a good investment for you. If the common-stock value goes down, the convertible bond keeps its fixed yield. But when the common-stock value rises, you might want to sell the bond and take advantage of the gain. For example, a company with common stock trading at $20 per share might issue a $1,000 convertible bond that pays 5 percent interest and may be exchangeable for 40 shares of common stock. The bondholder would not convert at the present time to shares because he or she would be able to buy those same 40 shares at $800 ($20 × 40 shares) in the current market. But if the shares increased in value to more than $25 per share, he or she could convert the bonds to shares, sell the shares, and make a profit. For example, if the common stock of the issuing corporation rises in value to $30 per share, it would pay to convert your $1,000 for 40 shares (as agreed), sell them for $1,200, and pocket the difference of $200 per bond. Until a decision is made to convert, the bond will pay $50 per year ($1,000 × 5 percent) in interest. As usual, however, there's no free ride. You must ordinarily sacrifice about 1 percentage point in interest yield in exchange for the convertibility feature. What's important to remember is that there is a limited downside risk but virtually a limitless upside potential.

What Factors Should You Consider When Purchasing Bonds?

When considering the purchase of any particular corporate bond, you must weigh two principal factors:

- The yield offered by the bond
- The safety of the investment

Unfortunately, these factors aren't as simple as they appear, so let's examine them in greater detail.

What Is the Yield as Applied to Bonds?

With regard to bonds, the very term *yield* can be confusing, as there are several types of yields associated with bonds.

The *coupon yield*, or *coupon rate*, is the interest rate stated on the bond itself. A $1,000 bond with a coupon yield of 7 percent will pay $70 interest each year.

The *actual yield* is the rate of return that the coupon yield actually produces when the cost of the bond is taken into account. If you purchase the bond above par, the actual yield is lower than the coupon yield; if you purchase the bond below par, the actual yield is higher. For example, a $1,000 bond with a 7 percent coupon rate bought at 82 (for a cost of $820) would produce an actual yield of 8.5 percent (7 percent of $1,000 = $70 ÷ $820). The same bond bought at 104 (for a cost of $1,040) would actually yield only 6.7 percent ($70 ÷ $1,040).

The *current yield* is the actual yield on the closing price of the bond on the bond market for a given day. When the price of the bond declines, the current yield increases; when the price of the bond increases, the current yield declines. For example, suppose a $1,000 bond with a 7 percent coupon rate closed on the trading market on Friday at $910. The current yield for the bond on Friday would be 7.7 percent ($70 ÷ $910).

Finally, *yield to maturity (YTM)* represents the total rate of return if the bond is held to maturity, taking into consideration the purchase price of the bond, the interest paid, and the redemption price. Any broker can refer to a standard reference book, which contains yield-to-maturity figures for almost any bond. The YTM is important because current yield does not reflect any difference between the current purchase price and the value at maturity. If you purchased a bond for $850 and held it to its maturity, you would receive the bond's face of $1,000. In other words, there was a capital appreciation of $150 in addition to the annual interest. The YTM takes all this information into consideration as part of its calculation. The rate plus prorated discount (or subtracting prorated premium) is divided by the average of the total of the face plus purchase price. For example, the YTM of a 7 percent, $1,000 bond that sold for $850 with 10 years to maturity would be calculated as follows:

$$YTM = \frac{coupon + prorated\ discount}{(face\ value + purchase\ price) \div 2}$$

$$= \frac{\$70(rate) + \$15(\$150 \div 10\ years)}{\$1,000(face) + \$850(purchase\ price) \div 2}$$

$$= \frac{\$85}{\$925}$$

$$= 9.2\%$$

In the Real World... Bonds and interest rates are like certain married couples—they can't get along with or without each other. To put it another way, they share an inverse relationship: when interest rates rise, the bonds you currently hold become less valuable; when interest rates fall, the bonds become more attractive. Why? Let's look at an example. Say a new bond floated by a corporation offers a 6.5 percent rate, competitive with current interest rates (the prime rate, mortgage rates, personal loan rates, etc.). Now two years later, the prevailing interest rate has fallen to 5.5 percent. Since new bonds are then issued at that rate, your bond becomes more valuable and could sell at a profit in the secondary bond market. In the opposite scenario, if interest rates rise to 7.5 percent, the value of your bond falls because it returns less than new bonds being issued at the higher rate. To sell it, you would have to offer it at a discount to what you originally paid.

Naturally, all things being equal, the higher the yields on a particular bond, the better buy that bond is likely to be. But all things are not always equal. Bonds also differ in their degree of safety. That brings us to the second dominant consideration in choosing a bond for purchase.

How Is Safety Applied to Bonds?

The degree of risk associated with the purchase of a particular bond depends on the strength of the issuing corporation. Of course, it's not easy for the average middle-income investor to analyze the performance of all the many bond-issuing corporations. For a full examination, it would be necessary to study the company's financial statements, its earnings projections, the track record of management, prospects for the industry, and many other factors.

Fortunately, you don't need to do all this research yourself. There are special advisory services that have assumed the task of analyzing and rating the safety of corporate bonds. These ratings can be obtained from reference books you can readily find at your public library or request from any brokerage house.

The two best-known rating services are Moody's and Standard & Poor's (S&P). They rate bonds according to two slightly differing scales. Starting with the highest-rated bonds, the two scales are as follows:

Moody's: Aaa, Aa, A, Baa, Ba, B, Caa, Ca, C

S&P: AAA, AA, A, BBB, BB, B, CCC, CC, C

The safest bonds—those issued by large, stable corporations showing excellent future earnings projections—are rated Aaa or AAA. Bonds rated AA, Aa, or A are issued by firms whose ability to pay interest and principal is quite strong, but the safety of these bonds is somewhat more vulnerable to changes in economic conditions.

As you move toward the lower end of the rating scale, yields are likely to be higher; the lower-rated firms must offer higher interest rates to induce investors to accept the greater degree of risk.

Most brokers will quote the standard bond ratings along with prices and yields when you inquire about possible investments. For maximum safety, you'll probably want to stick to bonds rated A and higher. However, even though a bond may have an AA or Aa rating when you purchase it, that rating is always subject to change, upward or downward. The only exception would be if you want to choose a low-rated, high-yield bond on a speculative basis. The types of bonds involving high risk are known as junk bonds, though Wall Street prefers to call them "high-yield bonds." If you are late on your credit card payments, a higher rate of interest will be imposed on you. The same goes for corporations that may be considered a credit risk. They must pay out higher-than-normal interest payments in order to attract investors.

You're probably wondering where junk bonds fit into the bond picture. In my opinion, they're not unlike junk food. Allow me to explain.

Junk bonds are those on the lower rungs of the ladder. These bonds have ratings of BB or lower and usually pay yields about 3 percentage points higher than A-rated bonds. They received their disparaging nickname in the late 1920s and early 1930s, when the Great Depression led to numerous defaults by bond issuers, and are today considered one of the major factors in the inadequate financing of major mergers and acquisitions.

Junk bonds offer neither the security of bonds nor the growth of stocks, and most have bad credit ratings. Yet there are those who will argue that presently junk bonds have done well. Perhaps a statement I heard about them will suffice. If you ask a drunk at 11 p.m. how he feels, the answer is "fine." The big question is how will he feel in the morning?

How Do You Learn about Bonds?

If you're interested in getting into the bond market, you should know how to read the bond quotations that appear on the business page of your daily newspaper. These are a good basic source of information about currently available bonds. Figure 3.1 provides a sample bond listing as it might appear in the newspaper. You'll find an explanation of the information each column provides below the sample listing.

Bonds make an excellent choice for many middle-income investors, especially those whose primary need is for income rather than growth.

People looking toward retirement, for example, are likely to find that bonds are available in so many different forms that they must be careful in their selections. Remember the importance of safety, and use the standard ratings as your guide. Also be sure you understand the details of the particular bond

Figure 3.1 Sample Corporate Bond Listing

ISSUE	DESCRIPTION		CURRENT YIELD	VOLUME	HIGH	LOW	LAST	CHANGE
J & E	6 ¾	028	7.6	28	90	88	89	+3

Issue: The abbreviated name of the corporation issuing the bond.

Description: A description of the bond. This bond has a coupon yield of 6¾ and matures in 2028.

Current Yield: The annual interest on a $1,000 bond divided by today's closing price for the bond. In this case, 6¾ percent of $1,000 ($67.50) divided by $890 = 7.6 percent.

Volume: The number of $1,000 bonds traded that day.

High: The highest price of the day; in this case, 90 percent of par, or $900 for a $1,000 bond.

Low: The lowest price of the day; in this case, 88 percent of par, or $880 for a $1,000 bond.

Last: The day's closing price; in this case, 89 percent of par, or $890 for a $1,000 bond.

Change: The difference between today's closing price and yesterday's. Since today's closing price of $890 is 3 points higher than it was the previous day, yesterday's closing price must have been 86, or $860.

issue you are considering before you buy. The educated investor can do very well in today's corporate bond market.

And on the topic of learning, education is what you get when you read the fine print; experience is what you get when you don't.

It's a Wrap

- Bonds are forms of debt issued by a corporation.
- In general, corporate bondholders enjoy more safety than corporate stockholders. On the other hand, stockholders may share in unlimited potential profits, whereas the bondholder's return (interest rate) is fixed.
- When interest rates rise, bonds lose value. When interest rates fall, bonds become more attractive.
- Most bonds today are "callable." That means corporations can recall them if interest rates rise. However, it's sometimes possible to purchase "call protection" as insurance against this.

- Bonds offer several types of yields—coupon rate, actual yield, current yield, and yield to maturity—which you should know before purchase.
- Ratings issued by Standard & Poor's, Moody's, and other advisory services can help you to analyze the safety of corporate bonds.

"Seize the moment. Remember all those women on the **Titanic** *who refused dessert?"*

CHAPTER 4

Gold, Silver, and Diamonds—Investment or Enjoyment?

"The golden rule: he who has the gold, rules."

Do I Need to Read This Chapter?

- Am I looking to introduce an entirely different type of asset into my portfolio?

- Does my portfolio include foreign holdings that could be balanced by investment in precious metals and jewels?

- Will gold really shield me in times of upheaval?

- Do I understand the risks involved in buying and holding this type of investment?

- What types of gold investments are available?

- How about silver and diamonds as investment performers?

Gold has been used as money since biblical times. It has several characteristics that have made it desirable as a medium of exchange. Gold is scarce. It is durable. More than 95 percent of all the gold ever mined during the past 5,000 years is still in circulation. And it is inherently valuable because of its beauty and its usefulness in industrial and decorative applications.

It is our fundamental right as Americans to own gold. Unlike many other countries around the world, we are able to hedge and secure our currency by owning a percentage of our savings in gold; and as our national debt explodes to all time highs, this metal emerges as a secure investment against inflation. As of 2007, the United States has a $63 trillion fiscal gap, meaning that the amount is the difference between the country's projected tax receipts and its future expenditures. Gold is one of the few safe-haven investments to protect against unchecked government spending.

The traditional portfolio is invested primarily in traditional financial assets—stocks, bonds, mutual funds, and the like. Adding gold to a portfolio introduces an entirely different type of asset. The point of diversification is to protect the total portfolio against fluctuation in the value of any one particular class of asset. Gold does exactly that. With more American investors seeking opportunities in foreign markets, this form of diversification is particularly applicable. Indeed, gold is an excellent hedge against foreign exchange volatility.

The economic forces that determine the price of gold are different from, and in many cases opposite to, the forces that determine the prices of stocks (equity) and bonds (debt). The value of an equity depends on the earnings and growth potential of the company it represents. The value of the debt security depends on safety, yield, and the yields of competing fixed-income investments.

Remember that phrase by Thoreau about marching to a "different drummer"? Gold is like that, as it doesn't conform to the more predictable patterns of mainstream financial instruments. Investors must be prepared for this.

In short, the value of gold depends on a wide variety of factors: worldwide supply, fabrication demand, central bank sales and purchases, currency movements, political turmoil, and inflationary expectations. The effects of all these factors are somewhat complex and variable. But the important point to remember is simply that they cause the price of gold for the most part to move independently of the prices of financial assets, including stocks and bonds.

Why Is Gold Considered an Investment?

Gold has long been referred to as the "doomsday metal" because of its traditional role as a bulwark against economic, social, and political upheaval and the resulting loss of confidence in other investments, even those guaranteed by national governments. Yet when gold hit an all-time high of $825 on January 21, 1980, and fell only 5 days later to $634 per ounce, people realized that the world wasn't coming to an end.

Let me illustrate. It was wise in the 1970s to hold gold because high interest rates coupled with a high inflation rate could not provide a real rate of return. It is obvious that if you received an interest rate of 17 percent with an inflation rate of 16 percent, your true return would be only 1 percent. Therefore, gold became an investment as a store of value. But as the inflation rate dropped over the years, gold lost much of its appeal. However, between July 1, 2003 and November 30, 2006, the price of gold increased by 85 percent. As of April 2007, its price hovered around $680 per ounce.

Gold is not for the faint of heart or for people who love predictability. Its value can fluctuate daily, owing to economic and political conditions, such as those in the Middle East. When interest rates in the United States fall, the dollar grows weaker in relation to other currencies. As a result, foreign businesspeople find U.S. investment less attractive, and some of them turn to gold instead. This forces the price of gold higher. When interest rates in the United States rise, the reverse can occur.

Why Is Gold Considered Risky?

The value of gold is volatile, and so investing in it carries a definite degree of risk. Any number of events that investors cannot control can influence the price of gold. Many government actions, such as a decision by the U.S. Treasury to sell some of its vast gold holdings, can cause a sharp drop in the price of gold. Even a soaring gold price can carry risks for the investor. If the price of gold becomes prohibitively high, industrial users of the metal may turn to substitutes. This could quickly increase the supply of gold relative to demand and so force the price down. On the other hand, gold could rise because of a sudden demand. For example, if a country has "too many dollars," it may, in the near future, become an active participant in buying gold.

There's one more drawback to investing in gold. Gold is a non-income-producing asset. That is, it earns profits only when it is sold for a price greater than its purchase price. Gold earns no interest while it sits in your vault.

Should you go for gold or rule it out of your portfolio altogether? If you can answer yes to each of these questions, gold may be right for you:

1. Do I have no need of current income?
2. Do I have the time and interest to watch the market and sell my gold at an advantage?
3. Am I prepared to trade off short-term income from other assets in exchange for gold's long-term, but not guaranteed, profit potential? (This is what is known as opportunity cost.) Another sensible test is to look at how you feel about investing in real estate. Gold is a similar investment—it's easy to get into but sometimes difficult to leave.

I personally feel that it takes a lot of "brass" to speculate in gold today. It is not all glitter, because its opportunity cost can be high. If you are more concerned with current income than with future gain, then gold is definitely not the investment for you.

Despite these drawbacks, gold can be considered a good investment for some. During its strong periods, gold has been known to increase in value many times over a short span of weeks or months. And, of course, gold has a strong aesthetic and emotional appeal. Unlike most other investments, gold can serve not only as a source of security for the future, but also as an ornament to be worn today.

What Do the Numbers Mean?

Pure gold is known as *24-karat (24K)* gold. In this form, it is too soft to be made into jewelry. Therefore, it is generally mixed with other metals, such as zinc, copper, nickel, or silver, for additional strength. The number of karats marked on an item of jewelry indicates the ratio of gold to other metals contained in the piece. The higher the karat rating, the more gold the item contains (and the higher in price it is likely to be). For example, using 24K as pure gold, 18K gold contains 18 parts pure gold and 6 parts other metals (24 − 18); 14K gold contains 14 parts gold and 10 parts other metals (24 − 14), which means that 14K jewelry is only 58 percent gold.

What Are the Options for Investing in Gold?

See Table 4.1 for an overview of the types of gold investments in the following discussion.

Table 4.1 Types of Gold Investments

	Bullion	Coins	Shares and Funds	Certificates
Who should invest?	Conservative investors prepared to hold large amounts of gold for years	Conservative investors who wish to own small amounts of gold	Aggressive investors	Conservative investors, particularly those interested in buying at regular intervals
Where to purchase?	Large banks, coin dealers, stockbrokers	Most banks, stockbrokers, coin dealers	Stock brokers, financial planners, by mail from no-load and low-load funds	Brokers and large banks
What is the smallest investment?	Tiny bars weighing 1 gram (0.032 ounce); more typically, 1 ounce	0.1-ounce coin, more typically 1 ounce	The price of one share of an individual company	$250 in systematic buying programs that let you subsequently invest as little as $100 a month
Advantages	Low markup on large bars (2 to 3 %)	Ease of buying and selling; portability	Maximum gains when gold prices rise; possible dividend income; no storage costs; diversification and professional management in funds; ease of buying and selling	Low dealer markup (3 to 3.5 %)

Continued

Table 4.1 Types of Gold Investments—cont'd

	Bullion	**Coins**	**Shares and Funds**	**Certificates**
Disadvantages	Cost of storage (usually in a bank vault) and insurance; high cost of selling	Higher markup than on bars based on minting charges; cost of storage and insurance	Maximum losses when gold prices fall; risk of loss if a mine becomes unprofitable or because of political unrest (as in, say, South Africa)	Annual storage fee

Gold bullion. When you buy gold bullion (that from Engelhard and from Johnson-Matthey is the most widely traded), you are buying gold in the form of bars that are 99.9 percent pure gold. You can actually take physical possession of the gold bars, or you can buy gold through a bank or broker that stores the gold in its own secure facilities. Although you can buy as little as an ounce of gold bullion, a minimum of 10 ounces is usually required, with a kilo bar (32.15 ounces) being the standard. When you buy gold bullion from metal brokers, you must pay certain charges (2 to 4 percent over the spot price) apart from the ounce-for-ounce value of the gold. In addition, some banks may charge a storage fee as high as 1 percent of its value per month for holding your gold.

You may choose to have gold bullion stored by a bank or broker. There's nothing wrong with that, but you must make certain that it is in a totally "nonfungible" storage program. This means that your gold is not combined with the assets of others but rather held separately and labeled with your name. Under such an arrangement, you have legal title to the gold, and it cannot be considered part of the assets of the bank or dealer which could be tied up by creditors in case of a liquidation.

Gold coins. Coins are a popular form for the purchase of gold. They are not only valuable but attractive, and since they are small and portable, they can be kept in a safe in your home or in any bank vault. Most gold coins are minted to weigh 1 ounce, but some weighing as little as 0.1 ounce are available. Expect to pay between 4 and 17 percent beyond the value of the gold to cover the expense of minting and retailing coins.

Gold stocks. These are shares in companies whose business is gold mining. The purchase of gold stocks is a way of betting on the future price of gold without actually dealing in the metal itself. Owning gold stocks has some advantages over owning gold directly. Securities are more liquid than the metal, and no assaying or storage costs are involved. However, shares in gold-mining companies are "leveraged instruments." That is, the value of the stock is affected disproportionately by the value of the product being sold. When the value of gold rises, the value of the stock rises even faster; when the value of the gold falls, the value of gold stocks falls faster and farther. In addition, most gold stocks pay no dividends; when the gold originates in a foreign country, it may be subject to international risks.

Gold certificates. If you want to buy a small amount of gold (minimum $2,500) and do not want to take delivery, certain banks and brokers will allow you to make a purchase and receive a certificate of ownership rather than the gold itself. In essence, you are buying title to gold held at a bank or broker on your behalf. A yearly fee of about ½ percent is usually charged. The main advantage of this way of buying gold is that you do not need to have the gold assayed when you decide to sell it. This makes your assets more liquid.

What Is the Relation between Gold and Silver?

Is *silver* (the poor person's gold) a better investment as a precious metal? Whereas gold's primary role is monetary, silver's is industrial. Silver has many more commercial uses than gold, and its value has outshined gold. From July 2003 to December 2006, the price of silver increased by more than 200 percent, over twice the increase of gold for the same period.

How Do You Purchase Silver for Investment Purposes?

As with gold, there are several ways to buy silver. One way is to buy junk silver, which consists of a bag of pre-1965 U.S. dimes, quarters, or half dollars with a face value of $1,000 and a market value based on the price of silver for the day. Silver bullion is available in 1,000-ounce bars, while silver certificates are receipts for the purchase of silver, held at a bank in your name. Like gold certificates, silver certificates have the advantage of being highly liquid and posing no storage or security problems, so your investment will remain intact.

How Do Diamonds Compare with Gold in Today's Economy?

A diamond, it has been said, is nothing more than a piece of coal that under pressure made good. As an investment, it has a great deal in common with gold. Both gold and diamonds tend to be costly in terms of brokers' fees and sales markups, but each offers the investor safety as a hedge against inflation. But diamonds are also a good hedge against depression. Have you noticed what happens when you give a diamond to a depressed spouse?

For people with substantial wealth who wish to concentrate a lot of that wealth in a small space, diamonds can be a sound investment. Unlike gold, diamonds don't demand continual monitoring of a highly volatile market; diamond prices don't fluctuate widely.

How Do You Purchase Diamonds?

If you do decide to buy diamonds as an investment, regard it as a long-term proposal, not a get-rich-quick scheme. Buy gems weighing from 1 to 3 carats and have them evaluated by an appraiser from the Gemological Institute of America. Since the certification will state the "four Cs" (color, cut, clarity, and carat), it is easy to determine the stone's fair price by consulting a grading table.

Color refers to how white or yellow a diamond is. The color of a diamond is rated alphabetically from D to Z. The closer a diamond is to the D grade, the whiter its color and the more valuable the stone. *Cut* refers to the shape of the diamond and the skill with which it has been crafted. The brilliance and beauty of a diamond depend largely on how accurately the diamond cutter did his or her job. Note that round diamonds are generally most stable. *Clarity* refers to the number and size of the flaws (or "inclusions") contained in the stone. Diamonds range from internally flawless (F) to imperfect (I-3). *Carat* is the unit of weight for the gem, with 1 carat equaling 200 milligrams ($\frac{1}{142}$ ounce). The value of a diamond increases dramatically as its size increases; a 2-carat stone will usually be worth more than twice as much as a 1-carat stone of comparable quality.

What Are the Major Drawbacks to Investing in Diamonds?

1. Most diamonds appreciate in value less than 8 percent a year.
2. Like gold, diamonds are non-income-producing; no interest or dividends are paid on them.
3. Diamonds are relatively difficult to liquidate.
4. The jewelry value of a diamond is much higher than its investment value because of heavy retail markups, which range from 40 to 300 percent, with 100 percent being the average. A diamond bought from a jeweler for $8,000 is likely to yield only about $4,000 if you decide to sell it to another jeweler later.
5. Diamonds have high storage and insurance costs.
6. About 85 percent of the world's diamond market is controlled by the DeBeers-Central Selling organization, headquartered in London. Therefore, the price of diamonds is dependent on the activities of a single group.

How Would You Summarize Investing in Precious Metals or Gems?

If you want to try your hand at investing in gold, silver, or diamonds, go ahead; if you have educated yourself and follow the market carefully, you may do very well. But most people will probably derive more benefit and happiness from the beauty and sentimental value of gold, silver, and diamond objects than they will from their investment value.

And on the topic of happiness, the reason people find it so hard to be happy is that they always see the past better than it was, the present worse than it is, and the future finer than it will be.

It's a Wrap

- Gold, silver, and diamonds probably have more drawbacks than advantages as investment options for the average, middle-income American.
- Gold is not an automatic bulwark in times of economic and social upheaval.
- Gold and precious metals carry a high "opportunity cost" if the money you invest in them could be diverted to other assets that produce more immediate income.
- There are several ways to invest in gold: bullion, coins, shares and funds, and certificates. Silver, whose primary role is industrial rather than monetary, offers similar investment options.
- Diamonds can be a sound buy for experienced investors. Diamond prices are less volatile than those of precious metals.

"Majority rule only works if you also consider individual rights. You cannot have five wolves and one sheep voting on what to have for dinner."

CHAPTER 5

Money Market Accounts—The Parking Lot

◆◆

"The idea is to make a little money first and then to make a little money last."

Do I Need to Read This Chapter?

- Am I looking for a place to temporarily invest idle cash?

- Do I want a relatively safe investment that usually pays slightly higher yields than bank savings accounts and certificates of deposits (CDs)?

- Am I interested in an account where I can write checks and earn interest?

- Do I understand the major types of money market accounts, including tax-frees?

- Have I considered a money market direct account (MMDA)?

- Are my money market investments insured? Safe?

As far as I am concerned, the money market is nothing more than a parking lot, a temporary area for buying and selling high-yield, short-term instruments of credit. In the money market, securities such as jumbo certificates of deposit and short-term commercial loans are bought and sold. Since these securities carry higher-than-normal interest rates, they make money grow quickly. But they usually require large investments that only wealthy individuals or large institutions can afford. That's where money market funds come in. First made available in 1974, money market funds offer the smaller investor a chance to take advantage of the interest rates prevailing in the money markets by pooling people's money.

How Does a Money Market Account Work?

Money market funds operate by combining many small investors' funds to accumulate the kind of money needed to buy costly money market instruments. Since the instruments purchased by the fund have different maturities, the fund earns interest on a daily basis. Each investor receives his or her share of the interest by means of a regular statement, usually issued monthly. The amount earned on an investment varies continually as the prevalent interest rates in the money market rise and fall.

Money market funds are managed by investment firms and brokerage houses. The management fee is deducted from the fund's earnings, but usually no redemption charges are imposed on the fund. Most firms transact business by mail, so a money market fund headquartered in Illinois, for example, may have shareholders in any of the 50 states. A minimum deposit is required to open a money market account; $1,000 is typical. You can add to your investment at any time, and your funds are completely liquid—you can make withdrawals whenever you wish.

Another important point about this type of investment: because of the liquidity of a money market fund, it is an ideal way to invest idle cash that might otherwise find its way into a low-paying passbook savings account. For example, placing the proceeds from the sale of securities into a money market fund until you've decided upon your next investment venture is a good way of earning continuous higher interest on your money. Certain money market funds are a part of a larger group of other types of funds (known as *family of funds*). The advantage is that keeping your money "in the family" permits you to move it easily from one investment to another as financial conditions change, without ever leaving the "group."

How Do I Start?

If money markets seem right for you, the first step is to decide which category is most suitable. Money market funds can be broken into three categories based upon the type of instruments in which the funds invest:

1. *General money market funds.* These invest primarily in nongovernmental securities, such as bank certificates of deposit, commercial loans, and banker's acceptances. Of the three types of funds, general money market funds usually pay the highest interest rates.

2. *Government-only money market funds.* These invest only in securities issued by the U.S. government or by a federal agency. Such funds boast a somewhat higher degree of safety than the general money market funds, but they pay a little less.

3. *Tax-free money market funds.* These purchase only short-term, tax-exempt municipal bonds and are especially suitable for investors in high tax brackets. Although this type of money market fund is exempt from federal tax, it could still be subject to state and local income taxes since most states do not exempt taxes on municipals issued out of state. If you reside in a high-income-tax state, search out those municipal money market funds that purchase investments only within your state of residency. For example, a fund may obtain only New York securities so that all the income earned will be "triple tax free" to New York investors.

How Do Money Markets Issued by Banks Work?

Banks entered the money market field in 1982 with their version of the money market fund: the *money market deposit account.* The MMDA was authorized by Congress in order to stem the $200 billion tide of withdrawals that banks claimed had been lured away by money market funds.

The MMDA is similar in many ways to the money market fund. It too is based on the pooling concept, allowing small investors to earn interest rates otherwise reserved for the large institutional investors or wealthy individuals.

Like a money market fund, an MMDA initially requires a minimum deposit as well as a minimum balance. However, as of 1986, federal regulations no longer mandated a minimum MMDA balance. Thus banks became free to enforce a minimum balance rule at their discretion, so don't blame the government if your bank requires a high minimum balance.

Finally, as with a money market fund, an MMDA is a good way to invest cash for a short period.

What Are the Major Differences between the Money Market Fund and the MMDA?

When you invest in a money market fund, you become a shareholder in the fund. You and the other shareholders receive all the income earned by the fund's investments, less a small management fee (usually about ½ percent annually). When you invest in an MMDA, on the other hand, you are not a shareholder but simply a depositor. Investors in MMDAs do not necessarily receive all the interest generated by their investments, but receive whatever interest rate the bank chooses to pay. Furthermore, the bank is free to invest your money any way it sees fit, even in investments that have little or nothing to do with the money market. Therefore, you have no guarantee that the interest rate you receive will truly reflect the money market rate.

Note, too, the differences in the way the money market funds and the MMDAs usually advertise the interest rates they pay. Money market funds normally advertise the current simple interest rate being earned by the fund. This yield, which is not guaranteed, can change daily as conditions in the money markets change. By contrast, banks often promote MMDAs by advertising the effective yield rate, which is usually a fraction of a point higher than the simple interest rate because of compounding. However, the effective yield rate can be misleading since it assumes that the bank will be giving compound interest on an unchanging interest rate for a full year.

Consider these differences when deciding between money market funds and MMDAs. They can be significant:

1. With an MMDA, you have a person-to-person relationship with a bank officer whom you know, in contrast to the rather anonymous through-the-mail relationship usually offered by the money market funds. For some investors, dealing with a personal banker is psychologically important.
2. The money market fund may be preferable if you plan on making frequent withdrawals from your account. You may be permitted unlimited withdrawals by check from the fund. With an MMDA, there is normally a limit of three checks per month. However, in most banks you can make deposits or withdrawals 24 hours a day by means of the bank's automated teller machines. You cannot do this with the money market fund.
3. With an MMDA, you may lose up to a month's interest if you close out your account anytime within a given month. With a money market fund, this cannot happen because of the daily payments of interest.

Are the Money Market Fund and the MMDA Safe Investments?

As with any form of investment, safety is a factor to consider. Your investment in an MMDA offered by a bank or a savings and loan institution is insured by the federal government up to a maximum of $100,000. If safety is of overriding importance to you, choose an MMDA over a money market fund. However, you should realize that the money market funds have an excellent safety track record. This is because they invest only in short-term instruments issued by such secure institutions as government agencies, large corporations, and major banks. Remember, the shorter the maturity of an investment, the lower the risk. Why is this? If interest rates should rise rapidly, funds holding long-term maturities would find it more difficult to liquidate their low-yielding holdings. Furthermore, the Securities and Exchange Commission regulates money market funds very strictly.

Given their relative safety and numerous advantages, money market funds have earned their place as one of today's most popular options.

And on the topic of safety, it is better to be wounded than always to walk in armor.

It's a Wrap

- Money markets are an excellent place to park your money temporarily—and sometimes for the longer haul.
- The principal you invest in money markets is safe, although not federally insured (unless you are investing in a money market deposit account at a bank).
- Money markets allow you to withdraw your money at any time with no penalty.
- Money markets earn interest rates that reflect current market conditions.

"Every morning in Africa a gazelle wakes up. It knows that it must run faster than a lion or it will be killed. Every morning a lion wakes up. It knows it must outrun the slowest gazelle or it will starve to death. It doesn't matter whether you are a lion or a gazelle—when the sun comes up, you'd better be running."

CHAPTER 6

Mutual Funds—The Basics

◆◆◆◆◆◆◆◆◆◆◆◆◆◆◆◆◆◆◆◆◆◆◆◆◆◆◆◆◆◆◆◆◆

"The things that come to those who wait may be the things left by those who got there first."

Do I Need to Read This Chapter?

- Am I thinking about getting started in mutual funds?

- Is there a way around price fluctuation in the mutual fund arena?

- Do mutual funds have advantages over direct stock purchases?

- What key factors should I examine when evaluating individual funds and families of funds?

- What are the different kinds of stock-based mutual funds?

- What are the different kinds of bond-based mutual funds?

For the past seven years in this new century, we have experienced stock market record-breaking rises and stock market plunges that today are still causing anxiety among investors. If you feel uncertain about the market but would like to take some active part, a mutual fund may be ideal. In 2006, investors added their 10 trillionth dollar to mutual funds up from 3 trillion just 10 years earlier. This country's 80 million baby boomers are coming close to their retirement years, and mutual funds are the most popular investment for savings during retirement.

How Does the Mutual Fund Work?

It begins by having a large number of investors putting their money together in a pool that will be managed by knowledgeable investment professionals. The price of a share in the mutual fund is determined by the value of the fund's holdings. As the value of the stocks owned by the fund increases, the share price increases, and the investors make a profit. If the value of the stocks decreases, the shares are worth less, and investors suffer a loss. The price of a share in a mutual fund (determined by dividing the net value of the fund's assets by the number of shares outstanding) is usually announced once or twice a day. The mutual fund also earns dividends that may be paid directly to investors or reinvested to buy additional shares in the fund.

Therefore, mutual funds can make money for their investors in three distinct ways:

1. The shareholders receive dividends earned through the investment that the fund possesses.
2. If a security in the fund's portfolio is sold at a profit, a capital gains distribution will be made by the fund to its shareholders.
3. If the value of the fund's portfolio increases, the value of each share also increases.

Mutual funds are normally created and managed by brokerage houses. As you'll learn, there are many kinds of mutual funds, depending on the types of stocks invested in, the degree of risk involved, the financial goals of the fund, and other factors.

A way to take care of market fluctuations in the mutual fund arena is through dollar cost averaging (DCA). The investor invests into the mutual fund the same amount of money at regular intervals (monthly, for example). This system allows the investor to purchase more shares when prices are low and fewer shares when prices are high.

What Is Dollar Cost Averaging?

DCA can limit your market risk by investing the same sum of money monthly regardless of any stock fluctuations. As prices fall, your fixed amount of money buys more shares. If prices should rise, your amount would purchase fewer shares. But in the long run, DCA results in your buying more shares at low prices than you do at high prices. This method uses time to the best advantage, since, over time, several market cycles can occur. The best way to understand DCA is to think of it as an installment plan for the investor or as an automatic purchase plan. Arrangements can be made to have this predetermined monthly or quarterly withdrawal come directly from your checking or savings account into the investment of your choice.

Dollar cost averaging sounds ideal, doesn't it? In most ways, it is. However, you should be aware that DCA is not without its problems. If the same amount is invested each month, its inflation-adjusted value will decrease over the years. Also, it does not guarantee that you will protect your investment from losses. If the overall economy and the market are down, you will wind up with a loss for that period of time.

Although dollar cost averaging can work with any investment, it is especially well suited to mutual funds, because funds have a diversified portfolio and can bounce back quickly from declines. Table 6.1 presents an example. For the investment shown, the average price of a share was $11.25. But the investor using the dollar cost averaging method paid only $8.89 on average. This means that the average cost per share was $2.36 less than the average price.

Table 6.1 How Dollar Cost Averaging Pays Off

Month	Regular Investment	Share Price	Shares Acquired
January	$200	$10	20
February	200	5	40
March	200	10	20
April	200	20	10
Total	$800	$45	90

Average share cost: $8.89 ($800/90)
Average share price: $11.25 ($45/4)

Table 6.2 Average Annual Rates of Return

Total Return		Average Annual Rate
3 Years	**5 Years**	
15.76%	27.63%	5%
19.10	33.82	6
22.50	40.26	7
25.97	46.93	8
29.50	53.86	9
33.10	61.05	10
36.76	68.51	11
40.49	76.23	12

One more point on market fluctuations: many funds advertise how high their total return was for a period of time. If you are more interested in knowing the average annual rate of gain rather than the total return, which is the compounded average annual rate, examine Table 6.2.

What Are the Advantages of Mutual Fund Ownership?

Mutual funds offer seven important benefits to prospective stock market investors:

1. *Diversification and risk control.* Money invested in a mutual fund is used to buy shares in many different stock issues. This reduces your investment risk since the failure of one or two companies out of many will not have a devastating effect on your portfolio. It would be impossible for an individual investor to achieve a comparable degree of diversification without having a very large sum to invest in a variety of stocks. Also, with a small investment amount, you will find that by "doing it yourself" your transaction costs (commissions) will be very high because you will be transacting in small dollar amounts. Remember that diversification takes both time and a great deal of knowledge.

2. *Professional management.* Few investors have the time, energy, or expertise to keep track of all the many factors affecting the stock market, including changes in interest rates and the money supply, new developments in technology,

legal and political developments, and foreign competition. Mutual fund companies have the resources to monitor these developments, for they employ staffs of researchers whose sole task is to keep track of business and economic trends that may affect the performance of securities in the fund's portfolio. This expertise works to your benefit when you invest in the fund. And one more point on management and decisions regarding the terms *value* and *growth*. A value approach by fund managers is based on the theory of finding corporations whose underlying values are underappreciated, or in other words, their value is less than what they believe it should be. Sometimes they may purchase bankrupt companies or those in serious financial difficulty if they determine the firm has the potential to gain solvency. They seek to earn their profit if and when the market learns of the new, higher value of the company.

Growth fund managers are interested in revenue and earnings, seeking out those companies that outpace other corporations similar in nature. They want companies that have a potential for large increases in earnings.

3. *Fund-swapping option.* Many investment firms sponsor more than one type of mutual fund. The firms usually allow their investors to move money from one fund to another by means of letters or phone calls. This is a convenient way to take advantage of changing investment conditions. You enjoy definite advantage by investing in a fund that is part of a family of funds. Literally, hundreds of fund families are offered today; entire books, magazines, and newsletters (available at any public library) are devoted to identifying and ranking them.

   • Determine which fund families interest you; then ask for their literature and study their offerings.

   • Pay special attention to the types of stocks each fund invests in, the degree of risk involved, and the financial goals of the fund.

All fund families have the same basic structure: Each is a group of mutual funds with differing investment objectives, managed by the same company. Each allows you to move your money from one fund to another (by written notification, by telephone, or, in some cases, even by Internet access), thus offering you maximum flexibility with a minimum of paperwork and lost time.

4. *Moderate cost.* Many mutual funds require only a small initial investment, with management fees averaging ½ percent of your investment annually. By buying or selling in large blocks, the mutual fund pays a brokerage

commission that is but a fraction of what you, the small investor, might have to pay. Also, certain types of securities should be bought only in large amounts. For example, Treasury bonds produce the best prices on trades of $1 million or higher—far more than most of us can afford—but such trades are no problem for the mutual fund. For more information, see the discussion of load and no-load funds in Chapter 7.

5. *Automatic deposits and reinvestments.* You can usually arrange for automatic investments to be made in your mutual fund account by specifying a dollar amount to be withdrawn from your bank account on a regular basis. This provides a painless way of building your investment portfolio month by month. Also, you can have all dividends, interest, and capital gains earned by your investment automatically reinvested in additional shares in the fund, another painless way of keeping your investment growing.

 Some funds may charge a high fee for reinvesting dividends. Make certain that your monthly statement says that the offer is at "net asset value" and not that the reinvestment of the dividend was at the "offering price."

6. *Ease of withdrawal.* You can withdraw your funds by means of a letter authorizing the redemption of shares. You'll normally receive your money within seven days.

7. *Reduction of record keeping.* The fund handles all stock transactions for you, records any changes in your holdings, and provides periodic statements showing all transactions, dividend distributions, reinvestments, and capital gains.

Please note that I said "*reduction* of record keeping," not elimination of it. Yes, mutual fund ownership requires some paperwork on your part. If you do not identify the specific shares you are selling, the rule of "first in, first out" applies, meaning that the basis of the shares you are turning in will be considered to be the ones that you own for the longest period of time. This can be a major drawback since the early shares are often the lowest priced. Thus your taxable profit will be higher. Therefore, always keep a detailed record of how many shares you buy, the date of each purchase, and the cost per share. This also includes any dividend reinvestment.

What Are the Different Types of Mutual Funds?

Depending on your financial circumstances and your investment objectives, there are many types of mutual funds from which to choose. Let's consider the features of the most common types of funds: common-stock funds and bond funds.

Common-Stock Funds

Many funds invest in common stocks issued by corporations. Stock funds are often classified as either growth funds (holding riskier stocks that may pay low or no dividends but are expected to rise in value rapidly) or income funds (holding low-risk stocks that pay higher dividends but rise in value slowly). Different types include:

- *Aggressive growth.* Small-company growth funds, sector funds, precious metal funds, and others that seek maximum capital appreciation.

- *Long-term growth.* Funds whose main objective is long-term growth of capital; income is secondary.

- *Global/international.* Funds that invest worldwide, outside the United States only, and single-country funds. It is important to understand the difference between international funds and global funds. International funds invest only in securities of foreign countries, whereas global funds may invest in both foreign countries and the United States. Remember also that all investments involve risk, but to invest in foreign countries adds additional problems. For example, currency fluctuation is a risk in international and global funds that is not felt by other funds. Global and international funds investments are denominated in foreign currencies, and thus the value of the holdings depends on the relative strength of the dollar. A weakening dollar will boost the returns of these funds, while a strengthening dollar will reduce them. Other risks to be considered are political situations, economic instability, less liquidity, and a decreased availability of investment information.

Bond Funds

Bond funds invest in corporate or government bonds. These funds fall into several categories. High-grade bond funds deal in top-rated bonds with a high degree of safety and modest yields. Speculative bond funds deal in somewhat riskier bonds (with ratings in the high B's) that often pay higher yields. Junk bond funds carry both the greatest degree of risk and the greatest potential yield. And municipal bond funds invest in tax-free bonds issued by state and local governments.

Just as "turnover rate" can tell you a lot about a stock mutual fund, "duration" is a key factor when evaluating a bond mutual fund. *Duration* measures the sensitivity of a fund to interest rate abuses. It is stated in years and forecasts the up or down movement of the market value of the fund resulting from a 1 percent shift in interest rates. Naturally, the shorter the duration, the less volatile the fund's value.

For example, in a short-term fund, the duration may be 2 years, which would mean that a 1 percent rise in interest rates would cut the market value of the mutual fund by 2 percent (1 percent × 2 years). A long-term fund with a duration of 10 years would lose 10 percent in value if rates rose by 1 percent.

The concept is to think of duration as a multiplier rather than a time frame. In the long-term example, it would take 10 years for the added income to make up for the lost capital. Ask the company or your broker for the duration of its bond fund portfolio.

And on the topic of time, time does not go. Time stays. We go.

It's a Wrap

- Mutual funds may be ideal for investors who want the action of the stock and bond markets without having to choose and monitor individual stocks and bonds themselves.

- With mutual funds, your money has the chance to grow in three ways: through dividends, capital gains, and increase in share value.

- Investments made regularly, known as dollar cost averaging, help you ride out fluctuations in the markets.

- Mutual funds offer an easy way to diversify your money, control risk, and benefit from professional money management at a reasonable cost.

- Computing taxes owed on earnings from mutual funds can be complicated. Always keep detailed records of your purchases.

- There are as many types of stock mutual funds and bond mutual funds as there are stocks and bonds.

"Be careful of the toes you step on today because they may be attached to the backside you may have to kiss tomorrow."

CHAPTER 7

Mutual Funds—
Spreading the Risk

◆◆◆◆◆◆◆◆◆◆◆◆◆◆◆◆◆◆◆◆◆◆◆◆◆◆◆◆◆◆◆◆◆◆◆

"If you risk nothing, you risk everything."

Do I Need to Read This Chapter?

- Do I have a basic knowledge of mutual funds, but want to know more?

- Is my portfolio properly diversified for my age and investment goals?

- Do I understand the difference between load and no-load funds?

- How do mutual fund investments affect my taxes?

- Have I been double-taxed on mutual funds without realizing it?

- Am I aware of the best time of year to invest in mutual funds?

- What information can I glean from the daily mutual fund listing in the newspapers?

How Do You Choose a Mutual Fund?

In order to choose a mutual fund that is best for you, consider these factors:

1. *Past performance.* It is more likely that a fund with a good performance record will repeat its good record than that a company with a poor performance will turn itself around.

2. *Expenses.* The less a fund takes out of your payments (management fees, commissions, etc.), the better off you will be since more money is being invested on your behalf.

3. *Risk.* Risk comes in two forms. The first type of risk is the possibility that rising interest rates will bring down the value of the bond. As you are aware, higher interest rates have a direct reverse effect on fixed-rate securities such as bonds. Thus, short-term bond funds are less risky than intermediate- or long-term bond funds. The second area of risk involves credit risk—the risk that the issuer of the bonds will not pay. Funds that invest in government securities are therefore considered very safe.

4. *Management.* Good management is, of course, essential for profit. Look at the portfolio turnover of your funds (turnover rate is explored further at the end of the chapter). This will tell you how often a manager sells the instruments in the fund and buys new ones. Remember that the more the selling and buying, the more commissions that have to be paid. Also to be considered with respect to high portfolio turnover is that the manager may be buying instruments, not on their merits, but rather in anticipation of short swings in the market. This is a situation that is risky and may not work in the long run.

5. *Your goals.* Did you buy the fund for your child's education? For retirement? The goal you set up will determine the type of mutual fund you will want to purchase. Thus a time horizon is very important for your financial decision making, as you may need the money in 8 years (short term) for your child's education but in 25 years (long term) for your retirement. For a long period, up-front load is not as important as a large annual maintenance charge.

 One of the great things about mutual funds is the diversification opportunities they offer. And the key to diversification, in turn, is to assess your investment needs by age and family situation. As your needs change over time, so do the types of funds that are best for you:

1. When you are young, growth funds are usually best. Your financial needs are often modest, and you can afford to take a higher risk in exchange for maximum growth potential.

Continued

2. As you and your family grow older, diversification among various types of funds is desirable. Both stock funds and bond funds belong in your portfolio in middle age. For maximum diversity, try a five-prong approach: domestic and international stock funds, domestic and international bond funds, and money market funds. In this way you enjoy the potential benefits of three types of financial instruments—stocks, bonds, and cash—in both domestic (United States) and global markets.
3. When you are nearing retirement age, current income becomes paramount. Bond funds are probably your best choice at this point.
4. Investors of any age who find themselves in a high tax bracket should consider one of the tax-free funds that invest in municipal bonds or other tax-free investment. This type of investment can be free of federal, state, and/or local taxes.

What Are the Costs of Owning a Mutual Fund?

Depending on how they are purchased, mutual funds can be classified as either load or no-load funds. Let's look at the difference.

There are people who use self-service gas pumps, and there are those who prefer service; the same goes for mutual funds. If you are not certain about your current income needs, your risk involvement, or the price fluctuations of market investments, or if you simply don't have the time to be "involved," then the load fund is for you.

Shares in a *load fund* are sold through a stockbroker, who charges a sales commission that is a percentage of the purchase price (this is the *front load*). This commission—about three-quarters of which is kept by your individual broker while the balance goes to the sponsor of the fund—is deducted from your account before any investment is made. If you deposit $10,000 in a mutual fund that charges a load of 3 percent, only $9,700 will actually be invested in the fund. Depending on the performance of the fund, it could take several months or more for you to recoup the $300 commission. However, if you plan to remain in the fund for a number of years, the initial sales charge will become relatively unimportant over time. An annual management fee of about ½ percent of your investment is usually also charged.

What does your commission fee pay for? Primarily you are paying for the advice and services provided by your broker. As an investment professional, he or she should help you select the best fund or funds for your purposes and should keep you continually informed about when you should move in or out of a particular instrument. If your broker doesn't provide this kind of expert advice, consider changing brokers; after all, you're paying for it.

No-load funds are usually sold through the mail by means of advertisements in newspapers or magazines. No sales advice or investment services are offered with a no-load fund because no sales broker is involved, as shares are bought directly from the funds and not a broker; therefore, no up-front commission must be paid. However, a service charge is levied each year; and in addition, you may have to pay an exit or redemption fee (back-end load) when you withdraw from the fund.

No-load funds are allowed to have these fees because of a little-known regulation. In 1980, the Securities and Exchange Commission (SEC) added rule 12b-1 to the Investment Company Act, permitting mutual funds to charge shareholders for the cost of getting more assets into the fund. In other words, a fund could charge the investor for advertising, sales literature, and brokers' commissions on new fund sales. Fund managers felt that they were justified in charging these fees since, in the long run, fundholders would benefit as operating costs were spread over more assets. Thus expense ratios would go down, and all would benefit. What is considered an equitable expense ratio? A rule of thumb might be that no more than 1 percent annually for stocks and ¾ percent annually for bonds should be charged.

In the past, funds could hide these 12b-1 costs by scattering them throughout the entire prospectus (a booklet containing information to help evaluate the investment being offered), thereby hiding the fund's true costs. In 1989 the SEC enacted new rules that required funds to disclose all fees and expenses in one table near the front of the prospectus. This table must show all expenses (both direct and indirect) paid by the shareholders and must also disclose the cumulative expenses paid on a $100 investment (5 percent return assumed at the end of 1-, 3-, 5-, and 10-year periods).

Transaction Costs

All mutual funds have brokerage costs, which are costs incurred when stocks and bonds are bought and sold. These costs do not appear in any stated expense ratio, and so they are not easily available for investors to compare one fund's expense ratio with another's. Yet the more trading taking place, the higher the cost to the investor. Many reasons are acceptable, to a point, on active trading or higher commissions. The speed of transaction execution is an example. But excessive brokerage commissions on trading can be a red flag. If there is too much activity in the fund, commissions will be abundant. If your fund's entire portfolio changes over a year (100 percent), that is too much trading.

Also, it's almost always better to invest in a mutual fund after the fund makes its distribution, which is usually between September and December. Here's why: Funds buy and sell securities. When profits on trading exceed losses, the difference is passed along to the investor. This is known as a *distribution*, and you will owe tax on it. Thus, before buying any mutual fund during the last quarter of the year, ask when the next payout will be, and get an estimate of its per-share value. As a rule of thumb, if it is more than 5 percent of the net asset value (NAV), wait until after the payout to buy.

What Information Is Available?

Each newspaper that carries daily information about the value of mutual funds may list data in different ways. Figure 7.1 is a standard reading of mutual funds as listed in the financial section of your newspaper.

Figure 7.1 Sample Mutual Fund Listing

Name	NAV	BUY	CHANGE
Fund p	12.60	13.18	+.12
Fund r	6.18	7.15	−.15
Fund t	18.01	18.02	+.21
Fund x	11.14	N.L.	−.05

Explanations

NAV (bid): Net asset value per share (in dollars and cents).

BUY (ask): Price paid by investors plus commissions.

CHANGE: Change in NAV from yesterday.

Symbols

p: Fund imposes a 12b-1 charge.

r: Fund imposes a back-end fee (redemption price).

t: Used when both p and r are applied.

x: The fund's NAV has been reduced by a dividend payout.

N.L.: Signifies no front- or back-end load.

Let's look at an example. Yields reported on the same funds may produce different amounts. The yield in an advertisement you read is called the *SEC yield* because it is based on a strict conservative formula devised by the SEC and can be the only rate used for advertising. The problem with this yield is that the figure suggests income you would earn if you were in the fund for a full year and the fund kept paying at its current rate, which may not always be the case. However, some publications may cite the 12-month average yield, which represents the entire fund's income payout per share for the past year divided by the NAV. This method expresses what the fund actually paid to fund-holders over the past 12 months. Thus, think of yields and NAV as opposite sides of a seesaw. The interest income is in the middle and stays the same as long as the fund's holdings do not change. As the NAV goes up, the yield goes down. As the NAV goes down, the fund's yield from that same amount of income goes up.

It's easy to let your eyes glaze over when you study mutual fund literature. It's also easy—too easy—to concentrate on the fund's past performance, which cannot be guaranteed for the future. Here's an alternative technique that the pros use: pay special attention to the "turnover rate" when evaluating a mutual fund. It speaks volumes about the fund's management and philosophy.

The *turnover rate* refers to the dollar amount of stock the fund buys or sells in each year, calculated as a percentage of the average value of its stock holdings. A perfect 100 percent means that within a year, the management has turned over the entire value of its portfolio. That shows an extremely aggressive policy. A 25 percent turnover rate indicates a much more conservative, buy-and-hold concept. However, bear in mind that a high rate does not necessarily mean a bad policy or a low rate a good one; but in the long run, I would steer toward the lower turnover rate. Thus, turnover can yield information about very active fund managers (who are making profits for the fund or just churning the accounts) or inactive managers (who are steady in their investment policy or just sleeping at the helm of leadership).

And on the topic of information, I have noticed that when a person with money meets a person with experience, the person with the experience gets the money and the person with the money gets the experience.

It's a Wrap

- Factors such as past performance, expenses, risk, management, and your own financial goals can help you make your mutual fund choices.

- Your age and lifestyle can help you build a portfolio suited to current income and future growth.

- Load and no-load mutual funds are available.

- It is generally advantageous to buy a mutual fund after its distribution, which is usually made in the last quarter of the year.

"Anger is only a letter short of danger."

CHAPTER 8

Stock Market—Bulls, Bears, and Pigs

◆◆

"I made a killing in the market bust of 2001. I shot my broker."

Do I Need to Read This Chapter?

- Am I interested in buying stocks, but hesitant to begin?

- Exactly what happens when I buy or sell a stock?

- What's the difference between common and preferred stocks?

- Have I weighed the advantages and disadvantages of stock ownership?

- Can I buy stocks directly from a company without using a broker?

Just prior to October 19, 1987, everyone was witnessing a major surge in the stock market. Money was being made everywhere, and the golden bubble of prosperity just grew and grew. Then came the inevitable burst in 1987, again in 1989, and again with the big bang of high-tech stocks in 2001–2002. It is said that bulls can make money and bears can make money, but pigs get slaughtered. And that is exactly what happened.

There's no doubt that investing in the stock market can be one of the most exciting ways of making money. Nothing quite compares with the thrill of seeing the little-known stock you picked become a hot property, perhaps doubling in price—and then doubling again and again. Microsoft, Google, and many of the other high-tech stocks are good examples. But as with any investment, the potential risks are equal to the rewards. Enron and WorldCom show the negative potential of stocks as well as the greed of their CEOs, Ken Lay (Enron) and Bernie Ebbers (WorldCom). Therefore, middle-income investors who want to play the market owe it to themselves to become fully informed before getting involved. This chapter should be only the beginning of a continuing process of education for anyone interested in becoming a successful stock market investor.

Never forget that whenever you buy a stock, there is someone selling it. You may buy the stock because you believe that the investment is good and the price will rise. However, the person selling that same stock may believe the opposite, so only one of you will be correct. Think of it in these terms, and you will become a more realistic and conservative player.

How Does the Stock Market Work?

A share of stock represents a unit of ownership in a corporation. When you buy stock, you become a part owner of the business. Therefore, you benefit from any increase in the value of the corporation, and you suffer when the corporation performs badly. You're also entitled to share in the profits earned by the corporation.

Stocks are bought and sold in marketplaces known as stock exchanges. The exchange itself does not buy or sell stock, nor does it set the price of stock; the exchange is simply a forum in which individuals and institutions may trade in stocks. Stock exchanges play a vital role in a capitalist economy. They provide a way for individuals to purchase shares in thousands of businesses, and they provide businesses with an important source of capital for expansion, growth, and research/development.

The New York Stock Exchange (NYSE) is both the best-known and the largest exchange (over 1,300 members). Only members may trade shares on a stock exchange, and only individuals may become members, although a member may be a partner or an officer in a brokerage firm (known as a *member firm*). To become a member, you must buy a membership, or "seat," from another member or from an estate. The price of a seat varies greatly depending on the volume of business being transacted, from a low of $35,000 to well over $1 million in the past years.

Most brokerage firms own seats on an exchange, with one of the firm's officers designated as a member. In their role as brokers, members carry out clients' orders to buy or sell certificates on the floor of the exchange. In communication with other exchange members, brokers can carry out buy-and-sell transactions right on the exchange floor. Current sale prices on each stock being traded are constantly updated and made available to all members. Thus the exchange operates as a kind of auction market for the trading of securities.

How Does an Investor Purchase Stock?

Here, in two steps, is what happens when an investor decides to buy or sell a particular stock. First, an account executive at the brokerage house receives the buy or sell order, which may take any of several forms:

Round-lot order. An order to buy or sell 100 shares, considered the standard trading unit

Odd-lot order. An order to buy or sell fewer than 100 shares

Market order. An order to buy or sell at the best available price

Limit order. An order to buy or sell at a specified price

Stop order. An order designated to protect profits or limit losses by calling for sale of the stock when its price falls to a specified level

Good till canceled (GTC) order. An order that remains open until it is executed or canceled by the investor

Second, after the order is received, it is sent to the floor of the stock exchange. The brokerage firm's floor broker receives the order and executes it at the appropriate trading post. Confirmation of the transaction is reported back to the account executive at the local office, who notifies the investor. Remarkably, the entire process may take as little as two or three minutes.

Not all stocks are traded on the organized exchanges. Those that are not are traded "over the counter" in the so-called unorganized exchange. Not a physical place, this unorganized exchange consists of thousands of brokers and dealers who trade in about 50,000 different unlisted stocks through telephone or telegraph communication. A computer system, known as the National Association of Securities Dealers Automated Quotations (Nasdaq), is used to provide instant bid and ask prices on stocks.

Figure 8.1 Sample OTC Stock Listing

STOCK	BID	ASK	BID CHANGE
EILEEN	7.25	8	+.50

Stock: The abbreviated name of the issuing company.

Bid: This is the price at which dealers are willing to buy the stock—in this case, $7.25 per share.

Ask: This is the price at which dealers are willing to sell the stock; it is always higher than the bid price. In this case, it is $8 per share.

Bid Change: This is the difference between the bid price today and the bid price at the close of the previous day. Since today's bid price is up .50 from the previous day's close, the bid price yesterday was $6.75 per share.

In the over-the-counter market, transactions are negotiated privately rather than on an auction basis. An investor wishing to purchase a particular unlisted security consults a broker, who contacts other brokers dealing in that stock. The broker offering the stock for sale at the lowest price receives the offer.

Prices of over-the-counter stocks are quoted as both bid and ask prices. The bid price is the final price offered by a buyer, while the ask price is the final price requested by a seller. Trades are normally made when the bid and ask prices approach one another. (See Figure 8.1.)

What Kinds of Stocks Are Available?

There are two kinds of stocks: common and preferred.

Common Stock

Each year, hundreds of new issues of stock, known as *initial public offerings (IPOs)*, are sold to the public. Although human life ends at the hands of the undertaker, it begins for common stock at the hands of the underwriter, who sells the stock, at a fixed price, to a group of initial buyers, who in turn "farm out" the investment until it reaches the "street," which is you, the investor.

Don't Forget IPOs have their fans and detractors. If you're anxious to make big money on an IPO, then the letters stand for *immediate profit opportunity*. If you're a skeptic, the acronym has only one meaning—*it's probably overpriced.*

A share of common stock represents a unit of ownership, or equity, in the issuing corporation. Each share of common stock usually has a par value, which is a more or less arbitrary value established in the corporation's charter and which bears little relation to the stock's actual market value. The market value is influenced by many factors, including the corporation's potential earning power, its financial condition, its earnings record, its record for paying dividends, and general business conditions.

Ownership of a share of common stock carries certain privileges:

1. *A share in earnings.* Each year, the board of directors of the corporation meets to determine the amount of the corporation's earnings that will be distributed to stockholders. This distribution, known as the *dividend*, will vary depending on the company's current profitability. It may be omitted altogether if the company is earning no current profits or if the board elects to plow back profits into the business.

2. *A share in control.* Holders of common stock have the right to vote on matters of corporate policy on the basis of one vote per share held. However, the small investor with only a few shares of stock has little or no practical influence on corporate decisions.

3. *A claim on assets.* In the event of the company's liquidation, holders of common stock have the right to share in the firm's assets after all debts and prior claims have been satisfied.

There are four main categories of common stock, each of which is best for a particular investment strategy and purpose:

1. *Blue chip stocks.* High-grade, or blue chip, stocks are issued by well-established corporations with many years of proven success, earnings growth, and consistent dividend payments. Blue chip stocks tend to be relatively high priced and offer a relatively low-income yield. They are a relatively safe investment.

2. *Income stocks.* Income stocks pay a higher-than-average return on investment. They are generally issued by firms in stable businesses that have no need to reinvest a large percentage of profits each year.

3. *Growth stocks.* Issued by firms expected to grow rapidly during the years to come, growth stocks have a current income that is often low, since the company plows back most of its earnings into research and expansion. However, the value of the stock may rise quickly if the company performs up to expectations.

4. *Speculative stocks.* Speculative stocks are backed by no proven corporate track record or lengthy dividend history. Stocks issued by little-known companies or newly formed corporations, high-flying "glamour" stocks issued by companies in new business areas, and low-priced "penny stocks" may all be considered speculative stocks. As with any speculative investment, there is a possibility of tremendous profit but a substantial risk of losing all as well. The good news is that a speculative stock cannot fall below zero, so the most you can lose is everything.

Preferred Stock

Preferred stock, like common stock, represents ownership of a share in a corporation. However, holders of preferred stock have a prior claim on the company's earnings as compared with holders of common stock—hence the name *preferred stock*. Similarly, holders of preferred stock have a prior claim in the company's assets in the event of a liquidation, but they have no voting privileges.

Preferred stock also has certain distinctive features related to dividend payments. A fixed, prespecified annual dividend is usually paid for each share of preferred stock. This fixed dividend may be expressed in dollars (for example, $10 per share) or as a percentage of the stock's par value. It must be paid before dividends are issued to holders of common stock.

However, preferred stock dividends are not considered a debt of the corporation, unlike, for example, the interest due on corporate bonds, because the firm is not obligated to meet its dividend payments. If the corporation is losing money, the board of directors may decide to withhold the dividend payment for a given year. To protect stockholders against undue losses, most preferred stock is issued with a cumulative feature. If a dividend is not paid on cumulative preferred stock, the amount is carried over to the following period, and both current and past unpaid dividends must be paid before holders of common stock can receive any dividend.

More and more investors are considering dividend reinvestment plans (DRIPs), which are direct stock-purchase plans. You might say DRIPs are getting splashier all the time. Like any form of stock ownership, they have pros and cons:

1. DRIPs allow you to purchase shares of a company without any brokerage commission. How? You are buying *directly* from the company, not through a stockbroker.

2. With traditional dividend reinvestment plans, you had to purchase your first shares through a stockbroker before purchasing additional shares directly from the company. Today's DRIPs allow you to buy your first share, and all following shares, directly.

3. Getting into DRIPs is simple, as seen by the ever-increasing number of companies that offer them.

4. However, getting out of DRIPs is another story. You may have to pay a fee to terminate your DRIP as well as tackle the tedious task of attempting to figure your cost basis of shares you have acquired at various different prices.

What Are the Advantages and Disadvantages of Stocks?

Like any other investment, stocks have distinct advantages and disadvantages. Some of these should already have become apparent. Let's take a systematic look at them. First, the advantages of investing in stocks:

1. *Growth potential.* When a company has the potential for growth in value and earnings, so does its stock. If you pick the right stock or group of stocks, you can profit significantly and relatively quickly. History shows that, as a whole, the stock market has had an upward trend in values, with years of gain outnumbering those of decline by better than 3 to 1.

2. *Liquidity.* Stocks traded on the major exchanges can be bought and sold quickly and easily at readily ascertainable prices.

3. *Possible tax benefits.* Growth stocks, which pay low or no dividends so that company profits can be reinvested, provide an effective tax shelter. As the corporation's value grows, so does the value of the stock, which is a form of tax-deferred income since no taxes need be paid on these gains until the stock is sold.

Now the disadvantages:

1. *Risk.* There can be no guarantee of making money by investing in stocks. Companies may fail, stock prices may drop, and you may lose your investment. Remember the saying of one concerned investor: "I am not so concerned with the return *on* my investment as I am with the return *of* my investment."

2. *Brokerage commissions.* Most investors need the help and advice of a stock-broker when they become involved in the market. However, high broker commissions can largely erode profits. Since one fee is charged when you buy stocks and another when you sell them, you are, in effect, forced to pay twice. Unusually well-informed investors should look into the use of a discount broker, who provides little or no investment counseling but charges reduced commissions when trading stocks.

3. *Complexity.* The stock market is complicated, and the amount of knowledge needed to be consistently successful is tremendous. Investors who lack the patience, time, or skill to inform themselves about the market often buy and sell on impulse, thereby minimizing their profits and maximizing their losses. If you get into the stock market, be prepared to devote the time and work necessary to make intelligent decisions instead of haphazard ones.

And on the topic of stocks, what keeps most people out of the stock market is the supermarket.

It's a Wrap

- Playing the stock market requires attention, concentration, and good information. (For more on the latter, please see the next chapter.)
- There are four types of common stock: blue chip, income, growth, and speculative stocks.
- Preferred stocks confer certain advantages in regard to earnings and dividend payments.
- Stocks offer growth potential, liquidity, and possible tax benefits.
- Stocks also involve commission payments and risk.
- Dividend reinvestment plans allow you to buy stock directly from issuers, thus bypassing brokers and their commissions.

"If you always tell the truth, you will never have to remember what you said."

CHAPTER 9

Stock Market Information—Where to Get It

◆◆

"It's not the bulls and the bears on Wall Street that make you lose money; it's the bum steers."

Do I Need to Read This Chapter?

- Am I eager to jump into the stock market, but feel a little short on general preparations?

- Am I totally clear on "P/E," "100s," and all the other shorthand notations for stocks in the financial pages?

- Can I identify and analyze the five key indicators in judging a stock's value?

- Do I understand the key stock market indexes?

- Have I developed the thick skin and commonsense attitude required to play the market?

Now that you know the basic characteristics of the different kinds of stocks, let's take a look at some of the things you should know to get started in stock market investing. People will spend 5 to 10 hours in comparison shopping for a television that cost $300 but will put $5,000 into a stock after a 5-minute phone call from a broker. The next time you want to buy a stock, spend time learning about the market and its offerings. Pretend you are shopping for a TV. Remember this advice: "Buy on rumor. Sell on news." Facts are your most important asset.

How Do You Learn about Investing in the Stock Market?

An investor's most important tool is information: information about stock prices, movement in the market, and likely business trends. Without plenty of sound information, investment decisions are pure guesswork. The first place to look for information about any stock is the financial pages of your newspaper, and the best place to start is with the columns listing the current stock prices on one or more of the major organized exchanges. Figure 9.1 provides

Figure 9.1 A Sample Stock Page

HIGH (1)	LOW (1)	STOCK (2)	DIV (3)	P/E (4)	100S (5)	HIGH (6)	LOW (6)	LAST (7)	CHANGE (8)
44	16	EWS	2.50	9	69	35.25	34	35	+.50

1. **High and Low**. These are the highest and lowest prices paid for the stock during the previous year (over 52 weeks). This entry shows that the highest price paid for EWS stock during the previous year was $44 per share; the lowest price, $16 per share.

2. **Stock**. Stocks are listed alphabetically by an abbreviated form of the corporate name.

3. **Dividend**. The rate of annual dividend is shown; it is generally an estimate based on the previous quarterly or semiannual payment. This entry shows that EWS is paying an annual dividend of $2.50 per share, or about 7 percent yield (2.50 ÷ 35).

4. **Price/Earnings Ratio**. This is the ratio of the market price of the stock to the annual earnings of the company per share of stock. As you'll learn later, this is an important indicator of corporate success and investor confidence.

5. **Shares Traded**. This is the number of shares sold for the day, expressed in hundreds. In the example shown, 6,900 shares of EWS stock were traded. The figure does not include odd-lot sales. *Note*: If the number in this column is preceded by a "z," it signifies the actual number of shares traded, not hundreds.

6. **High and Low**. These are the highest and lowest prices paid for EWS stock during the trading session (that is, the business day). The highest price paid for EWS stock today was $35.25 per share; the lowest price, $34 per share. Stock prices are shown in dollars and cents.

7. **Closing Price**. This is the final price of EWS stock for the day. In this case, it was $35 per share.

8. **Change**. The difference between the closing price of the stock for this session and the closing price for the previous session. Since EWS stock closed at $35 per share, up 50 cents from the previous close, yesterday's closing price would have been $34.50.

explanations of the information you'll find in those columns and what it means for you as a prospective investor. It shows a typical listing for a stock traded on one of the major exchanges.

Newspaper listings are useful, but consider them just a starting point for getting information and analyzing the value of a particular stock. Prudent would-be investors should also consult a corporation's annual report, newspaper and magazine articles about the business, stock market newsletters, and columnists' comments. And the advice of your broker can also be helpful.

What Statistics Should You Know to Evaluate Stocks?

The following statistics are the "big five" when it comes to judging the value of a stock's offering:

1. Earnings per share
2. Book value
3. Price/earnings (P/E) ratio
4. Yield
5. Rate of return

These are the building blocks, so let's examine them one by one:

1. *Earnings per share.* The current earnings-per-share figure is one basic measure of the success of a corporation. It is computed by taking the corporation's net profit after taxes, subtracting any preferred-stock dividends, and dividing the remainder by the number of outstanding shares of common stock. For example, suppose MASTCA Corporation earned a net profit of $4,300,000 last year, paid a dividend on preferred stock of $300,000, and has 800,000 outstanding shares of common stock. The earnings per share for the corporation are $5:

$4,300,000	Net profit after taxes
− 300,000	Dividend on preferred stock
$4,000,000	
÷ 800,000	Outstanding shares of common stock
= $5	Earnings per share

2. *Book value.* This is one measure of the value of the assets of the corporation. It is computed by taking the value of the assets, subtracting amounts due to creditors and preferred stockholders, and dividing the remainder by the number of outstanding shares of common stock. To take another simple example, suppose MASTCA Corporation owns assets valued at $30 million, has debts totaling $10 million, and has 800,000 shares of common stock outstanding. The book value of MASTCA Corporation is $25 per share.

$30,000,000	Assets
−10,000,000	Debts and value of preferred stock
$20,000,000	
÷ 800,000	Outstanding shares of common stock
= $25	Book value per share

3. *Price/earnings (P/E) ratio.* This important index allows you to compare the market price of the stock to its demonstrated earning power. A low P/E ratio—say, under 7—shows that the company has high earnings relative to the current market price of its stock and suggests that the market has undervalued the stock. The stock is probably a good buy at its current price. Stocks with low price/earnings ratios can reward you in two ways:

- If they're undervalued, their prices should eventually go up.
- If the market as a whole slumps, they may not sink as much.

　　For cautious investors, stocks with a low P/E ratio make sense. A host of different studies have shown that, as a group, such stocks perform better, over the years, than a group with medium or high P/E ratios. Conversely, a high P/E ratio (15 or more) shows that the market expects large future gains from the company and has therefore driven up the price of the stock. The P/E ratio is computed by dividing the stock's market price by the company's earnings per share. If a company's stock is selling at $35 per share and the company has earnings of $3 per share, the P/E ratio is 35 ÷ 3, or 11.6, which is a bit lower than the average P/E ratio of 13.

4. *Yield.* This figure offers another indication of how reasonable the current price of a stock is. It is a percentage determined by dividing the current annual dividend per share by the current market price of a share. If a corporation is paying an annual dividend of $2.50 per share and the stock is selling at $35 per share, then the yield is 2.50 ÷ 35, or about 7.1 percent.

5. *Rate of return.* The rate of return on a given stock is a measure of the total profit you gain from holding that stock for a specified period of time.

Computing the rate of return involves several steps. First, find the total market value of your stock at the end of the period in question. Add to this figure the total amount of dividends earned by the stock during the period. Divide this sum by the total market value of the stock at the start of the period. Subtract 1, and multiply by 100. The resulting figure, expressed as a percentage, is your rate of return for the period.

Here's an example. Suppose you bought 100 shares of stock at $24 per share. You've held the stock for one year. The stock paid a $2-per-share dividend during the course of the year. At the end of the year, it has a market value of $25 per share. The rate of return for this stock is 12.5 percent, calculated in this way:

$2,500	Market value of stock at end of period
+ 200	Dividend paid during period
$,2,700	
÷2,400	Market value of stock at start of period
1.125	

$$1.125 - 1.0 = .125 \times 100 = 12.5\% \text{ rate of return}$$

What Are Stock Market Indicators?

It has been said that the stock market is a "leading" indicator, meaning that stock prices reflect expectations of future growth and profits. The market is not designed to show current conditions. Most market indexes will move in tandem, but there is a considerable difference in their performances in the long run. The reason is that the indexes are composed of different stocks. Below is a list of three of the most widely accepted stock market indexes and the types of stocks they include.

1. *Dow Jones Industrial Average (DJIA)*. In attempts to gauge or predict large-scale trends in stock market values, the Dow Jones Industrial Average is most often cited. The most frequently mentioned of four Dow Jones averages (covering industrial stocks, transportation stocks, utility stocks, and a composite average), the DJIA is a barometer of stock market trends based on prices of 30 large U.S. corporations listed on the NYSE. Every day, the fluctuations in the prices of these stocks are combined by adding up the prices of the 30 stocks and dividing the result by a designated factor of 0.3 (used to compensate for complicating situations, such as stock splits and

Table 9.1 DJIA Stocks, May 2007

Alcoa Inc	(AA)	Home Depot Inc	(HD)	Altria Group Inc	(MO)
Amer Intl Group Inc	(AIG)	Honeywell Intl Inc	(HON)	Merck Co Inc	(MRK)
Amer Express Inc	(AXP)	Hewlett-Packard	(HWQ)	Microsoft CP	(MSFT)
Boeing Co	(BA)	Intl Business Machines	(IBM)	Pfizer Inc	(PFE)
Citigroup Inc	(C)	Intel Cp	(INTC)	Procter & Gamble	(PG)
Caterpillar Inc	(CAT)	Johnson & Johnson DC	(JNJ)	AT & T Inc	(T)
Du Pont E I DE NEM	(DD)	J.P. Morgan Chase Co	(JPM)	United Tech	(UTX)
Walt Disney	(DIS)	Coca Cola Co	(KO)	Verizon Commun	(VZ)
General Electric Co	(GE)	McDonald's CP	(MCD)	Wal-Mart Stores	(WMT)
General Motors	(GM)	3M Company	(MMM)	Exxon Mobil CP	(XOM)

periodic substitutions in the list of stocks used). The 30 stocks that made up the DJIA during 2006 are shown in Table 9.1.

2. *Standard & Poor's Composite Index.* This index, better known as the S&P 500, began in 1957 and is presently one of the 12 leading economic indicators. Although the DJIA is much older than the S&P, many investors believe that the S&P better measures the performance of blue chip stocks because of its broad base of 500 stocks (compared with the DJIA's 30). These 500 stocks, which are traded on the New York and American Stock Exchanges and on the over-the-counter (OTC) market, are in turn broken up into subindexes (400 industrial, 40 public utilities, 40 financial companies, and 20 transportation companies) so that a broad base is represented. Unlike the DJIA, which measures the returns of a small sector of the stock market, the S&P 500 measures the performance of many relatively smaller stocks as well as the blue chip ones. Investors mistakenly think that this index would be composed of the 500 largest traded companies, but that is not the case. There is a committee of eight who hold a monthly meeting to decide which corporations stay and which ones go. Whereas the DJIA simply adds up the current day's prices of its 30 stocks in its index and begins its calculations from that total, the S&P is weighted by market value (number of shares multiplied by price). Thus each stock can influence the result in proportion to its market value. Another point is that the DJIA moves more dramatically than the S&P 500. In a broad market move, the S&P usually moves 1 point for every 7 points lost or gained by the DJIA.

3. *Nasdaq Composite.* This index, begun in 1971 by the National Association of Securities Dealers, traces thousands of stocks traded on Nasdaq (formally, the National Association of Securities Dealers Automated Quotations). Like the S&P 500, the index is market weighted so that the larger stocks will influence the index more than the smaller ones.

In summary, the only way to approach the stock market is with good, old-fashioned common sense:

1. *Avoid hot tips.* If a friend or your brother knows about a hot tip, so do hundreds of other people. Remember, hot tips can get you burned.

2. *Don't fall in love.* Don't get married to a stock even if it's your employer's stock that you have accumulated over the years. Weed out those stocks that are not meeting your objectives, even if it's the first stock you ever bought.

3. *Compare your portfolio.* Check on your total return by adding up the stock's price change and dividends for a specific period and then dividing the total by the price at the start of that period. Multiply the result by 100. This will give you a percentage, which is a fair comparison to other types of investments. Remember that with stocks you own; with bonds you lend.

4. *Have a bit of patience.* Except for wild speculation, take your time. Sell, not on the basis of the stock's performance over a short period of time, but rather on the concept of the long run. Remember that the longer the holding period, the more likely you will gain a profit in spite of the inevitable interim ups and downs. On the buy side, the same rule applies. Don't get bullied into purchasing something that "can't wait." Good investments can wait.

5. When stocks fall, they are cheaper, and it may be the time to buy, not sell. When stocks have increased and are high, it may be the time to sell. Don't let fear (stocks falling) and greed (stocks rising) make your decision for you.

6. Stock market terms in a falling market (taken with a grain of salt):
   P/E ratio. The percentage of investors wetting their pants as the market keeps crashing.
   Broker. Poorer than you were last year.
   "Buy, buy". What you said to your money in 2002.
   Standard & Poor. Your life in a nutshell.
   Market correction. The day after you buy stocks.
   Cash flow. The movement your money makes as it disappears down the toilet.
   Futures. If you trade this too much, you won't have one.

It is true that there is no way to tell where the market will be a year or two from now, but by keeping informed, you stand a better chance in this roller-coaster market we are now experiencing.

And on the topic of the market, did you know that Wall Street is a place where the day begins with good buys?

It's a Wrap

- Successful stock investments are based on sound information, not hot tips or guesswork.
- The five key indicators in judging a stock's value are earnings per share, book value, price/earnings ratio, yield, and rate of return.
- The three leading market indexes—the Dow Jones Industrial Average, Standard & Poor's Composite Index, and the Nasdaq Composite—attempt to measure the strength and direction of the U.S. stock market.

"By the time we make it, we have had it."

CHAPTER 10

Zero Investment

◆◆◆◆◆◆◆◆◆◆◆◆◆◆◆◆◆◆◆◆◆◆◆◆◆◆◆◆◆◆◆◆◆◆◆◆◆

"Dig a well before you are thirsty."

Do I Need to Read This Chapter?

- Do I need to save money toward a particular life event in the future, such as college tuition for my child?

- Am I aware of zero coupon bonds?

- Can I balance a predictable, long-term investment with a certain degree of risk?

- Am I interested in an investment with tax-deferred features?

I s there an instrument that lets you know exactly how much money you will have at a particular future date (whether it be for your child's education, your retirement, etc.) and, if administered correctly, becomes tax deferred or even tax exempt?

As you will see in the following pages, zero coupon bonds have some definite advantages over other types of long-term investments. They have become a good choice for pension funds and for a child's college savings. They are therefore an ideal investment for those of you who are more concerned about "outcome" than "income."

How Does the Zero Coupon Bond Work?

Bonds are debt obligations issued by a corporation or by a federal, state, or local government agency. When you buy a bond (usually at face value), you are buying a promise from the issuing institution to pay the amount of the face value of the bond at maturity. "Zeros" are sold at a price well below the face value. Thus, these bonds are appealing to the small investor because they can be bought for cheaper than ordinary debt obligations. The discount is usually from 50 to 75 percent.

For example, a zero with a face value of $1,000 (at 8 percent) may sell for just $456. You pay $456 today; at the time of maturity—10 years—you can redeem the bond for its full $1,000 face value. The extra $544 paid on redemption is the accumulated 10 years' worth of interest on your $456 investment.

&Don't Forget As the old saying goes, "Good things come to those who wait." If waiting patiently isn't your nature, zero coupon bonds are not a suitable investment for you. They are strictly for the long term. During the life of the zero, you clip no coupons and receive no interest payments (hence the term *zero coupon*). The entire interest payout comes at once—upon redemption.

Table 10.1 shows the price for a $1,000 zero coupon bond under various interest rates and maturity dates. Naturally, the longer the term of the bond and the higher the interest rate, the greater the discount at which the bond is sold. Note that the amounts are rounded to the nearest dollar.

If you're still in your twenties or thirties, you may purchase a big chunk of retirement money very cheaply by buying a long-term zero right now.

Table 10.1 The Cost of a $1,000 Zero Coupon Bond

	Maturity Date and Cost*					
Interest Rate	5 Years	10 Years	15 Years	20 Years	25 Years	30 Years
6%	$744	$544	$412	$307	$228	$170
7%	709	502	356	255	179	127
8%	676	456	308	208	141	95
9%	644	415	267	172	111	71
10%	614	377	231	142	87	54

* Actual price can vary because of availability, fees, and other factors affecting bond prices.

For example, at an 8 percent interest rate, you may buy a zero redeemable at $1,000 in 30 years for under $100. It's hard to imagine a better buy than that.

What Advantages Do Zeros Offer as an Investment?

 Zeros do offer several distinct advantages:

1. Call protection
2. Liquidity
3. Adaptability
4. Special suitability for tuition savings

Let's look at each of these in depth.

1. Zeros have *call protection*, meaning that it is unlikely that they will be called in for early redemption by the issuing company if interest rates should fall. (There'd be no advantage to the corporation in prepaying the interest on zeros unless there were special call provisions in the agreement.) Remember to be certain to find out whether the bond you wish to purchase is callable, and if so, ask about its "yield to call." *Yield to call* means that you will be guaranteed a set return if the bond is called in early. Also, if interest rates in the market should fall, with a conventional bond the interest payments you receive would have to be reinvested at a lower existing rate. You avoid this when you purchase zero coupon bonds because the interest is reinvested at the fixed rate (which was higher than the prevailing rate) at which you purchased them.

2. Zeros also offer *liquidity*. If, for some reason, you need to sell your bond before maturity, you can sell it on the so-called secondary market at the current rate. This may produce a gain or loss, depending upon interest rates at the time of the sale. For example, if interest rates are higher at the time you dispose of the bonds, you will take a loss. However, a lower interest rate will yield you a profit. And speaking about interest rates, another advantage of zeros is that you avoid the roller-coaster ups and downs of interest rates if a bond is kept to maturity. As stated above, the value of a bond will rise if interest rates fall and will drop if interest rates rise. With zero bonds,

no matter how much their value may fluctuate and fall, at maturity the bond will be redeemed at its face value. This gives you the assurance of knowing exactly what you will receive at a certain time in the future.

3. Most important, zeros *adapt* themselves very well to a variety of personal financial plans. Because you know exactly how much money you'll be receiving for your investment and exactly when the payout will occur, you can make long-range plans on the basis of your investment in zeros. Thus, they may become an alternative choice, in some cases, for your individual retirement account.

4. Zero coupon bonds are also an excellent way of saving for your child's college tuition. That just-born baby is certainly a joy today but financially a major cost problem years from now. (Someone has described a baby as making your days shorter, nights longer, bankrolls smaller, the past forgotten, and the future worth living for.) So true. You can invest in zeros that will mature at the time your child is ready for school and, at the same time, greatly reduce the tax bite on the interest if the transaction is done properly. Assume that under the Tax Reform Act only the first $1,700 of your child's unearned income will be taxed at his or her low rate, with the first $850 being exempt (because of the standard deduction). This means that by reporting the interest each year on the child's return, you will get that exemption 18 times (assuming an 18-year bond), for a total of $15,300. However, if the interest were to be reported in one lump sum only (as with some instruments), you would be able to use the $850 exemption only once. Also, by declaring the tax each year, you do not have to concern yourself about having a taxable lump-sum amount come due just when you are about to pay for your child's college tuition. (For more about taxes, see the following section on disadvantages.)

What Are the Disadvantages of the Zero Coupon Bond?

As a wise person once said, "Perfection is not of this earth." This is another way of saying that zero coupon bonds, good as they are, do have their disadvantages.

The degree of risk is one. If the company issuing the bonds is no longer solvent at the time of maturity, you may lose your entire investment. The possibility of default is a serious consideration with bonds of every kind, but the problem is especially significant with zeros. This is because you receive all interest payments at one time, upon maturity, whereas with other types of bonds you receive interest on a regular basis throughout the life of the bond.

A second disadvantage involves the markup that brokers add to the wholesale price of the bonds. The cost to purchase a zero is much higher (in percentage terms) than that of ordinary bonds because of the broker's markup, which is based on face value rather than cost. For example, a $30 commission on an ordinary $1,000 (face value) bond is 3 percent, but on the much smaller price of a zero it would be higher. It is very difficult for an investor to determine what the markup is on zero coupon bonds because the bonds are not sold "net." Brokerage houses buy them at wholesale and resell them to the general public at retail prices. The markup, which is used instead of a sales commission, will increase the price of buying the zero and will reduce the price you get when you resell.

The only way to know whether your broker is charging you a fair price is to shop around. Call other brokerage houses to see what the competition has to offer. Remember that the larger the broker's markup, the more the bond will cost, leaving you with a smaller yield. Also, prices of zeros change every day, so if you are seeking the best rate, do all your shopping on the *same* day in order to compare fairly.

You can minimize the markup disadvantage by comparing what brokers have to say. The way to do that is by asking each of them the following questions:

1. How much will I have to invest in order to get the bond (zero) that I want?
2. How much will that investment be worth at maturity?
3. What is the effective yield to maturity?

The broker who can give the lowest figure for question 1 and the highest figures for questions 2 and 3 will be getting you your money's worth.

As a humorous sidelight, those investors who were hurt in the 2001 market crash felt that people selling stocks are called brokers because after you take their advice, you are.

A third disadvantage involves taxes. Although you receive no cash payments during the life of the zero coupon bond, you are taxed as if you do, because interest on a zero coupon bond must be reported to the IRS each year. After 18 years, a zero bought for $2,000 might grow to $10,000 at maturity. To report the $8,000 interest, you do not take ⅛ of the $8,000 ($444 each year), but instead the interest as it actually accrues. During the first year, a $2,000 investment earning 8 percent would produce approximately $160 in interest. In the second year, your investment would not be $2,000 but $2,160 ($2,000 + $160), and $172.80 would be the interest that year. You do not have to personally compute this every year; you will receive a notice from the issuer or your broker informing you of the amount of interest to report to the IRS. The tax on this "invisible interest," also known as *phantom income*, can be considered a major drawback of zero coupon bonds, because you are forced to pay tax on income you haven't received and will not receive for many years. To avoid this problem, look into *zero coupon municipal bonds*, which are tax free.

Another area of taxes involving zeros is the tax basis of these bonds increasing as interest accrues. If you wait until they mature, there is no problem. But if you sell before the due date, your basis determines capital gain or loss. Many investors fail to add accrued interest to their original investment, thus forcing them to pay higher taxes. This rule applies to corporate zero, strips, and tax-free municipal zeros. Your broker can give you the amount of accrued interest annually so that you can add it to your basic cost.

What Are Zero Coupon Municipal Bonds?

The zero coupon municipal bond performs the same way that a corporate zero coupon bond does except that it is issued by a state or local government agency. Because it is a municipal bond, the interest you earn is exempt from all federal taxes and, in many cases, if the bond is issued within your state, from state and local taxes as well. The amount you receive at maturity is considered tax-free income that has accrued annually from the time of the issuance of the bonds.

You should realize that all bonds have an interest-sensitive basis. That means that when interest rates rise, bond values fall; and when interest rates fall, bond values rise. This can occur because of the lack of regular interest payments. For example, if interest rates should rise, the holder of zeros would not be able to reinvest the interest at the new higher rate. However, if interest rates should take a downward turn, earnings on the zero would continue to be reinvested at the older, higher rate.

Which Type of Zero Is Best for You?

If you're sold on zeros, don't rush out and buy the first one you find. Make your purchasing decision based on the taxable-equivalent yields paid by each type. (*Taxable equivalent* means the amount you have left after all taxes are paid.)

If quality is your primary criterion, the safety of Treasury zeros should be your choice, as there is no risk in a government obligation. If taxes are the prime concern because of your high tax bracket, look at municipal zeros. Although corporate zeros usually pay the highest yield, the market choice is small and the risk may be high.

You should consider the purchase of zero coupon bonds over a fixed rate when you need to have a predetermined amount of money on a certain date and you will not need to touch the instrument before maturity. Zero coupons will also be advantageous to the investor who does not wish to make decisions about reinvesting interest payments twice a year. It is said that you can just let the zero run on automatic pilot and thus avoid the semiannual decision on reinvestment that you would have to make with an interest-bearing bond. Tell your broker when you'd like your bonds to mature, and he or she can let you know when zeros that meet your future needs are available.

And on the topic of the future, today is the tomorrow that yesterday you spent money like there was none.

It's a Wrap

- Zero coupon bonds are extremely well suited to long-term savings, such as tuition needs.
- Zeros are appealing to the small investor because they can be bought far more cheaply than traditional types of bonds.
- Zeros offer the advantages of call protection, liquidity, and adaptability to a variety of personal financial plans.

- The disadvantages of zeros are high initial markup, risk of default by the issuer, and tax complications.
- For those seeking tax-deferred or tax-free investments, zero coupon municipal bonds should be considered.

"The wise person knows everything; the shrewd person everyone."

CHAPTER 11

Ginnie Mae—The Misunderstood Instrument

▶◆◆◆◆◆◆◆◆◆◆◆◆◆◆◆◆◆◆◆◆◆◆◆◆◆◆◆◆◆◆◆◆◆◆◆◆◀

"God gives every bird its food, but does not throw it in the nest."

Do I Need to Read This Chapter?

- Am I looking for an excellent, safe, long-term investment?

- Am I aware of Ginnie Maes? Of Ginnie Mae mutual funds and trust funds?

- Do I understand the relation between Ginnie Maes, current interest rates, and mortgage rates?

- What are Fannie Maes and Freddie Macs? Are they cousins to Ginnie Mae?

If I had to choose the most misunderstood financial instrument from among the many about which I write, I would pick the government-insured mortgage.

What Is a Ginnie Mae?

The Government National Mortgage Association (GNMA) was formed by Congress in 1968 as a branch of the Department of Housing and Urban Development. Its objective was to buy government-insured mortgages, similar to those guaranteed by the Federal Housing Administration (FHA) and the Veterans Administration (VA), from the banks that originally made the loans. By doing this, the GNMA provides the lending institutions with the money to offer additional mortgages.

After buying these FHA and VA mortgages, the GNMA groups them into units of a million dollars or more, known as *pools*. These pools are then sold to investment brokerage houses, with an additional guarantee against default added by the GNMA. The brokers, in turn, sell shares in these units of $25,000 or more. These shares are known as *Ginnie Mae pass-through certificates*. The name *Ginnie Mae* is a fanciful pronunciation of GNMA, and the term *pass-through certificate* comes from the fact that when an investor buys the certificate, the homeowner's mortgage payments are passed through to the investor.

How Does the Ginnie Mae Work?

To explain how the Ginnie Mae works, let's follow one mortgage as it is created with the borrower and ultimately winds up in the hands of the investor. Eileen takes out an FHA mortgage with the Woodridge National Bank. This bank combines about 50 other similar mortgages totaling approximately $1 million and sells these mortgages to the GNMA. This gives the Woodridge Bank its funds back so that it can continue to lend more money. The GNMA can either retain this pool of mortgages or sell it to investors. A brokerage house may purchase the pool, carve it up into smaller units, and sell them to its clients, the general public. It then moves out of the picture, leaving the original lender collecting Eileen's monthly payment and forwarding it to the investing public who just bought the Ginnie Mae. If Eileen should not be able to meet her mortgage payments, the bank will foreclose and the government will make good that portion of the default.

As you can see, the Ginnie Mae is a way of investing in a large pool of government-guaranteed mortgages simply by purchasing a share in the pool.

Are Ginnie Maes Safe?

Ginnie Maes are excellent, safe investments because the GNMA payments on both principal and interest on the mortgage loans are fully guaranteed by the federal government. This guarantee is in addition to the government guarantee that already covers FHA and VA mortgages, and so the degree of risk in Ginnie Maes is as small as you're ever likely to get. However, they are not considered obligations of the United States and are therefore subject to federal, state, and any local taxes.

&Don't Forget   Unlike Treasury bills or savings bonds, Ginnie Maes are not government instruments. The government's only obligation is to back up the promise of the Ginnie Maes to pay. What's going on? Don't worry—nothing shady. A two-step safety net is at work. The first obligation to make payment on Ginnie Maes rests with the financial institution that issues the certificates. The U.S. government is only a guarantor in the unlikely event of default.

How Is Income Paid to the Investor?

Income from Ginnie Maes is paid on a monthly basis. If you own a Ginnie Mae, you'll receive (around the fifteenth of each month) a check representing an installment of the repayment of the mortgages in the pool into which you've bought. A part of each check represents repayment on the principal on the loan; the rest is interest. An enclosed statement will tell you what portion of the check is interest and what portion is principal—something you'll need to know since the interest portion is taxable while the principal payments are not. During the early months of the repayment period, you'll mainly receive interest; later payments include a higher percentage of principal, which may be advantageous at times, but it might present a problem. The continual return of your principal can expose you to what is known as *reinvestment risk*. Normally, during times of falling interest rates, your payments accelerate, meaning that you will get money that will be reinvested at lower rates. Also, some people tend to forget that, with each month's payments they receive, a portion of their principal is included in the total amount. Many times this is ignored, and the total amount is spent as if it were all interest. Remember that when those checks stop coming, there is no principal left.

"No principal left" sounds ominous, doesn't it? Here's where a broker can help. If your broker holds your Ginnie Mae certificates, he or she can move the principal you receive into a cash management account. Thus you can reinvest in the Ginnie Mae when you have accumulated enough principal to do so.

There is a variation of this system by which you can arrange to have the principal remain intact and receive only interest payments. Younger investors may wish to consider this option since it provides for steady payments of interest on a fixed principal, which itself is paid in full at the time when the certificate matures. Older investors—retirees, for example—will probably prefer the usual interest-plus-principal repayment plan since they usually have a greater need for monthly income than for a large lump-sum payment at the end.

There is one major drawback to investing in Ginnie Maes—the impossibility of predicting their yield. The monthly checks you'll receive will vary in size, and the period over which the checks keep coming may vary also. The reason is that no one is certain when the mortgages will be paid in full. As you know, some people take a full 30 years to repay their mortgage loans; others sell their houses and repay the mortgages after only a year or two. Since no one can predict how long the homeowners in a particular pool will take to repay their loans, no one can predict exactly how long the payments will last or how large each monthly payment will be. Therefore, one month you might receive a large check that is an unexpected payoff of principal, but then subsequent checks might be smaller because you will be earning the same rate on a smaller principal.

When Does the Ginnie Mae Mature?

One rule of thumb brokers often cite is that Ginnie Mae mortgage pools are repaid, on the average, within 12 years. This means that if you buy a Ginnie Mae certificate, you can estimate that you'll continue to receive monthly checks for about 12 years, and those checks will be larger in the beginning than near the end since the amount of outstanding debt will be greater at that time. Neither prediction is guaranteed. For example, your certificate may continue to pay monthly checks for 15 years or more, or it may be entirely paid out within 5 to 8 years or less.

Bear in mind that the Ginnie Mae is *not* a financial instrument to speculate with for a short period of time.

When you purchase a Ginnie Mae, you are not involved with "Ginnie" for a quick romance; you are in for a long-term relationship. The reason is that the bid/ask spread on this instrument (the difference between what is paid for the instrument and its selling price) is very costly, and you could lose a great deal on a short-term basis. If something more short term suits your needs, it would probably be more beneficial if you bought a Ginnie Mae mutual fund even if it costs you about a half point in lower yields. At least you will have the confidence of knowing that you can get out at any time.

How Do Current Interest Rates Affect the Ginnie Mae?

Changes in the market interest rate on mortgages play an important role here. The interest rate you'll receive on your Ginnie Mae depends, of course, on the mortgage rate at the time the pool was established. If mortgage rates fall below that figure, it's likely that repayment of your Ginnie Mae will be accelerated. Do you remember those low interest rates of 2004–2006? An acceleration in repayment took place because homeowners who took out higher-interest-rate mortgages were eager to repay their mortgages and refinance their homes at the new, lower rates. So you will get back your money sooner and be forced to reinvest it elsewhere at the new, lower prevailing interest rates.

By contrast, if mortgage interest rates rise, the life of your Ginnie Mae is likely to be prolonged. Homeowners will be content to keep paying the relatively low rate of interest they locked in at the time they took out their mortgages, and you'll continue to receive checks for longer than the average 12-year repayment period.

As you can see, Ginnie Maes are not an ideal investment for those who must be able to predict their future monthly income with absolute certainty. If you can afford to be flexible, you can afford to consider Ginnie Maes.

There is a major secondary market in Ginnie Maes made up of shares in mortgage pools established at some time in the past. Like previously issued bonds, previously issued Ginnie Maes fluctuate in value owing to market conditions. Depending on the age of the certificate, the number of monthly payments that have already been made, and the interest rate considerations, you may be able to buy an older Ginnie Mae certificate at a considerable discount from its face value. A Ginnie Mae quoted at 90 sells for 90 percent of its face value; that is, a $25,000 certificate would cost $22,500.

If you are concerned about taking a loss when selling your Ginnie Mae, consider the following. If the certificate is sold prior to maturity and interest rates rise, your Ginnie Mae would be sold at a loss because it is a fixed-rate instrument. You can avoid any fluctuation by purchasing a Ginnie Mae certificate backed by an adjustable-rate mortgage pool. Since the rate of interest is adjusted on the certificate, the Ginnie Mae should trade at close to its original price.

What Other Factors Should You Know About?

In addition to the quoted price, there are two important factors to consider when you look at previously issued Ginnie Maes: the *pool factor* and the *pool speed*.

The *pool factor* is the percentage of the principal that remains unpaid in a particular mortgage pool. The higher the pool factor, the longer it will probably take for the loan repayments to be completed and the longer you will continue to receive checks. The *pool speed* is the relative speed with which repayment of loans in a particular pool is occurring. This will vary depending on economic conditions, the interest rate at the time the pool was established, and the geographic areas in which the mortgages were issued. If the pool speed is high, your Ginnie Mae checks will probably end fairly soon; if the pool speed is low, they will probably last longer.

Therefore, you can readily understand that for the following reasons, a Ginnie Mae is an investment worth looking into:

1. Your money is backed by the U.S. government even if the borrowers do not meet their obligations.
2. The loans are liquid and may be resold if necessary.

3. There is a monthly cash flow that slows debt repayment to go from borrower to bank, which services you, the investor.

4. You can reinvest your monthly income during periods of higher interest rates.

5. The yields are attractive and higher than those from Treasury obligations. Also, because mortgages compound every month rather than every six months, as with bonds, the yield is higher than what is stated.

How Can the Small Investor Purchase a Ginnie Mae?

Many people can't afford the $25,000 minimum investment required to buy a Ginnie Mae certificate. If you're one of these people, consider buying a unit in a Ginnie Mae mutual or trust fund. These units usually sell for $1,000 and can be bought and sold through brokers. Each fund has its own rules and procedures, as well as its own portfolio of mortgage holdings, which may affect the income you'll receive. When you invest in a Ginnie Mae fund, you may have to pay a sales charge and possibly an annual service or management fee.

How Do Freddie Macs and Fannie Maes Work?

When you investigate Ginnie Maes, you may hear references to two other forms of mortgage-backed securities: Freddie Macs and Fannie Maes.

Freddie Macs

Freddie Macs are issued by the Federal Home Loan Mortgage Corporation (FHLMC) and focus on conventional loans, which it purchases in quantity and then resells. A minimum of $25,000 is needed to invest in Freddie Mac *participation certificates* (PCs). The mortgages in the Freddie Mac pools are usually not government-insured loans, like the FHA and VA mortgages in which the GNMA specializes, but are privately issued, nonguaranteed mortgages. As a consequence, the FHLMC does not absolutely guarantee your investment as the GNMA does; instead, you are guaranteed "timely" payments of interest and "ultimate" repayment of principal. It's possible, then, that you might be kept waiting for some of your money when you invest in a Freddie Mac.

As with most forms of investment, the slightly greater risk with a Freddie Mac is counterbalanced by a higher rate of return—usually ¼ to ½ percent or more. Note also that the market for Freddie Macs is much smaller than that for Ginnie Maes, and so it might take a while to liquidate your holding if and when you decide to sell.

Fannie Maes

Fannie Maes are issued by the Federal National Mortgage Association (FNMA). The FNMA serves the secondary market by buying single and multifamily loans and then reselling them to investors by way of mortgage-backed securities. In most ways, Fannie Maes are similar to Freddie Macs, and as with Ginnie Maes, timely payments of both interest and principal are guaranteed. Unlike Ginnie Maes, which consist of mortgages insured by the FHA or guaranteed by the VA, Fannie Maes may include either government-backed loans or privately insured conventionals. In the latter case, the FNMA (rather than the government) stands behind the debt. If the term *privately insured* sends a chill down your spine, here's some reassurance. Do not overly concern yourself about the safety of either the FNMA or FHLMC, as both organizations are government-chartered companies, and their issues are considered to be "moral obligations" of the government. They also yield slightly higher interest rates than the GNMA.

A Common Disadvantage

The risk faced by an investor in Ginnie Maes, Fannie Maes, or Freddie Macs is not that the homeowners will not make their monthly payments, but just the opposite, that they might pay off their mortgages too rapidly if mortgage rates should fall. This can occur when homeowners sell, refinance, or exchange a high-interest mortgage for a lower-interest one. The trouble for the investor is that there is a sudden infusion of money because a prepayment by a homeowner will cause all interest payments on the mortgage to stop, and this repaid principal will then have to be reinvested, usually at a lower rate.

And on the topic of risk, "A ship in a harbor is safe, but that's not what ships are for."

It's a Wrap

- Ginnie Maes are government-insured mortgages that are pooled and sold in shares or pass-through certificates.

- Ginnie Maes are a good choice if you want an investment that is liquid, usually yields a monthly income, and is backed by the U.S. government.

- Ginnie Maes are not for investors who must predict their future monthly income with absolute certainty.

- Another form of Ginnie Mae investment is a Ginnie Mae mutual fund or trust fund, usually sold in $1,000 units.

- Fannie Maes and Freddie Macs are mortgage-backed securities that offer "timely" payments of interest and "ultimate" repayment of principal, though not necessarily on a fixed schedule.

- A drawback of all three investments is that homeowners often prepay their mortgages ("prepayment risk"). When this happens, it leaves investors uncertain of the maturity date of their investment.

"How old would you be if you didn't know how old you were?"

CHAPTER 12

Municipal Bonds— The Tax-Free Choice

"You work hard all your life to reach a high tax bracket, and then the government goes and lowers it on you."

Do I Need to Read This Chapter?

- Do I want, or need, tax-exempt income?

- Am I prepared to invest a fair amount of money, usually a minimum of $5,000?

- Do I understand the problems of investing in municipal bonds while collecting social security benefits?

- How can I eliminate the risk of buying municipal bonds?

- Do I know how to find the best bond values?

With proposals of new tax reform and the changing of some of the tax code in 2010, the desire for untaxed income has become stronger than ever. Since tax-exempt bonds yield about 85 percent of comparable taxable instruments, the investor in a high tax bracket has a chance to lock in excellent returns.

How Do Municipal Bonds Work?

Today, few local or state governments have on hand the vast sums of money needed to build schools, roads, water and sewer facilities, and other public works. Some towns, cities, and counties are finding it difficult to meet their daily operating expenses. But these social needs won't just disappear. In order to meet these expenses, communities borrow money by issuing vehicles known as municipal bonds (munis), which are tax free. More than 40,000 different governmental units and agencies are currently issuing municipal bonds. They include states, cities, towns, counties, and such agencies as highway departments and housing authorities.

What Types of Municipal Bonds Are Available?

Among the more popular varieties of municipal bonds available are the following:

1. *General obligation (GO) bonds.* These are backed by the full faith and credit of the issuing agency. Interest payments on GO bonds are supported by the taxing authority of the state or city government and are generally considered the safest form of municipal bonds.

2. *Revenue bonds.* These are usually issued by a government agency or commission that has been charged with operating a self-supporting project such as a highway or bridge. The money raised through the sale of revenue bonds goes to finance the project, and the income realized from the completed project (tolls, for example) is used to pay the interest and principal on the bonds.

Revenue bonds pay a slightly higher yield than GO bonds. You can guess why—there's more risk. If the project being financed by the bond should earn insufficient income, bondholders may be the ones left holding the bag. The taxpayers of the community are not responsible. Seems unfair? The fact is that if revenue bonds default, the courts are reluctant to auction off the bankrupt assets so that the bonds can be repaid. Municipal assets are viewed as being vital for the public welfare; thus their sale could place the community in jeopardy.

What Are the Advantages and Disadvantages of Municipal Bonds?

The advantages of municipal bonds are as follows:

1. *Tax exemption.* For the investor, the most important advantage of municipal bonds is the fact that they earn income that is tax free at the federal level. If you live in the state in which the bonds are issued, the bonds are usually free from state and local taxes as well.

2. *Safety.* Municipal bonds have historically been a very safe form of investment since states and cities, with their power of taxation, have normally been able to fully meet their debt obligations.

3. *High collateral value.* It's usually possible to borrow up to 90 percent of the market value of your municipal bonds from such lenders as banks and brokerage houses since municipal bonds are free of certain restrictions imposed by the Federal Reserve Board on the use of other bonds as collateral.

4. *Diversity.* Thousands of different municipal bonds are available to suit the requirements of individual investors.

5. *Marketability.* A large nationwide market for municipal bonds exists, making them easy to sell when necessary.

Despite these advantages, I firmly believe that you should never buy municipal bonds for speculation. Purchase them for the tax-free income they produce and only in anticipation of "what you can get *from* them, not *for* them."

If municipal bonds sound attractive—and there are many reasons they should—you must now do a preliminary "reality check":

1. *Investment.* Are you prepared to make a fairly sizable investment? A minimum of $5,000 is usually required.

2. *Yield.* Is your tax bracket high enough to reap the tax-exempt advantage? Remember, tax-exempt municipal bonds usually carry a lower rate of interest than taxable bonds. If you pay a fairly high tax rate, your tax savings will more than make up for the lower return. Those near the bottom of the tax rate tables, however, may be better off with another type of investment.

Continued

3. *Social security.* Are you collecting social security benefits? You may have a problem with munis, because while the interest you receive from these bonds isn't taxable for federal purposes, it may push your income higher and thus force you to pay federal income tax on up to 85 percent of your social security benefits.

Are Municipals Your Best Investment?

To determine whether or not you should invest in municipal bonds, you must figure out the taxable rate of return equivalent to that paid by tax-exempt municipals. For example, suppose you have a marginal income tax rate of 28 percent, and you are offered a tax-exempt municipal bond paying 6 percent interest.

You can use the following formula to help you determine the equivalent taxable yield (ETY) of any specific municipal bond you may be considering:

$$\frac{\text{Yield on muni}}{1.00 - \text{tax bracket}} = \text{ETY}$$

So:

$$\frac{.06}{1.00 - .28} = \frac{.06}{.72} = .083 \text{ or } 8.3\% \text{ETY}$$

First you take the difference between your marginal tax rate and 100 percent, and then you divide this into the rate paid by the tax-exempt bond. Since your marginal tax rate is 28 percent, the difference between this and 100 percent is 72 percent. Divide 72 percent into 6 percent, and you obtain a result of 8.3 percent. Thus, a tax-exempt interest rate of 6 percent is equivalent to a taxable interest rate of 8.3 percent for someone in the 28 percent tax bracket.

Table 12.1 shows several typical tax-exempt interest rates along with the equivalent taxable yield for investors in various tax brackets. For example, in the above situation, for an investor in the 28 percent tax bracket, a 6 percent tax-exempt yield is equivalent to an 8.3 percent taxable yield.

Table 12.1 Taxable-Equivalent Yields

Tax-Free Yield %	Federal Tax Rates				
	15%	28%	31%	36%	39.6%
3.50	4.12	4.86	5.07	5.47	5.79
3.75	4.41	5.21	5.43	5.86	6.21
4.00	4.71	5.56	5.80	6.25	6.62
4.25	5.00	5.90	6.16	6.64	7.04
4.50	5.29	6.25	6.52	7.03	7.45
4.75	5.59	6.60	6.88	7.42	7.86
5.00	5.88	6.94	7.25	7.81	8.28
5.25	6.18	7.29	7.61	8.20	8.69
5.50	6.47	7.64	7.97	8.59	9.11
5.75	6.76	7.99	8.33	8.98	9.52
6.00	7.06	8.33	8.70	9.38	9.93
6.25	7.35	8.68	9.06	9.77	10.35
6.50	7.65	9.03	9.42	10.16	10.76
6.75	7.94	9.37	9.78	10.55	11.18
7.00	8.24	9.72	10.14	10.94	11.59

This taxable-equivalent yield of 8.3 percent means that you would need a taxable instrument paying almost 9 percent to equal your 6 percent tax-exempt bond. By using this table, you will be able to determine the type of taxable return you would have to receive to exceed the tax-exempt return from your muni. Also, bear in mind that state tax is not considered in this example, so your yield is actually higher than 8.3 percent.

Are Municipals a Risky Investment?

As with any other investment, risk is a factor to consider in purchasing municipal bonds. Like corporate bonds, municipal bonds are rated by two major independent rating services: Moody's and Standard & Poor's. The AAA rating is the highest; the C rating is the lowest. In general, the lower the rating, the higher the yield. However, I don't recommend that you purchase bonds with a rating lower than A, since the slightly higher interest rate you may be offered on the lower-rated bond isn't worth the sacrifice in safety. Also, when financial

Believe it or not, you can virtually eliminate the risk in buying municipal bonds if they are covered by insurance. The secret (which isn't so secret) is to buy bonds that carry a third-party guarantee offered by companies such as the Municipal Bond Insurance Association. If the municipality should fail, the insurer will continue to make timely payments of interest and principal as agreed upon at the time of purchase. In addition, the insurance will add to the liquidity of the investment since potential buyers appreciate the greater safety of the insured bonds.

times are uncertain, investors will look for high-quality bonds even though they do produce a lower yield.

Here's how the insurance concept works. When a municipality issues muni bonds, the city's or state's credit is on the line. If bonds are somewhat lower rated, the municipality must pay higher-than-normal interest on the issued bonds. To save money, it may purchase insurance that guarantees that all payments of principal and interest will be made on time. It thus may appear that the insurance is free to the investor, but that is not true. Since the insurance raises the quality of the municipality's credit, the yield on the bond issued will be lower. And one more point, because the cost/yield difference between an insured and an uninsured bond is narrow, the insurance has become a "good buy."

Can Municipal Bonds Be Called Back?

Callability is a significant factor affecting the value of municipal bonds. Bonds that offer higher interest rates than what is presently being offered are most likely to be called in, because the issuer will want to redeem these costly older bonds and replace them with new ones paying lower yields. And this is so true today. When a bond is callable, it may be redeemed by the issuing agency prior to the maturity date, usually within 10 years after issue, and usually at a premium (2 percent)—$1,020 for each $1,000 face value of the bond. Of course, this places a lid on potential profits, which may be a significant loss to you if interest rates decline greatly after the bond is issued. Look what happened to the drop in interest rates from 2004 to 2006. Many bondholders could have had their higher-yield bonds called back.

Are There Strategies in Purchasing Municipal Bonds?

One method of diversifying a bond portfolio is a technique known as *laddering*. The idea is to purchase bonds maturing in different years. Therefore, if rates have risen when a bond matures, you will be able to reinvest the proceeds into an instrument paying the new high yield. Conversely, if interest rates should fall, a portion of your holdings will still earn interest at the higher (earlier) rates.

How Do You Find the Best Bond Value?

Okay. You're ready to buy municipal bonds. Surprise! Unlike stocks, they are not listed on any exchange, making it that much harder to gauge prices. Follow these guidelines, and you'll be a smart shopper:

1. Get quotes from several brokers before buying bonds. Prices of previously issued bonds vary greatly from dealer to dealer since each sets his or her own profit margin.

2. Be aware that the difference between what the broker pays for the bond (known as the *bid price*) and its selling price (known as the *ask price*) is the *spread*. Brokers don't charge commissions on bond trades, but make their money on the spread, which is quoted in basis points (hundredths of a percentage point).

3. *Remember*: The longer the maturity and the smaller the trade, the wider the spread.

4. Ask the broker what he or she would pay to buy back the bond on the following day. The answer will reveal any hidden charges such as fees and markups.

5. Consider buying new issues only. The issuer pays the dealer's markup on those, and so you'll get the best price no matter where you buy.

Bottom line: Seek out all information before purchasing.

And on the topic of information, the jawbone of an ass is just as dangerous today as it was in Samson's time.

It's a Wrap

- Tax-free municipal bonds can be a good choice for those in the 28 percent tax bracket and above.
- Tax exemption, relative safety, high collateral value, diversity, and marketability make municipal bonds worth considering.
- The downside of tax-free munis is high minimum investment requirements, lower yields, and the fact that they can be recalled by the issuer.
- Municipal bonds are rated from AAA (least risk) to C (most risk). Risk can be reduced by purchasing insured bonds and by laddering (buying bonds that mature in different years).

"Any government big enough to give you everything you want is big enough to take everything you have."

CHAPTER 13

Municipal Trusts and Funds—Tax-Free Alternatives

◆◆◆◆◆◆◆◆◆◆◆◆◆◆◆◆◆◆◆◆◆◆◆◆◆◆◆◆◆◆◆◆◆◆◆◆◆◆

"A government is the only vessel known to leak from the top."

Do I Need to Read This Chapter?

- Am I in a high enough tax bracket to need tax-free alternatives?

- Do I want to know more about municipal bond unit trusts? Municipal bond mutual funds?

- Am I looking to invest in units as low as $1,000?

A t one time, tax-free benefits were available only to the well-to-do because any purchase of municipal bonds under $25,000 was considered an "odd-lot" amount and would cost you extra brokerage commissions (as well as being harder to sell later). Under these conditions, the municipal bond market was strictly a high-priced investor's playground, and the cost of establishing a diversified portfolio of many municipal bonds was extraordinarily high. It was to remedy this situation that the municipal bond unit trust and the municipal bond mutual fund were developed.

What Are Municipal Funds and Trusts?

In some ways, the municipal bond unit trust and the municipal bond mutual fund are similar. Both offer a way for the small investor to buy a portion of a diversified selection of municipal bonds for as little as $1,000. Both offer investments that are free of federal income tax and, in some cases, state and local taxes (if you live in the state in which the bonds were issued). Also, both pay interest on a monthly basis, unlike the municipal bonds themselves, which pay interest only semiannually.

However, there are many differences between the unit trust and the mutual fund. Let's explore these differences so that you can decide which of the two might be worth considering as an investment for you.

How Does the Unit Trust Work?

A municipal bond unit, also known as a *unit investment trust (UIT)*, is established by a sponsor who purchases a substantial share in at least 10, but more often 20 or more, long-term bond issues, usually with maturities ranging from 10 to 30 years. The bonds bought by the trust are left intact and do not change once they have been purchased. Therefore, the yield of the trust remains the same throughout its life span, which has a predetermined length that ends when the bonds in the portfolio mature. When you buy a share in a unit trust, you are buying a portion of this fixed portfolio, and you can predict just how long your investment will last and how much it will pay each year. These units, also called *shares*, trade around $1,000 a unit. However, the exact value is based on what each issue in the portfolio is worth.

Unit trusts come in many types, which vary greatly according to length of maturity, degree of risk, tax-exempt status, and yield:

1. Examine your investment needs carefully to ensure that you choose a trust with the right combination of features for your needs.
2. Decide whether you want to buy your units directly from a sponsoring firm or indirectly through your broker.
3. In my opinion, it pays to work through your broker, who can offer you trusts assembled not only by his or her firm but by other companies as well.

Once all the units in a particular trust have been sold, no more can be issued. You can dispose of your units without incurring a penalty or sales charge by asking your broker or the sponsoring firm to redeem them. In most cases, unit trust sponsors constitute a secondary market for their own units and will guarantee to buy back your units at their current market value. Of course, this may or may not represent the same amount as you originally paid. If interest rates have risen since the trust was assembled, the rate being paid by the trust may no longer be competitive, and the market value of the units will be less than what you paid for them. On the other hand, if interest rates have fallen, you may profit when you sell your shares.

Remember the spread, as first discussed in the previous chapter on tax-free municipal bonds. The concept is the same when you are buying and selling units in a bond trust; you must take into consideration the spread between the bid price and the ask price. The bid price is what the broker pays for the bond; the ask price is the price the broker charges the investor for the same bond. The gap between the two is the broker's profit. It averages about 2 percent of the value of the bond and is expressed in basis points (hundredths of a percentage point). Each point of the spread reduces your yield by $\frac{1}{100}$ of 1 percent and costs you 0.01 percent.

Because the portfolio of a unit trust is basically fixed, managing the trust is very simple. Therefore, a very small management fee is normally charged. However, when you purchase units in the trust, you must pay a commission, which may range from 2 to 5 percent, depending on the company sponsoring the trust, the length of maturity, and other factors.

What would happen if one of the bonds in the trust should run into financial difficulties? Normally, the trustee may decide to sell that specific issue in the trust; however, unlike fund managers, trust managers are not permitted to add any new issues to a portfolio once it has been created. This tends to make trusts slower to respond when a bond's creditworthiness is in doubt. Also bear in mind the risk of early redemption. Many new issues are callable, meaning that the bonds can be called back after a specified period of time. This may occur if interest rates fall by more than 2 percentage points, so beware of high-yield projections. Every trust prospectus must inform you of which bonds in its portfolio are subject to call and their dates of possible callability.

Do you remember our discussion on insurance for munis in the previous chapter? If you're the type of investor who likes some insurance—and assurance—be warned that unit trusts and funds are normally *not* a good value. That's because the trust or fund is formed around many individual units, not just one bond. For example, a trust having 15 bonds that saw one of its bonds lose all its money would suffer a loss of only 6.6 percent. Since the cost of insurance over a 10-year period averages about 3 percent, you can see that you pay an extremely large premium to protect yourself from a minor loss.

How Does the Municipal Fund Work?

A municipal mutual fund is similar to a money market fund: Its shares are highly liquid. Each fund sells or redeems shares at its net asset value (NAV) at any time, with some funds permitting redemption by wire transfer and even allowing investors to move from one fund to another by telephone. Whereas a bond unit trust stands pat with its investments, the managers of a bond fund are constantly trading. Thus the fund as a whole never matures, but goes on indefinitely buying and selling bonds to take advantage of changes in the marketplace. Because of this continuous activity, a higher management fee, compared with that of the trust, is charged, usually about ½ percent annually.

Participation in a bond fund usually requires an initial investment of $1,000. Any time thereafter you can buy additional shares in the fund. You have the option of receiving a check for your monthly earnings or having them automatically reinvested to purchase additional shares in the fund. Whenever you wish, you can sell your shares back to the fund. However, since the value of the bonds in the fund's portfolio fluctuates over time, you may or may not get back your original investment when you sell your shares.

What Are the Basic Differences between the Trust and the Fund?

The differences between the municipal bond trust and the municipal bond mutual fund are summarized in Table 13.1

However, you should be aware of how sensitive municipals are to interest rates. In times of stable interest rates, their after-tax yields are better than

Table 13.1 The Municipal Bond Trust and Fund Compared

Factors	Unit Trust	Mutual Fund
Yield	Fixed	Varies with market conditions
Life of investment	Ends when bonds mature	Unending; constantly changing portfolio
Average maturity of bonds held	10 to 30 years	3 years or less
Purchase	Fixed number of units offered	Shares always available for purchase
Portfolio	Same bonds (15 to 20 issues) held to maturity	100 or more bonds actively managed
Disposal	Units sold through brokers, as with stocks	Shares sold back to fund

those of most investments (for the high-tax-bracket investor); and should interest rates decline, they can add capital gains as well. It is when rates move upward that the bonds may become a problem, because capital losses can occur upon their sale.

Another problem that funds and trusts are currently experiencing involves two distinct areas: (1) the questionable quality of the bonds bought by funds and trusts looking to boost their yields and (2) the threat that bond-rating agencies might lower the grades on many munis because of the ever-growing financial strains that may cripple state and local governments. Therefore, a word of caution. Look toward safety when considering muni funds or trusts, staying only with those that invest at least 90 percent of their portfolio in the bonds rated A or higher. You can get this information from the company's annual report by requesting a copy from your salesperson or by writing the company.

In the Real World... Not sure which is better for you, a unit trust or mutual fund? Follow this rule of thumb: The unit trust is a better choice if you are certain that you want to hold on to the investment for at least 5 years. If you think you may need to liquidate your holdings sooner than that—or if you anticipate shifting to other investments fairly frequently—the mutual fund is preferable. Either investment, however, is a good way for the small to medium-sized investor to get into municipal bonds with a diversified, professionally selected, tax-free portfolio of holdings.

And on the topic of taxes, Form 1040, the tax return we all file, could just as easily have been numbered 1039 or 1041. The IRS has assured the American public that the number 1040 was a random selection. Still, some taxpayers insist it's not a mere coincidence that in Coventry, England, Lady Godiva, covered only by her long hair, rode naked through the streets protesting the high, oppressive taxes imposed by her husband, the Earl of Coventry, in the year 1040.

It's a Wrap

- Municipal bond unit trusts and mutual funds make it possible for the small investor to buy a portion of a diversified selection of municipal bonds for as little as $1,000.

- Municipal bond unit trusts vary greatly in terms of their length of maturity, degree of risk, tax-exempt status, and yield.

- Municipal bond mutual funds are similar to money market funds.

- Insured unit trusts and funds offer poor value, because you must pay a large premium to protect yourself from a minor loss.

- Municipal bond unit trusts are generally preferable to municipal bond mutual funds for those planning to hold the investment for at least 5 years.

- Given the volatility of interest rates and markets, it's wise to stick with muni funds and trusts that invest in bonds rated A or better.

"A fine is a tax for doing wrong. A tax is a fine for doing well."

CHAPTER 14

Treasuries Are a Treasure

◆◆◆◆◆◆◆◆◆◆◆◆◆◆◆◆◆◆◆◆◆◆◆◆◆◆◆◆

"Everybody wants to eat at the government's table, but nobody wants to do the dishes."

Do I Need to Read This Chapter?

- Am I seeking a safe, secure, short-term investment, perhaps as an alternative to a CD?

- Am I aware of the different ways to buy Treasury obligations, including at my bank?

- Would I benefit from direct deposit of interest, discount, and principal payments generated by my Treasury investments?

- Are Treasury bills right for me?

- How about Treasury notes, bonds, and TIPS?

The U.S. Treasury Department has one of the biggest jobs imaginable—providing money for the enormous financial needs of the federal government. No wonder that the laws that are created are called "bills." Much of the money the Treasury raises comes from the sale of securities to the general public and institutional investors. These securities are known as *Treasury obligations* and consist of Treasury bills, notes, and bonds.

In a low-interest economy, many people move away from their traditional certificates of deposit and switch to other investments. If you want a short-term investment, safe and secure, look at the alternative to the CD, the Treasury bill, and its longer-term brother and sister, the Treasury note and bond.

What Is the Best Method of Purchasing Treasury Obligations?

Treasury obligations are tax exempt at the state and local levels and are backed by the "full faith and credit" of the United States. The credit risk involved in this form of investment is considered practically nil. In comparison with similar obligations issued by corporations, Treasury obligations usually pay a yield that is one or two percentage points lower. However, many people are willing to accept the slightly lower yield in exchange for absolute safety. As the saying goes, you can eat well or sleep well, but you can't do both.

Buying Treasury Issues by Direct Purchase

This method has a certain amount of convenience, because you are buying directly from your brokerage house or bank. You will pay a nominal fee, of course, for that convenience. Commercial book entry, available through most financial institutions and brokers, may be most appropriate if you want a third party to manage your account or if you plan to sell your securities prior to maturity. In the commercial book-entry system, your account records are maintained on the books of the third party you select. Interest and maturity payments are made directly to the third party, who disburses the funds to your account.

If you purchase Treasuries from a bank or brokerage house, you are not covered by the government's guarantee because they may not be in your name. However, the bank or brokerage firm will be covered since the assurance reverts to the registered owner. That may not be a problem as long as financial conditions are sound, but if your bank or brokerage firm should develop financial difficulty, you may have a problem in securing your money. Therefore, have your name on the instrument as registered to you if you purchase Treasuries from banks or firms.

Buying Treasury Issues Directly from the Government

In my opinion, the best way to purchase Treasury obligations is directly from the government (without a fee) through any of its 12 Federal Reserve banks or their various branches.

You may buy Treasury securities in person or by mail, by submitting a competitive or a noncompetitive bid. These bids are called *tenders*. Most competitive bids are made by institutional investors, such as commercial banks and brokers, purchasing large amounts of securities. Competitive bidders must specify the percentage yield they are seeking to two decimal points.

When a competitive bid is made, there is a risk of bidding too high and not getting an allotment of the security, since the Treasury usually will accept the lowest bids.

Virtually all individuals submit noncompetitive tenders, which do not require that a yield be specified. These individuals agree to accept the average yield and equivalent price determined by the accepted competitive tenders. Since the Treasury usually accepts all noncompetitive tenders, these bidders do not risk rejection of their bid.

Tenders must be submitted before 12 p.m. on the auction day. Auctions are not open to observers. Auction results are announced by the Treasury in the late afternoon of the auction day and can be found in the financial section of newspapers the next day. Shortly after they are announced by the Treasury, auction results are also available on the Federal Reserve's 24-hour recorded message or on the Web at treasurydirect.gov.

Treasury securities are issued in book-entry form only. Under the Treasury Direct System, you establish an account master record when you submit your first tender form. You may review your account master record at any Federal Reserve bank or branch, or request that a statement of account be mailed to you. It consists of name, address, phone number, Treasury Direct account number, tax information, and payment instructions. It also provides detailed information on all your Treasury securities maintained in the Treasury Direct System. Whenever a change is made to the account information, you will receive a copy of the updated record.

Whenever you purchase a new Treasury security, a statement of account is sent to you, listing the description and price associated with each security and specifying the amount and date of the next interest payment. The statement of account simplifies your record keeping and offers flexibility since changes can be made quickly.

The Treasury Direct System uses the direct-deposit payment method, whereby interest, discount, and principal payments are electronically deposited into your account at the financial institution you designate. Direct deposit reduces the risk of late payments resulting from lost or stolen checks, ensures that scheduled interest or principal payments will be made to the designated financial institution on the payment dates, and allows your funds to earn interest from the payment date if the bank account is interest bearing. However, your first purchase with the Treasury will not follow the preceding scenario. Instead, you will get your discount by check.

Thus, in most cases it is better to go "Treasury Direct" because:

- It is offered *free of charge* at Federal Reserve offices throughout the country.
- It allows all interest and maturity payments to be deposited on time and automatically into an account of your choice through *direct deposit*. Direct deposit eliminates the possibility of destroyed, lost, or stolen checks.
- It provides a *single master account* for all Treasury securities holdings having the same registration, simplifying your record keeping. You are mailed a statement of account after any transaction or change that affects your master account, including reinvestments.
- With it, you have the *option of reinvesting* in other Treasury securities being offered at the same time your current holdings mature.

The concept of Treasury Direct has proved to be quite successful with the investing public, but this system does have certain drawbacks. During this decade, the U.S. Treasury put out new rules to overcome some of the Treasury Direct program's problems:

- The investor is now able to authorize the Treasury to debit his or her account when a security is purchased rather than having to send a check before the auction.
- The investor can reinvest his or her maturing Treasuries by simply making one call to 800-943-6864, which is open 24 hours a day.
- The investor will now need only one form to purchase as many different types of Treasuries as desired instead of having to use a separate form for each different issue.
- The investor can now sell his or her Treasury prior to maturity by going directly through the Chicago Federal Reserve Bank. Under the old ruling, you first had to authorize the Treasury to send your securities to a broker or bank if you wished to sell them before they matured. This procedure could take weeks to complete.

For forms and information, try the Bureau of the Public Debt's Web site (publicdebt.treas.gov).

Beginning in 2006, investors who enrolled in the Treasury Direct program for purchasing securities by mail are now able to buy securities over the Internet.

When you buy a Treasury obligation, you can have its ownership registered in any of four ways:

Single owner. For example, Robert Tollin (social security number 100-10-1000).

Two owners. For example, Robert Tollin (100-10-1000) *and* Heather Tollin (200-20-2000)

Joint tenancy. For example, Robert Tollin (100-10-1000) *or* Heather Tollin (200-20-2000)

Guardian or custodian for a minor. For example, Heather Tollin (200-20-2000), guardian (or custodian) for Robert Tollin, Jr. (300-30-3000). Treasury obligations cannot be registered solely in the name of a minor.

Buying Treasury Issue through the Secondary Market

The third and last method of purchase is to go to the secondary market and buy Treasury issues just as you would any stock or bond. However, this secondary market method does have a hidden transaction cost based on the bid/ask differential (the spread), to which a retail markup may also be added.

If you purchase in the secondary market, you should keep posted on the market value of the Treasury issue. Newspapers carry the Treasury price quotation each day.

What Are Treasury Bills, and How Do They Work?

Treasury bills, like other marketable Treasury securities, are debt obligations of the U.S. government and are backed by the government's full faith and credit. A bill is a short-term investment issued for a year or less. Investors buy bills at a discount from par (or face) value. The difference between the purchase price and what the investor receives at maturity is interest.

For example, a $10,000 bill may be bought at issue for $9,400. In this case, the investor receives $10,000 when the bill matures; therefore, the interest is $600. The interest is determined by the discount rate, which is set when the bill is auctioned.

Like other marketable Treasury securities, bills can be purchased directly from the Treasury. Buying a Treasury bill directly from the Federal Reserve is like one of those recipes that looks complicated but really isn't. Most of the "ingredients" are minor, like salt and pepper. By following these steps, you'll save yourself the brokerage or bank fee:

1. Bring your payment for a T-bill in the denomination you prefer to a branch of the Federal Reserve bank, making certain that it is received prior to 12 p.m. Eastern Standard Time on the day of the auction.

2. The payment must be by cash, a certified personal check, a bank check, or a matured U.S. Treasury note or bond, and it must be for the full face value of the T-bill.

3. When the auction takes place, the interest rate for the bills sold that day is set, and the amount of the discount to which you are entitled is determined accordingly. You are then sent a check (within four banking days of purchase) for the amount of the discount.

4. If no Federal Reserve bank is nearby, you can send for an application by writing either to the Bureau of the Public Debt, Division of Customer Services, or to your local Federal Reserve bank. Request the booklet *Basic Information on Treasury Securities—Treasury Direct.*

5. If you do not have an application, you can send a letter with a certified check and the following information: your name, address, social security number, and daytime phone number; a statement saying that your bill is

noncompetitive; the amount (face value) you wish to purchase; the maturity of the bill; and your account number at your bank (for direct deposit).

Do You Receive a Certificate When You Purchase a T-Bill?

The sale of Treasury bills is recorded in book-entry form, meaning that you will not be sent a certificate. The securities are held through the Federal Reserve records in a Treasury Direct account that will be opened when you purchase the securities. Thereafter, all future Treasury transactions will be entered in that account when an order is placed on the tender form. When the maturity date of the T-bill arrives, you can redeem the bill for its face value. And since you received the interest (in the form of the discount) in advance, the yield is actually higher than the nominal interest rate.

How Is Interest Paid, and What Are the Tax Consequences?

Suppose you buy a $10,000 T-bill with an interest rate set by auction at 6 percent. After paying your $10,000, you'll receive by mail (see the previous discussion of Treasury Direct) a check for the 6 percent discount, or $600. Thus the effective price of the T-bill is just $9,400. Since you've received $600 income in advance on that $9,400 investment, your true yield is 6.4 percent. To summarize:

$$\$10,000 \times .06 = \$600 \qquad \text{Discount sent to you}$$
$$\$10,000 - \$600 = \$9,400 \qquad \text{Net cost}$$
$$\$600 \div 9,400 = 6.4\% \qquad \text{True yield on an annual basis}$$

Also, you can take the $600, invest it somewhere else for the rest of the year, and further increase your income.

For Federal Reserve income tax purposes, the $600 is considered ordinary income to be reported at the time the T-bill matures, not at the time you receive it. For example, if you bought a 1-year T-bill in January 2008, you'd receive your full discount ($600) immediately. However, this amount would not be considered income until January 2009 when the T-bill matures. Therefore, the $600 would not have to be declared for tax purposes, nor taxes paid on it, until as late as April 2010.

 For most of us, state and even local taxes have a tax impact. However, T-bills have no state or local tax. Therefore, beyond the calculation for the true yield of a Treasury bill, you must factor them as well to get the actual yield. In the preceding example, if your state and local tax totaled 7 percent, your true yield would be even higher. To calculate, subtract the tax from 100 percent (100 − 7 = 93). Then divide the remainder into the T-bill's calculated yield (6.4 ÷ 93 = 6.9). Thus the above 6 percent T-bill has an actual yield of 6.9 percent.

What Happens at the Time of Maturity?

When it's time to redeem your T-bill, if you bought it through a bank or a broker, you'll follow the procedure arranged at the time of purchase. If you bought it directly from a Federal Reserve bank, the Treasury Department will make a direct deposit for you into your bank. This procedure smoothes the way for you by having the interest payments and proceeds (when the security matures) automatically deposited into your account at any bank of your choosing.

If for any reason you have to cash in your T-bill before it matures you can now go directly through the Chicago Federal Reserve Bank. The amount of proceeds will vary from day to day because the maturity value of the bill is affected by (1) the interest rates prevailing on the sale date, (2) the number of days remaining before the T-bill matures, and (3) the bank or brokerage fee.

What Are Treasury Notes and Bonds?

Treasury notes, like T-bills, pay interest rates determined by auction. However, they are not sold at a discount. Instead, they pay interest every 6 months at a rate fixed at the time of purchase. In this respect, they resemble corporate bonds.

Treasury notes also have a longer life span than T-bills (up to 10 years from the date of issue) and are offered in multiples of $1,000.

Like corporate bonds, Treasury notes can be bought and sold on the secondary market by both brokers and banks. The U.S. Treasury doesn't buy back Treasury notes, but you can exchange notes of one denomination for those of another. The market price for a Treasury note will fluctuate, depending on changes in interest rates. You can find current prices in the financial pages of your newspaper. However, the actual price you'll pay a broker—or the amount you'll receive when selling your note—will differ from the price shown, because of the broker's fee and the slightly higher cost involved in buying or selling odd-lot amounts (which include purchases of less than $1 million worth of Treasury notes).

In August 2005, the Treasury announced the reintroduction of the 30-year bond and held its first auction of the bond in 5 years in 2006. Bids for the auction can be placed through a broker or financial institution or directly from the Treasury through the Treasury Direct System, in which account holders can place noncompetitive bids for 30-year bonds today.

The 30-year bond now will diversify Treasury's funding options, expand its investor base, and stabilize the average maturity of the public debt. Before the reintroduction of the 30-year bond, the 20-year TIPS was the longest-dated marketable security issued by the Treasury.

The 30-year bond has long been a favorite of fixed-income market participants seeking to match assets to future liabilities, and it serves as an important benchmark by which other long-dated securities are measured. But it is possible to lose on a Treasury obligation. The reason is that Treasury bonds tend to fluctuate in price on the secondary market more than Treasury notes do. Study the following example as an illustration.

Suppose that the $1,000, 30-year Treasury bond you bought last year appears on your statement valued at only $970. What happened to the remaining $30? Nothing really, as you will get back your $1,000 at maturity, and so no risk is involved. But there is a risk on the secondary market (where Treasury obligations are traded) if you decide to sell the bond before it matures in 30 years. The proceeds from the sale are based on the market value of the bond, which depends on the direction of interest rates. When these rates rise, bond prices will tend to decrease. For example, if you bought a 30-year, 6 percent Treasury bond for $1,000 today and in 3 years interest rates should rise to 7 percent, the market value of your T-bond would be less than the $1,000 face value. The reason is that buyers would rather purchase a T-bond with a 7 percent return for the same $1,000 than buy your 6 percent bond.

What Are TIPS?

TIPS don't refer to gratuities. In 1997, the government introduced a new type of Treasury obligation known as the *Treasury Inflation Protection Securities*, or TIPS. They were designed to protect the investor against future inflation. As you are aware, Treasuries are absolutely safe in the face of their value, but during inflationary periods, their value loses ground. Thus, the government came up with TIPS, whose principal is adjusted daily to keep up with increases in the consumer price index (CPI). You can buy TIPS through Treasury Direct, banks, or brokers. TIPS are issued in 5-, 10-, and 20-year maturities, with $1,000 as a minimum purchase and in investment increments of $1,000. TIPS can be held to maturity or sold before maturity. Their interest income and growth in principal are exempt from state and local income tax but are subject to federal income tax. Payments based on the adjusted value are made to the investor twice a year. For example, if inflation becomes 4 percent for the year, the principal value of a $10,000 TIP would rise to $10,400. However, there are always disadvantages. TIPS offer a much lower coupon rate and have a difficult tax computation. The inflation adjustments to the principal are considered taxable income even though you do not receive it annually. You do not get this inflation adjustment in cash, as it is added to the bond's underlying value and paid only when you cash the bond in. Thus you are paying tax on money you have not yet received. TIPS work best for tax-deferred accounts [IRAs, 401(k)s] that can be set up through brokers and employers.

TIPS have a fixed interest rate that is layered on top of their variable rate which follows inflation. For example, if you purchased a $10,000 TIP at an interest rate of 3 percent and during the year it was determined that there occurred a 4 percent inflation rate, the computation would be:

First year: $10,000 × 3% interest = $300

Second year: $10,000 × 4% inflation = $400

$10,400 × 3% interest = $412

This compounding continues over the life of the bond.

&Don't Forget With TIPS, your principal can only be passed upward, never decreased due to deflation.

Where Can I Learn More about Treasury Issues?

For more information about any Treasury obligations, write to the Bureau of the Public Debt, Department A, Washington, DC 20239-1000, and request the Treasury Direct Package. Also, the Department of Treasury Web site (www.ustreas.gov) offers bond-pricing tools for downloading. One example of what's available: The Current Redemption Value tool has you enter the denomination of your bond, its issue date, type of series, and redemption date. It then generates the current redemption value and the amount of interest the bond has accrued.

There is a wealth of information about these instruments.

And on the topic of wealth, it is good to have money and the things that money can buy, but it is also good to check up once in a while and make certain you haven't lost the things that money can't buy.

It's a Wrap

- The federal government raises money by selling securities known as Treasury obligations, available as T-bills, notes, bonds, and TIPS.
- Treasury issues are exempt from state and local taxes and offer virtually no risk.
- Treasury issues can be purchased through commercial banks and brokerage houses, directly from the government, or through the secondary market.
- Treasury Direct offers safe, convenient, direct deposit of interest, discount, and principal payments generated by Treasury investments.

"Yesterday's political promises are today's taxes."

CHAPTER 15

U.S. Savings Bonds— Safety First

◆▬◆◇◆◇◆◇◆◇◆◇◆◇◆◇◆◇◆◇◆◇◆◇◆◇◆◇◆◇◆◇◆◇◆◇◆◇◆▬◆

"Patriotism is not so much protecting the land of our ancestors as preserving the land for our children."

Do I Need to Read This Chapter?

- Am I interested in an affordable, long-term investment with relatively low yields but unmatched safety?

- Do I know about the newer, easier way to buy U.S. bonds?

- Am I aware of changes in how savings bond interest is calculated and credited?

- If I'm buying bonds as a gift for children, do I understand how their tax liability works?

- Am I aware of the pros and cons of savings bonds used for college tuition?

When I was in public school, World War II was under way and the sale of war bonds was very popular. Every adult bought them. Children could purchase, in small amounts, freedom stamps (10 cents or 25 cents) that were then pasted into a "victory book." When this book was filled ($18.75), it was turned in to the bank and exchanged for a savings bond with a face value at maturity of $25. Well, things have certainly changed. Years ago savings bonds were purchased to help our country finance and win World War II, but today they're purchased for completely different reasons.

U.S. savings bonds have been sold by the Treasury for more than 60 years. In that time, these bonds kept their appeal because they are affordable and safe. They also offer certain tax advantages and have changed with the times as the interest rate environment has changed. Savings bonds are intended for investors who want to save for the long term, and yet the bonds are flexible enough for those who must have funds available if needed.

How Do EE Bonds Work?

The EE bond is a nonnegotiable security against the credit of the U.S. Treasury–nonnegotiable because once it is purchased, it cannot be resold to anyone else but may be sold back only to the government at a fixed price. However, you are permitted to transfer the bond, to someone else by using Form PD3360 to register it in the person's name. This form is available at any Federal Reserve district bank.

Series EE bonds are sold at half their face value and are available in denominations of $100, $200, $500, $1,000, $5,000, and $10,000. Thus savings bonds are available for as little as $50, making them a practical choice for the investor with only a minimal amount of money to set aside. Also they:

- Earn a fixed rate of interest and are adjusted each May 1 and November 1, with the new rate effective for all bonds issued in the six months following the adjustment.
- Increase in value every month rather than every six months.
- Have interest that is compounded semiannually and not subject to state and local tax.
- Must be held a minimum of one year, but you can redeem them anytime after that time period.

A 3-month interest penalty is applied to bonds held less than 5 years from the issue date. This rewards longer-term bond holders who benefit from higher 5-year rates over the full life of the bond. For example, if you buy a bond and redeem it 24 months later, you'll get back your original investment and 21 months of interest. The value of the bond would be based on the announced rates applied over the initial 21-month period.

Since Series EE savings bonds are sold at half face value, the Treasury guarantees that new issues of Series EE bonds will double in value by 20 years from

Table 15.1 Original Maturity for Series EE Bonds

Issue Date	Original Term
1/80–10/80	11 years
11/80–4/81	9 years
5/81–10/82	8 years
11/82–10/86	10 years
11/86–2/93	12 years
3/93–4/95	18 years
5/95–5/03	17 years
6/03–present	20 years

the issue date. This is referred to as the original maturity date. Table 15.1 shows the original term for Series EE bonds.

If you are buying a bond as a gift in the form of a paper savings bond and you don't know the social security number of the bond recipient, you may use your own. The social security number printed on the paper savings bond does not establish tax liability or ownership. It is used only to find records if the savings bond is lost, stolen, or destroyed, should the owner not have a record of the serial number.

On paper savings bonds issued or replaced after August 1, 2006, the first five digits of your social security number or employer identification number will be masked and replaced with a series of asterisks. This is being done to protect your privacy and to prevent the information from being used for identity theft.

The annual limit on the amount of Series EE bonds an individual may buy is $15,000 issue price ($30,000 face amount). This limit applies to the amount of bonds that may be purchased in the name of any one person in any one calendar year; it has no effect on cumulative holdings. Purchasing bonds in co-ownership form effectively doubles the limit if neither co-owner has purchased other bonds.

How Do You Purchase Savings Bonds?

The registration on a savings bond (owner's name) is conclusive of ownership. Bonds may be registered in the names of individuals in one of three ways: single ownership, co-ownership, or beneficiary form (see Table 15.2).

Table 15.2 Registering Savings Bonds

Category	Example	Rights
Single ownership	123-45-6789 Steve Gindi	Only the registered owner may cash the bond in. On the death of the owner, the bond becomes part of the owner's estate.
Co-ownership	123-45-6789 Steve Gindi or Dale Gindi	Either may cash the bond without the knowledge or approval of the other. On the death of one co-owner, the other becomes the sole owner of the bond.
Beneficiary	123-45-6789 Steve Gindi P.O.D.* Dale Gindi	Only the owner may cash the bond during his or lifetime. The beneficiary, if he or she survives the owner, automatically becomes the sole owner of the bond when the original owner dies. In order to redeem the bond, the beneficiary must present a certified copy of the registered owner's death certificate.

* Paid on death.

If you use your funds to buy a bond in your name and the name of another person as co-owners, *you* must report tax on the bond interest.

If you buy a bond in the name of another person who is the sole owner of the bond, *the person for whom you bought the bond* must report tax on the bond interest.

If you and another person buy a bond as co-owners, each contributing part of the purchase price, *both you and your co-owner* report tax in proportion to the amount each paid for the bond.

If you and your spouse, who live in a community property state, buy a bond that is community property, and if you file separate returns, *both you and your spouse generally* each report one-half the tax.

Are Bonds Right for Me?

It is undeniable that U.S. savings bonds do not match the rates of other, more competitive financial instruments. However, and especially if interest rates rise, they do provide an acceptable yield along with their unmatched safety—safety not only for their guarantee of principal and interest, but also for their repayment should they be stolen, lost, or destroyed.

If any of these three situations occurs, simply file Form PDF 1048. These bonds can be replaced by notifying the Bureau of the Public Debt, PO Box 7012, Parkersburg, WV 26101-7012.

What Role Do Bonds Play in Plans for College?

About 20 years ago, a new education savings bond program began. Known as the Technical and Miscellaneous Revenue Act of 1988 (TAMRA'88), it permitted qualified taxpayers to exclude from their gross income all or a part of the interest earned on savings bonds bought after that date. This tax-free income (federal, state, and local) is permitted if the proceeds of the bonds are used only for a child's college fees, which do not include room, board, or books. This program sounds great, but is it? Not really—because the conditions that must be met are quite numerous and will, in essence, disallow this tax loophole for most people. Read on and see if you qualify.

In order to get this tax-free income, the following conditions must prevail:

- Qualified higher education expenses must be incurred during the same tax year in which the bonds are redeemed.

- You must be at least 24 years old on the first day of the month in which you bought the bond(s).

- When using bonds for your child's education, the bonds must be registered in your name and/or your spouse's name. Your child can be listed as a beneficiary on the bond, but not as a co-owner.

- When using bonds for your own education, the bonds must be registered in your name.

- If you're married, you must file a joint return to qualify for the exclusion.

- You must meet certain income requirements.

- Your postsecondary institution must qualify for the program by being a college, university, or vocational school that meets the standards for federal assistance (such as guaranteed student loan programs).

Qualified Expenses

Qualified educational expenses include:

- Tuition and fees (such as lab fees and other required course expenses)
- Expenses that benefit you, your spouse, or a dependent for which you claim an exemption
- Expenses paid for any course required as part of a degree or certificate-granting program
- Expenses paid for sports, games, or hobbies—but only if part of a degree or certificate program

Note: The costs of books or room and board are not qualified expenses.

The amount of qualified expenses is reduced by the amount of any scholarships, fellowships, employer-provided educational assistance, and other forms of tuition reduction.

You must use both the principal and interest from the bonds to pay qualified expenses to exclude the interest from your gross income. If the amount of eligible bonds you've cashed during the year exceeds the amount of qualified educational expenses paid during the year, the amount of excludable interest is reduced pro rata. For example, assuming bond proceeds equal $10,000 ($8,000 principal and $2,000 interest) and the qualified educational expenses are $8,000, you could exclude 80 percent of the interest earned, (.80 × 2,000=$1,600), which would equal $1,600.

Income Limitations

The full interest exclusion is only available to married couples filing joint returns and to single filers. Modified adjusted gross income includes the interest earned under a certain limit in each case. These income limits apply in the year you use bonds for educational purposes, not the year you buy the bonds. Exclusion benefits are phased out for joint or single filers with a modified adjusted gross income that exceeds the limit. For the tax year 2006, for single taxpayers, the tax exclusion begins to be reduced with a $63,100 modified adjusted gross income and is eliminated for adjusted gross incomes of $78,100 and above. For married taxpayers filing jointly, the tax exclusion begins to be reduced with a $94,700 modified adjusted gross income and is eliminated for adjusted gross incomes of $124,700 and above. Married couples must file jointly to be eligible for the exclusion.

Another Education Savings Option

Aside from the Education Tax Exclusion, there is another way to use savings bonds to pay for your children's education expenses. Interest income on bonds purchased in a child's name alone or with a parent as beneficiary (not co-owner) can be included in the child's income each year as it accrues or can be deferred until the bonds are redeemed. In either case, the child will be subject to any federal income tax on the interest.

Parents may file a federal income tax return in the child's name and social security number, reporting the total accrued interest on all bonds registered to the child. The intention to report savings bond interest annually, i.e., on an accrual basis, must be noted on the return. The decision to report accrued interest annually applies to all future years.

No tax will be due unless the child has a total income in a single year equal to the threshold amount that requires a return to be filed, and no further returns need to be filed until that annual income level has been reached. For children under the age of 18, unearned income over a specified threshold amount for that age group will be taxed at the parent's rate. If the child is age 18 or older, income will be taxed at the child's rate.

With this approach, the tax liability on the bond interest is determined on an annual basis so that when the bonds are redeemed, only the current year's accrual will be subject to federal income tax. Make sure you keep complete records when using this system.

 &Don't Forget It is wonderful to give our children a financial future, but sometimes we are so anxious to give our children what we didn't have that we forget to give them what we did have.

Series I U.S. Savings Bonds

A Series I bond (the *I* stands for *inflation*) is an appreciation-type savings security issued after August 1998 that is a contract between the owner and the

United States. Under the contract, the owner lends money to the United States, and the United States must repay that money with interest when the bond is redeemed. You can cash Series I bonds anytime after 12 months. The interest stops accruing 30 years after issue. Interest accumulates monthly (with semiannual compounding) and is paid when the bond is redeemed. Interest earnings are inflation indexed. The I bond earnings rate is a combination of two separate rates: a fixed rate of return (set by the Treasury Department) and a variable semiannual inflation rate (based on changes in the nonseasonally adjusted consumer price index for all consumers).

A social security number (SSN) is needed to buy a bond. However, if you're buying a gift and don't know the recipient's SSN, you can use your own. Using your SSN doesn't mean you will have the tax liability when the bond is cashed. The bond owner will be asked to provide his or her social security number for tax purposes when cashing the bond. You can purchase I bonds in paper from a financial institution or in electronic format (Treasury Direct) (see Table 15.3),

Buying I Bonds through Treasury Direct

- Purchased at face value in amounts of $25 or more to the penny.
- $30,000 maximum purchase in one calendar year.
- Issued electronically to your designated account.

Table 15.3 Where to Buy I Bonds

Treasury Direct	This is the easiest, fastest way to buy electronic I bonds. No paper bonds are issued. You have access to your account 24 hours a day, 7 days a week.
	You can set up an automatic purchase schedule of as little as $25 a month.
Banks and other financial institutions	The bond is printed to your instructions and mailed to you within 15 business days. Your bond's issue date reflects the date of purchase so that no interest is lost.
Internet banking systems	You can purchase paper bonds through online account access with many local financial institutions. See if a financial institution in your area offers this service.
Payroll savings plan	You can buy I bonds through the payroll savings plan. Payroll for paper savings bonds and payroll electronic bonds are available.

Buying Paper I Bonds

- Purchased in denominations of $50, $75, $100, $200, $500, $1,000, $5,000, and $10,000.

- $30,000 maximum purchase in one calendar year.

- Issued as paper bond certificates.

- If you redeem I bonds within the first 5 years, you will forfeit the 3 most recent month's interest. There is no penalty on redemption after holding them over 5 years.

How I Bonds Have Done in This Century

I bond rates consist of two parts: an inflation rate that is adjusted every six months and a fixed rate that stays the same for the life of the bond. Here's a look at fixed rates for I bonds issued since 2000:

Date		Fixed rate
2000	May 1	3.6%
	Nov. 1	3.4%
2001	May 1	3.0%
	Nov. 1	2.0%
2002	May 1	2.0%
	Nov. 1	1.6%
2003	May 1	1.1%
	Nov. 1	1.1%
2004	May 1	1.0%
	Nov. 1	1.0%
2005	May 1	1.2%
	Nov. 1	1.0%
2006	May 1	1.4%

Source: U.S. Bureau of Public Debt.

Who Can Own I Bonds?

You can own I bonds if you have a social security number and you are a

- U.S. resident, or you are a U.S. citizen who lives abroad.

- Civilian employee of the United States regardless of where you live.

- Minor (under age 18). Unlike other securities, minors may own U.S. savings bonds.

Redeeming I Bonds

When an I bond is 12 months old, you can redeem it and receive the purchase price of the bond plus any accrued interest. However, if you redeem an I bond before it is 5 years old, you will lose 3 months of accrued interest.

I bonds are nontransferable. If you purchase a bond at an auction or find a bond belonging to someone else, you can't redeem it. The registration on the bond is a contractual relationship between the owner and the U.S. Treasury.

You can cash your I bonds at most local financial institutions. When you present the bonds, you'll be asked to establish your identity. You can do this in either of two ways:

- By being a customer with an active account open for at least six months at the financial institution that will be paying the bonds
- By presenting documentary identification, such as a driver's license

If you're not listed as the owner or co-owner on the bonds you're redeeming, you'll have to establish that you're entitled to redeem the bonds. It's good to check with your financial institution before presenting the bonds for payment to find out what identification and other documents you need.

How Do I Bonds Compare with TIPS?

Which will better meet you needs—I bonds or TIPS? Table 15.4 compares the virtues of each.

If Your Bond Is Lost or Stolen

If you order a bond and don't receive it within 15 business days, contact the institution where you bought it. The institution will try to find out why you didn't receive your bond and will help you fill out a claim form to request a replacement bond. If you don't receive a bond you bought through a payroll savings plan, contact your employer's payroll office to obtain a claim form.

Table 15.4 Comparison of TIPS and Series I Savings Bonds

	TIPS	I Bonds
Type of investment	Marketable—can be bought and sold in the secondary securities market.	Nonmarketable—cannot be bought and sold in the secondary securities market. Registered in names of individuals or, for paper bonds only, their fiduciary estates.
How to buy	At auction through Treasury Direct, through Legacy Treasury Direct, or through banks, brokers, and dealers.	Electronic: Anytime online from Treasury Direct. Paper: most banks, credit unions, or savings institutions.
Purchase limits	Auction: Noncompetitive bidding—up to $5 million. Competitive bidding—up to 35% of offering amount.	Electronic: $30,000 per social security number per calendar year. Paper: $30,000 per social security number per calendar year.
Par amount/face amount	Minimum purchase is $1,000. Increments of $1,000.	Electronic: Purchased in amounts $25 or more, to the penny. Paper: Offered in 8 denominations ($50, $75, $100, $200, $500, $1,000, $5,000, and $10,000).
Inflation indexing	Inflation adjustments measured by CPI-U published monthly.	Semiannual inflation rate (based on CPI-U changes) announced in May and November.
Discounts/face amount	Price and interest determined at auction.	Electronic: Purchased in amounts of $25 or more, to the penny. Paper bonds issued at face amount (a $100 I bond costs $100).
Earnings rates	Principal increases/decreases with inflation/deflation. Coupons calculated based upon adjusted principal. Fixed coupon rate.	Earnings rate is a combination of the fixed rate of return, set at the time of purchase, and a variable semiannual inflation rate.
Coupons/interest	Semiannual interest payments at the coupon rate set at auction. Inflation-adjusted principal is used to calculate the coupon amount.	Interest accrues over the life of the bond and is paid upon redemption.

Continued

Table 15.4 Comparison of TIPS and Series I Savings Bonds—cont'd

	TIPS	I Bonds
Tax issues	Semiannual interest payments and inflation adjustments that increase the principal are subject to federal tax in the year that they occur, but they are exempt from state and local income taxes.	Tax reporting of interest can be deferred until redemption, final maturity, or other taxable disposition, whichever occurs first. Interest is subject to federal income tax but exempt from state and local income taxes. Interest can also be claimed annually.
Life span	TIPS are issued in terms of 5, 10, and 20 years.	Earn interest for up to 30 years.
Disposal before maturity	Can be sold prior to maturity in the secondary market.	Redeemable after 12 months with 3 months interest penalty. No penalty after 5 years.

If you lost your bond or if it was destroyed, fill out Form PDF 1048 and mail the completed form to:

Bureau of the Public Debt

PO Box 7012

Parkersburg, WV 26106-7012

Death of a Savings Bond Owner: Who Owns the Bond?

- If only one person is named on a savings bond and that person is deceased, the bond becomes the property of his or her estate.
- If both people named on a bond are deceased, the bond is the property of the estate of the person who died last.
- If one of the two people named on a bond is deceased, the surviving person is automatically the owner as if the survivor had been the sole owner from the time the bond was issued.
- Upon death of the owner, any surviving person named on the bonds as beneficiary becomes the new owner. As the new owner, this person is required to include on his or her tax return the interest earned on the

bonds for the year the bonds are redeemed or disposed of in a taxable transaction or the bonds reach final maturity, whichever occurs first.

And on the topic of death, be mindful of an old proverb. "Hurry and eat, hurry and drink, for this world is like a wedding feast from which we must soon depart."

It's a Wrap

- U.S. savings bonds are affordable, long-term investments that emphasize safety over yield.
- Series EE bonds are sold at half their face value and mature in 30 years.
- Interest on EE bonds is credited every six months.
- Savings bond interest is federally tax deferred and tax exempt at the state and local levels.
- Savings bonds can play a role in long-term college tuition savings, but be aware of the drawbacks.
- Series I bonds are based on a fixed rate of return and a variable, semiannual inflation rate.

"While standing at the edge of a cliff, a step backward is really a step forward."

CHAPTER 16

Life Insurance—The Risk Protector

◆◆◆◆◆◆◆◆◆◆◆◆◆◆◆◆◆◆◆◆◆◆◆◆◆◆◆◆◆◆◆◆◆◆◆

"For 3 days after death, hair and fingernails continue to grow but phone calls do taper off."

Do I Need to Read This Chapter?

- Have I thought about the need to protect my dependents when I die?

- Am I under the false illusion that my kids under age 21 need life insurance?

- Do I understand the different types of life insurance?

- Am I aware of the pros and cons (mostly cons!) of insurance as an investment?

- Can I decipher the ratings (like AA or Ba3) given to insurance companies?

- Have I determined, free of sales pitches, the best life insurance for my situation?

What Is the Purpose of Life Insurance?

The basic purpose of life insurance is to offer financial protection to your loved ones in the event of your death. The benefit it provides is one that you hope you won't need—at least not soon—but that most people would be foolish to do without. Remember that:

1. Life insurance is usually the major source of liquidity to beneficiaries.

2. Life insurance proceeds, in most states, are exempt from the claims of the deceased's creditors.

3. Life insurance proceeds are usually not subject to probate, thus eliminating both probate expenses and probate delays.

4. The beneficiaries receive the value of the policy and do not declare that money as income; thus it becomes, in most cases, tax free.

Because beneficiaries avoid probate and receive the face value of the policy tax free, be certain to name contingent beneficiaries. If not, and your primary beneficiary predeceases you, the insurance proceeds of your policy upon your death will become part of your will and will end up in probate court.

Also, naming young children as beneficiaries may not always be a smart move. An insurance company will not pay proceeds upon death to a minor. The money will be held until a court-approved guardian is established. A needless delay!

When speaking to a salesperson, make the following points clear:

1. Insure yourself for 7 times your annual income, after taxes, if your family is completely dependent on what you earn.
2. Raise that figure to 10 times your annual take-home pay if you have young children.
3. Naturally, if you and your spouse both work, you can combine your efforts to the stated needs.

Should I Buy Life Insurance for My Children?

Speaking bluntly, I do not believe in life insurance for children. If your son or daughter is a famous movie or rock star, bringing into the family huge sums of money, then I can accept the notion of insurance. But if your child is just a normal kid, you don't need it. The absolute purpose of life insurance is to provide (in the case of death) for your dependents. Children do not have dependents.

Also, the argument by insurance salespeople that a child insured today will be insured forever holds no basis. The scenario goes something like this: "What happens to your son or daughter if he or she should be stricken with some dread disease and become uninsurable?" The answer is simple. You should purchase, under your policy, a rider insuring the child to age 25. Also, I have heard of salespersons touting the concept of using such a policy as a method of saving for the child's college education. Don't buy that idea. You would be far better off with most other financial instruments that do not charge for the added expenses of mortality (life insurance costs) and commissions. Stay away from insuring children.

What about the Investment Benefits of Life Insurance?

It pays to understand the different types of life insurance and their values as investments.

Many life insurance policies contain investment features that can be used to provide additional income for you and your family. You probably won't want to buy life insurance primarily for its investment value—other forms of investments are generally more lucrative—but the investment benefits can be a significant secondary reason for buying insurance, as well as a factor in choosing among the available policies.

Let's consider the most popular forms of life insurance today with special attention to their investment potential: (1) term insurance, (2) whole life insurance, and (3) universal life insurance.

How Does Term Insurance Work?

Term life insurance offers the greatest amount of financial protection at the lowest cost in premiums. This is because when you buy term insurance, you buy the possible death benefit only; there is no savings or investment of a specified sum if you die during the life of the policy (the "term" from which this type of insurance gets its name). Term policies are usually issued for a specific period of years, after which the insurance coverage can be renewed but only at a higher premium rate.

Two variations on the term insurance policy are the *decreasing term* policy, in which the premiums remain the same but the amount of the death benefits decreases as you get older, and the *level term* policy, in which the amount of the death benefit remains the same but the size of the premiums increases over time.

Term insurance is popular in instances where the need for life insurance protection is temporary or where other, more costly forms of insurance are unaffordable. For example, term insurance may be an ideal choice for a young family with children, where insurance protection is vital but the family income may still be modest. As the family grows older and the parents' careers take wing, the family income will probably increase, and other types of policies may become more attractive. Although the premiums of term will eventually become more expensive than the cash-value policies mentioned in the next few pages, term has the advantage of being far less costly at the time in people's lives when large amounts of coverage are most needed.

How Does Straight Life Insurance Work?

Also known as *whole life insurance, straight life insurance* offers a specified death benefit (the face value of the policy) in exchange for an unchanging premium payment. The size of the premium depends mainly on your age at the time you purchase the policy; the younger you are, the lower your annual premium will be, but once bought, the annual cost to you never changes. At the time of your death, the face value of the policy will be paid to your beneficiary.

Unlike term insurance, straight life insurance includes an *investment feature.* Part of your premium payment is placed in a savings fund and invested by the insurance company. As the years pass, the amount of money in this fund will grow, both from your contributions and from the company's investment earnings. This growing sum is known as the policy's *cash surrender value.* It is quite small at first but, after a number of years, can become a substantial amount of money. The cash surrender value of your policy can benefit you in two ways. First, if you terminate the policy, you can receive the cash surrender value as a lump sum (unlike term insurance, in which you walk away with nothing). Second, while the policy is in force, you can borrow against the cash surrender value even if you may not qualify for other types of loans. This provision can be useful, for example, when college tuition bills come due.

The investment value of straight life insurance gives it an advantage over term insurance. However, it is considerably more costly. The amount of savings you'll accumulate through your insurance policy is probably smaller than the amount you could save through other investment plans. And, of course, in order for your beneficiary to receive the death benefit, you must continue to pay premiums until you die. This can be a financial strain, especially for older people whose earnings have fallen after retirement. So consider the pros and cons carefully before opting for a straight life policy.

Another factor to consider is the term *cost*. This is the difference between what you pay in premiums and what you will get back. If you buy term insurance, you will pay a premium and get nothing back; thus your cost for insuring your life is the premium. If there is a cash surrender value, as in the other types of life insurance, your cost is smaller than the premium. Cost can also be reduced by dividends in the "participating" policies, but not all policies carry this feature. Thus, in order to evaluate the costs of different policies, you need to compare the premiums, cash surrender values, and dividends, if any.

How Does Universal Life Insurance Work?

Because of much criticism about insurance companies' low returns on whole life policies, the concept of *universal life insurance* was born. Unlike deferred annuities, the universal life policy is bought mainly for its insurance feature. It was first introduced in 1979 as a type of life insurance that combines insurance protection (in the form of term insurance coverage) with a savings plan that builds tax-deferred income at highly competitive rates. This income becomes taxable only when the policy is surrendered. The holder of a universal life policy chooses the amount of life insurance protection he or she wants, and part of the premium goes to cover that protection. The insurance company invests the rest of the premium payments in various high-yielding instruments. Watch out for these yields, though. Although high, they are usually "gross" rates, meaning that administrative and other costs have not been considered in the computation. The insurance company's investment managers usually decide on the investment policy, and so your growth or yield is determined by their decisions. If the managers make a series of bad investment decisions, the cash value of your policy will decline. This doesn't happen with straight life insurance, in which cash values are protected using a fixed interest rate, so that you know in advance just what your policy's cash surrender value will be at any time.

Another important feature to consider is that this type of policy is very flexible. At any time, the amount of insurance coverage may be increased or decreased, the size of the premiums can be adjusted, and the accumulated cash value can be withdrawn by means of an automatic policy loan.

An interesting option that is offered with some universal life policies, known as a *vanishing premium,* allows you to discontinue your payments after a certain period of time. Assume you are 40 years old. You will pay a larger premium for a fixed number of years (I'll use 25 years as an example). After the twenty-fifth year, the earnings on the premiums will have accumulated, and the premiums will be paid from the earnings. So by the time you are ready for retirement, you no longer have to worry about paying life insurance premiums. Remember that the death benefit does not decline when you stop paying premiums.

One last point. If the earnings on the universal life policy are more than what the company had projected, you may find that the death benefit actually increases. The reason is that by tax law, the cash value of the policy cannot be allowed to come too close to the policy's death benefit. If this should occur, the death benefit must be increased or the policy will lose its tax-favored status.

Therefore, when you shop for universal life insurance, it's very important to compare the investment policies of different insurance companies. Some are more successful than others. Also find out about the fees charged by the companies you're considering. Some charge heavy sales commissions, while others charge large surrender fees (known as *back-end loads*) in the event you decide to cancel your policy. Here's an easy and accurate way to assess the relative costs of similar policies. Ask your insurance broker, or the insurer itself, for *cost indexes* that encompass the factors detailed earlier. Then compare the index number given for each policy. The lower the cost index number, the less the policy will cost you. It's as simple as that. Did you know that old insurance agents never die? It's against their policy.

For a summary of the three types of life insurance programs, see Table 16.1.

Why Is It Important to Know about Insurance Company Ratings?

The issue of the financial strength of an insurance company to meet its obligations is a most important item for the investor to understand. The role of a rating agency is to evaluate an insurance company's financial position and its ability to pay policyholder claims. Insurance customers and prospective customers can benefit greatly from seeing these evaluative ratings so that they can compare one company with another. Thus the consumer can better determine which companies possess the stability and financial resources needed in today's economy and then select the best company according to its product, its service,

Table 16.1 Summary of Life Insurance Programs

Features	Type of Insurance Programs		
	Term	Whole Life	Universal Life
Premium	Lowest cost; increases in cost at the end of each term	Fixed premium; reinvestment of interest reduces payments; insured for life	Flexible premiums; insured for specified period
Cash value	None	Some cash value	Varies with amount invested
Objectives	Protection for a limited time period to cover specific and temporary risks	Protection for life with cash value for insured	Life insurance protection plus high rate of return on savings component

and its performance. The three leading independent analysts are A. M. Best, Standard & Poor's, and Moody's. Although they have common characteristics in their evaluations, adopt the same accounting methods, and issue letter grades (including the use of modifiers), their rating methodologies differ. Each has its own basic approach to evaluating the data and performance of insurance companies.

Information can be obtained by calling these firms directly:

Standard & Poor's:	(212) 208-1527
Moody's:	(212) 553-0377
A. M. Best:	(900) 555-2378

In the Real World...

As times change, so do life insurance projections and yields. When approaching any type of insurance-investment relationship, you must be realistic. For example, many policies bought in the 1980s had interest rates projected at 12 percent (and higher)—at that time, the current rate. Twenty-eight years later, these projections are no longer valid, and policyholders may find that their idea of using cash surrender value to supplement their retirement income is at risk. Also, people who bought vanishing-premium policies may discover that, because of lower yields especially since 2003, they have to continue making premium payments long after the period of "no premiums" has expired.

What Other Types of Insurance Policies or Options Are Available?

Although an enormous array of choices exist—too many to delve into here—the "second-to-die" policy and the accelerated death benefit (ADB) option should be mentioned.

Second-to-Die Policy

Under the 1981 Economic Recovery Tax Act, an unlimited federal marital deduction was allowed at the first death. That meant that all federal estate tax payments would not be levied until the death of the surviving spouse. This was not always the case. Prior to 1981, estate taxes were levied on 50 percent of the assets left to the surviving spouse—an immediate tax. A new type of insurance arose from this procedure. Known as the *second-to-die* policy, it is used primarily for paying estate taxes, adding to a lowering inheritance, reducing insurance premiums, and caring for children with special problems.

The concept works in this way: Instead of one policy on one spouse's life or one policy on each spouse, there is one policy insuring both lives payable at the death of the second insured. It is much cheaper than having two policies and more efficient. However, there are certain disadvantages to such a policy. Income may be needed immediately after the death of the first insured, especially if there are large debts to be paid. Also, in the light of so many second marriages, individuals may want to leave their estate directly to their children and not to the surviving spouse.

In the Real World... Before signing up for any second-to-die policy, I strongly recommend that you speak with your attorney and ask if a second-to-die is advantageous to your specific circumstances.

Accelerated Death Benefits

Accelerated death benefits (ADB) are defined as a portion of the life insurance proceeds that are paid to a given policyholder prior to the death of the policyholder if he or she should become terminally ill. Most companies require that your life expectancy be 12 months or less from the time you apply for accelerated death benefits and that you must have a "dread disease."

Oftentimes consumers tend to confuse accelerated death benefits with viaticals or life settlements. There are important differences between the two types of plans that ultimately permit a life insurance policyholder to obtain funds related to a life insurance policy in advance of his or her death.

Under a *viatical settlement plan*, a third party provides the original life insurance policyholder with funds in advance of death in exchange for the right to receive the actual policy proceeds upon the insured's death. Pursuant to the terms and conditions of a viatical settlement agreement, the original insured releases his or her interest in the ultimate proceeds from the life insurance policy in consideration for the receipt of a lump-sum payment during the insured's lifetime.

On the other hand, under a provision allowing for accelerated death benefits within the confines of a life insurance policy, no third party is entering the scene effectively purchasing the ultimate interest in that policy. Rather, when contracting initially with the insured, the insurance carrier includes a proviso in the policy that allows the insured during his or her lifetime to obtain at least a partially accelerated payment of what otherwise would be death benefits. The insured is not contracting away any rights to actual death benefits that may remain after any accelerated payment is made.

You can usually find information about the ADB on a rider in your policy or in the insurance handbook. Cost for the ADB rider is minimal, but the good news is that some companies will not bill you unless the option is used. Check around for different policy carriers and how they handle the cost on this part of your life insurance contract.

What Should You Remember about Choosing a Policy?

On the basis of the brief descriptions in this chapter, if you consider your objectives, you will now be able to choose the best type of policy for you. Term insurance is your choice if your needs require large amounts of insurance and you cannot afford cash-value policies. Consider straight life or universal life only it you can afford the higher premiums. Remember that you should not forsake important coverage for investment yield. Also, the tax-deferred features of the investment-type policies are of most benefit to people in high tax brackets. If you are not in a high tax bracket, you may be better off in a taxable investment paying a higher rate even though the interest is subject to tax.

And on the subject of taxes, the point you must always remember is what the government gives, it must first take away.

It's a Wrap

- The chief purpose of life insurance is to provide for your dependents in the case of your death.
- Generally speaking, minors do not need life insurance.
- Term life insurance provides a death benefit only. Its cost usually rises as you age.
- Straight or whole life insurance provides a specified death benefit in exchange for a premium payment that never changes. It also accrues a lump sum called a cash surrender value.
- Universal life insurance combines term coverage with a savings plan that builds tax-deferred income.
- Insurance companies are objectively rated to evaluate their financial position and ability to pay claims.

"Marriage is like a hot tub. Once you get used to it, it's not so hot."

CHAPTER 17

Real Estate as Security and Investment

◆◆

"A lot of homeowners have discovered that trees grow on money."

Do I Need to Read This Chapter?

- Am I curious about real estate as an investment?

- Do I understand its unique risks?

- Am I thinking of selling my home?

- Am I aware of real estate investment trusts?

Real estate has been on the fastest roads to riches during this first decade of the twenty-first century.

What Are the Benefits of Investing in Rental Property?

When you buy real estate for use as rental property, you can benefit by the purchase in at least three ways: it provides current income; it provides tax benefits through business expense deductions and depreciation; and, if you like, it can provide a place to live when you retire.

Let's consider the tax benefits that result from offering property you own for rental purposes. First, any expenses you incur in operating the rental property are deductible from your income as business expenses. These might include repair and maintenance of the house or property, interest payments on a mortgage, or an occasional trip to inspect the property if it is outside your own residential area.

Second, depreciation can be deducted from your income as well. This is the annual decline in value of any property which results from its increasing age; the decline is determined according to a fixed schedule, depending on the nature of the property. This is a noncash deduction since you are not actually expending any money; yet you reap tax benefits just as if you were.

Interestingly, real estate values usually increase each year rather than decrease, despite what happens in "soft" markets such as in the early 1990s. Therefore, you could say that you benefit twice: the actual resale value of your real property will generally grow, while you get a tax deduction because of the theoretical decrease in the value of your property over time.

Real estate, then, offers decided advantages to the canny investor. But like any other investment, it carries risks as well. The greatest is the risk of buying a property whose rental or resale value is minimal. It has been said that the three most important rules of real estate investment are location, location, and location, and that saying is pretty sound.

There are plenty of places in the world where no one is living and where no one will ever want to live. If you buy one of them, your chance of renting or selling property is small; and mortgage payments, taxes, and other expenses will still have to be met. So above all, make sure you know the property before you buy.

&Don't Forget Experts will tell you that nothing can replace firsthand knowledge of a property. Examining it "up close and personal" is the only way to judge actual value. Never buy property you haven't personally visited and inspected. Photos or videotapes shown by an agent are no substitute; you'll never see the drawbacks of the property that way.

Real estate is such a major undertaking that you must tread very carefully before investing. Remember, above all, that property doesn't offer the liquidity of most other investments. Therefore, consider these two questions carefully before taking the real estate plunge:

- What are the tax benefits of selling a home?
- Is there an alternative to a direct real estate purchase?

What Are the Tax Benefits of Selling a Home?

Another important aspect of real estate investments is the selling of your home and its tax ramifications. When you sell your home and a profit is realized, you will get two favorable tax treatments: You will be able to postpone the tax on the profit indefinitely if you purchase another primary residence within two years. Also, you will receive a one-time tax exclusion up to the allowable maximum as long as the property was held as a primary residence for two of the past five years.

Do's and Don'ts of Real Estate Investing

1. Never buy property solely for its depreciation value. If a piece of real estate isn't a good investment in its own right, its tax benefits will not make it worthwhile.
2. Don't buy commercial property if you're a beginner in real estate investing. Single homes and smaller apartment houses are safer investments and more reliable sources of income.
3. Buy property within your community, where you know property values and can anticipate trends. Your chance of success in the real estate field decreases as the distance from your home base increases.
4. Use as little cash as possible when buying real estate for investment purposes. Make a small down payment, and take out the longest fixed-rate mortgage offered. In this way, you are repaying a smaller mortgage payment each month.
5. Don't invest in real estate unless you can reasonably foresee an annual profit from your investment (after deducting expenses and taxes) of at least 15 percent. The property itself should have a reasonable prospect for appreciation of about 10 percent annually.
6. Remember that renting can mean headaches for you as a landlord. The property must be maintained according to health and safety standards set by local governments, and complaints from tenants can be annoying. You might consider having a professional manager operate your property, but his or her fee, ranging from 6 to 10 percent of the rent, will cut heavily into your profit.

Is There an Alternative to a Direct Real Estate Purchase?

If you're interested in real estate investment but somewhat hesitant to get involved directly, consider a real estate investment trust (REIT). It is the simplest and most direct way to invest in real estate. Like a mutual fund, a REIT pools money from many investors, who buy shares in the trust's portfolio. However, rather than investing in stocks or bonds, a REIT invests in real estate.

Purchasing a REIT could be looked at as investing your money in real estate by the share instead of by the brick. When you receive shares in a trust, you are buying a stock that trades on a stock exchange just as any other stock does. Income from rent or interest on the mortgages is paid as dividends to the shareholders. These securities are required by law to pass through 95 percent of the income they generate to shareholders in the form of dividends. When the property is sold, capital gains will be given to the stockholders as a special dividend; or the sale may increase the earnings per share, thus raising the value of the stock.

What Are the Pros and Cons of REITs?

REITs have a number of advantages for investors. They allow small investors to participate in real estate investments that would otherwise be unavailable. Shares in a REIT are liquid and can normally be sold at or near their full value. They allow you to easily trade what is traditionally an illiquid asset and are easier to buy and sell than physical property.

As long as a REIT meets certain requirements, it pays no corporate tax. Thus, while other investments, such as mutual funds, pay after-tax dividends, the REIT can distribute pretax dollars. *One additional point*: Under the old law, pension funds were not permitted to invest in REITs. However, in 1993 this ban was lifted.

Naturally, REITs have their disadvantages. Management and operating fees reduce the net earnings of the trust and the amount of investor distributions as well. The tax benefits normally associated with real estate ownership—including deductions for depreciation, interest, and maintenance costs—are absorbed by the trust rather than passed on to individual investors. REITs normally do not have to pay taxes. However, you, the investor, do, since most dividends received from these trusts are taxable at regular rates. There is an exception.

Dividends paid out to shareholder's equity (which represents a return of capital) are not taxable. Also, remember that any loss occurring from your REIT can be used to offset capital gains you made during the year and that any loss over gain can be deducted from your income for up to $3,000 annually.

REITs fall into two basic categories. Chances are that one will appeal to you much more strongly than the other, based on your investment needs.

1. *Equity*. These REITs get their income from rental and lease payments and at times from the sale of property (capital gains). They have excellent growth potential. This type of REIT should be chosen if you feel that there will be higher inflation. Remember that the higher the inflation, the greater the chance that your property values will increase and rents will rise.

2. *Mortgage*. If you feel that inflation will remain low, then the mortgage REIT's yields will look very attractive against a background of stable or even falling interest rates. All REITs, like bonds, rise in value when interest rates fall as investors run to higher-yielding securities. But because they are highly leveraged, these mortgage REITs will react much more intensely to interest rate movements than the equity REITs.

You'll want to make sure that the objectives of the trust match your own investment plans before you get involved.

To REIT or Not to REIT?

By now you probably realize that REITs are more complicated than, say, savings accounts. Think about these six points as you decide whether REITs are right for you:

1. How do you know which REIT to buy? A little research based upon demographic and economic trends could certainly help. For example, a REIT involved in regional apartments would involve knowing about vacancy rates and rents, new apartment construction, and affordability of homeownership. As an example, because of the very high cost of residential homes, only a third of San Francisco's population can afford a house. Therefore, a REIT for apartments in this location might make an ideal investment.

2. Make certain you examine the proxy statement to see what management's stake has in its own investment. The people who are in charge of the REIT must have a substantial position in it. If you find that management had a large share and then sold it recently, the red flag is up. If the REIT is new, the prospectus will show the management's track record in other ventures.

3. Be careful about selecting trusts that use large amounts of short-term debt to finance long-term mortgages. If short-term rates go up, your holdings could face serious trouble.

4. Examine the reports about the costs of administration. Total management fees and other charges should not exceed 1 percent of gross assets a year. Try to choose a REIT that is "self-administered," meaning that the managers are employed by the trust.

5. Avoid newly formed REITs. As far as I am concerned, the trust should have a track record of at least three years. Also, look for a dividend growth of at least 10 percent annually.

6. If you want to see how well your REIT is doing, look at its FFO growth. FFO stands for *funds from operations*, which is net income (income excluding gains or losses) from the sale of the property with depreciation added back in. The major difference between a REIT and a stock of a company is that earnings per share are not the major concern for the REIT investor. Rather REITs use FFO.

Over the past four decades, home values in the United States have soared, with few other investments showing such a comparable growth. If the U.S. economy continues to prosper, real estate will continue to benefit. As long as you know what you're buying, the chances are that you can do very well.

And on the topic of real estate, by the time you finish paying for a house in the country, it's no longer the country.

It's a Wrap

- Real estate has distinct advantages for the canny investor.
- Real estate investment offers some great tax benefits, but never buy a property for that reason alone.
- You should net a 15 percent annual profit, after expenses, to make a real estate investment worthwhile.
- If you're interested in a mutual fund–type investment in properties, you should consider REITs.

"Acquiring real estate is like sex. You should get a lot when you're young."

CHAPTER 18

Condominiums and Co-ops—A Living Investment

◆▬◆◆◆◆◆◆◆◆◆◆◆◆◆◆◆◆◆◆◆◆◆◆◆◆◆◆◆◆◆◆◆◆◆◆◆▬◆

"Rents are so high, leases are breaking tenants."

Do I Need to Read This Chapter?

- Would you love your own space, yet can't afford to buy a house?

- Would you prefer to live in a townhouse or apartment, with much of the maintenance and repairs done by others (albeit for a fee)?

- Do you understand how condominium ownership works?

- Do you know if cooperatives, or co-ops, are available in your area? If so, are you acquainted with their pros and cons?

Chapter 17 discussed real estate and homeownership. You may want to consider buying a condominium or cooperative apartment as an alternative.

What Is a Condominium?

A *condominium*, or *condo*, is an arrangement in which you own your own dwelling unit, usually an apartment but sometimes an individual house, row house, duplex, or other unit. Therefore, you have the same control over your property as does the owner of a conventional house. However, you also own a share of the common properties used by all the owners in a particular building or complex, including the land, the lobby, the heating and electrical system, and the parking lots, as well as any community facilities such as a golf course, recreation hall, or swimming pool. In these areas you do not have full control. Control (including maintenance) of the land and amenities (pool, tennis court, etc.) lies in the hands of the owners' association, and your input into the decisions of the association is limited to the size of your shareholding. You must pay a monthly maintenance fee, which covers your share of the operating costs. In addition, you must pay your own property taxes and any mortgage you need to buy the apartment, just as most homeowners do.

Since you are the owner of your condominium unit, the finances of condominium ownership resemble those of buying a house. You must arrange for your own financing, generally by taking out a mortgage from a bank or other financial institution. Mortgage money for condominiums is usually readily available, sometimes at interest rates slightly lower than those charged for home mortgages. Like a house, a condo is a tax-wise investment. The portion of your mortgage payments devoted to interest payments is deductible.

Also, since you own your condominium unit, you have the right to sell the apartment without the permission of the board, providing that the board has been allowed to exercise its right of first refusal. You also have the right, in most cases, to rent out your apartment, as long as you follow the rules of the condominium association, but management also has the right to charge fees for this privilege. These fees can become excessive and can create a deterrent for rentals.

What Are the Advantages and Disadvantages of Condominium Ownership?

As you can see, condominium ownership can offer some important benefits. Here are some of the other advantages of owning a condo unit:

- It usually costs less to buy a condominium than to buy a private home, and as already mentioned, condo financing is often easier to arrange.

- Condominium projects are professionally maintained, thereby alleviating much of the anxiety of owning your own home. This can be especially important for the elderly, who may want to escape chores such as painting, shoveling snow, and trimming hedges.

- Safety and security are usually tighter in a multiple dwelling such as a condo apartment complex than in an isolated private home—another important consideration for older people in particular.

- Finally, the sharing of costs among a large group of owners permits luxuries that individual homeowners usually can't afford—swimming pools, tennis courts, golf courses, and the like.

This is not to say that condo ownership is without drawbacks or pitfalls. Here are some cautionary notes to consider before making a condo purchase:

- When investigating a particular condominium project, check the quality and condition of the property carefully. Make sure the plumbing, electrical, and heating systems are in good working order. The developer should be willing to certify the condition of the structure. If the condominium is in a newly built development, don't rely on assurances that special facilities, such as a pool or golf course, will "soon be available." If these amenities aren't in place and operating when you buy, you may never see them.

- When you own a condo, all decisions concerning the common properties of the condominium project are made by a management committee and ratified by a vote of the individual owners. The weight of your vote depends on the size of your unit; the bigger your apartment, the more votes you'll have. Nonetheless, the wishes of the majority of owners will normally prevail. Can this become a problem? Yes, if decisions are made that affect living conditions at the condo in ways you don't approve, the prohibition of pets, for example.

- The maintenance fee you pay is not permanently fixed. It may increase because of ordinary price inflation or have to be boosted if the maintenance budget initially set by the developer was unrealistically low. Also, weather damage to common property, such as the havoc that Hurricane Katrina caused in 2005, may play a role in raising maintenance costs. This is something to consider carefully before buying in climate-risk areas.

- Monthly carrying charges (for, say, building maintenance of lobbies, driveways, systems, services, etc.) can be lower than they are for co-op apartments of similar size, because there is no building mortgage to amortize. But not owning common property may not always be an advantage. If a condo building needs money for major repairs, such as a new elevator or expansion of social areas, and there is no cash reserve available, each condo owner is assessed for the cost of the repair.

What Is Needed in Order to Own a Condo?

Every investment involves much paperwork, and you must be extremely careful to understand the many documents needed in condo ownership;

- The declaration or master deed will describe the physical details of your condo ownership. The deed contains the conditions and restrictions of ownership.

- The condo association's bylaws are also an important document for you to examine, as they contain all the rules and regulations of the condo.

- The condo management agreement (if the project is managed by a professional management company) will disclose who operates the condo, what managers' duties are, and what rates the management company charges.

- The title insurance commitment, or an abstract certified to date, will disclose whether the seller has clear title to the condo (free of any mortgages or liens). This document is essential when you are contemplating the purchase of a condo.

- The purchase agreement (offer) is the most important document in your condo transactions, because once it is signed by you and accepted by the seller, it will govern every aspect of the purchase, including condition of the property, repairs to be made, construction of amenities, and simple things such as color of paint, fixtures to be included, and appliances. Verbal descriptions are not binding, and so any representations must be in writing. Therefore, you should employ experienced counsel well in advance of signing any papers.

As you can see, condo ownership can be ideal for many people. But be sure to understand the terms of the arrangement before getting involved:

1. See that the maintenance fees are spelled out.
2. Read the rules and restrictions carefully.
3. Have the condition of the property checked out thoroughly.
4. Above all, be sure you're dealing with an established, reputable developer. Talk to friends, or ask at your bank. If anything you hear makes you doubt the reliability of the seller, back off.

What Is a Cooperative?

As the name implies, the *cooperative*, or *co-op*, is considered to be a cooperative living arrangement with people who have a common interest (union membership as an example) and who run the building as a corporation. A cooperative differs from a condominium in several ways. When you buy a co-op, you buy a share or a number of shares in the corporation that owns and manages the land and the buildings. These shares entitle you to occupy a particular apartment for a specified term. However, you do not own the apartment, as you would when buying a condo.

As a co-op owner, you must pay a monthly maintenance fee, which includes not only your share of the cost of maintaining the building and grounds (like the condo maintenance fee) but also your share of the mortgage costs and taxes on the entire property, which are paid by the corporation as a whole. Note that you can deduct from your income, for tax purposes, the portion of your monthly maintenance fee which goes to pay for interest on the corporate mortgage and property taxes. In addition, of course, you may have to make payments on the mortgage loan you took out to purchase your shares in the co-op. If you get a co-op loan, unlike a condo loan, you will not have to pay a mortgage recording tax, because buying a co-op is not considered a real estate investment, but rather is deemed ownership of shares in a corporation.

What Other Differences Should the Investor Know Of?

There are other differences between a condo and a co-op. When decisions affecting the management of the development must be made, condo owners have voting power weighted according to the size of the units they own. A co-op owner has a single vote per share, and the number of shares he or she has is usually determined by the size and value of the apartment owned. A condo owner may sell the unit to anyone (although the management usually has the first right of refusal). By contrast, the corporation that manages the co-op has complete control over the buying and selling of apartments. You may be required to sell your apartment only to the corporation; you will certainly have to obtain permission before you can sell it to anyone else.

Thinking of buying a co-op to rent out as an investment? It may not be possible. The reason is that many co-op boards can deny their shareholders permission to sublet. Although this may not sound fair, many owners feel that they want to live in a building where "outsiders" cannot come and go as they please.

Co-op boards have the right to reject applicants without giving them a reason for nonacceptance. The only method of protest is to prove that the decision was based on race, creed, color, sexual orientation, marital status, or disability. Also, some co-ops will charge their shareholders a fee (known as a *flip charge*, usually 2 to 4 percent of the selling price) when they sell their apartments.

Finally, the co-op board will probably also have to approve any major alterations a shareholder wishes to make in an apartment. However, as with a condo, any appreciation in the value of a co-op apartment during the period of ownership will be of benefit when the time comes to sell.

Will Co-op Ownership Bring Restrictions or Possible Liabilities?

The strict control over the property held by a co-op's management can be both an advantage and a disadvantage to the individual owner. On the one hand, it restricts your freedom to do as you like with the apartment. On the other hand, as a voting shareholder in the corporation, you may like the idea that the corporation can limit and control the uses to which the property is put and, to some extent, the people who move in. In fact, this feature of the co-op has been used by many wealthy people as a way of preventing those whom they consider "undesirable" from becoming their neighbors.

There is one more important difference between condo and co-op ownership. When you buy shares in a co-op, you are investing in a corporation; in effect, you become business partners with the other co-op owners. This means that you can be held responsible for the solvency of the enterprise. And if a co-op owner defaults on his or her maintenance payments, you and the other co-op owners will have to help make up the difference. Therefore, the reliability of those buying shares in the co-op should be an important consideration in deciding whether or not to get involved. That is the reason that lenders such as banks usually charge more for a co-op loan than for a condo loan. This extra potential liability adds to the charges. In contrast, condo ownership means responsibility only for your own unit, and a default on a condo loan cannot be passed on to the other condo owners.

On balance, the condominium is probably a more favorable choice for most people than the co-op.

The Building Where I Rent Is "Going Co-op" — What Should I Do Next?

Co-op conversions have slowed greatly from their frantic pace in the past decade. However, if you're an apartment renter, you may find one day that the owner of your building has decided to "go co-op" — that is, to attempt to convert the building from rentals to co-ops, with the former owner as the manager of the newly formed corporation. If this happens, you will, of course, be faced with the decision of whether or not to purchase shares in the co-op. If you decide that you do wish to purchase, on the basis of your financial situation and how well you like your apartment, fine. If for some reason you prefer not to join the co-op, you should be aware of the rights you have as a renter in a building going co-op. It is impossible to list these rights here, as they will vary from one state and city to another because of local laws, but you can find out about them by contacting any local realtor or attorney who specializes in real estate.

As you can see, a condominium or a co-op can be a worthwhile investment. Both provide tax advantages that renting cannot offer, and with both arrangements you own a property (either the actual dwelling unit or a share in the co-op) that has a good chance of growing in value while you use it. Therefore, if you're currently renting the home in which you live and buying a house is either impractical or just not your cup of tea, look into the local condo and co-op markets. Both are options well worth considering.

And on the topic of real estate ownership, for what I paid for my townhouse today, 100 years ago I could have bought the town.

It's a Wrap

- Both condominiums and cooperatives can be worthwhile investments.
- As alternatives to single-family homeownership, both provide tax advantages that renting cannot offer.
- Condo owners hold title to their actual units (apartments, townhouses, or whatever), whereas co-op owners hold shares in the building corporation.
- Co-ops tend to have more stringent restrictions on financing, subletting, and other factors than condos do.

"If you don't make changes today, your tomorrows will be like your yesterdays."

CHAPTER 19

Mortgages—The Finances of Homeownership

"Love your neighbor—but don't pull down the fences."

Do I Need to Read This Chapter?

- Are you moving up to homeownership and want an overview of your financing options?

- Are you a current owner interested in refinancing?

- Do you wonder if you will qualify financially for a mortgage?

- Are you clear on the tax benefits and implications of holding a mortgage, especially where "points" are concerned?

- Are you considering a home equity loan, which entails borrowing money against your house?

For most people, buying a home, condo, or co-op entails taking out a mortgage to help meet the cost of the purchase. You are normally required to pay a percentage of the purchase price in cash; this is called a *down payment*. The remainder of the purchase price is covered by the mortgage, with your title to the house used as security for the unpaid balance on your mortgage. This means that if you are unable to repay your mortgage, the lender has the right to foreclose—that is, to take possession of the property. Most mortgage loans are made by banks and savings and loan associations, though other institutions and individuals may sometimes offer mortgages.

Mortgages have become financial "products" with all sorts of variations. If you ask the following questions, the answers will provide you with the basics of every type of mortgage:

1. What is the *origination fee?* This is a one-time charge that the lender will add as a cost of the mortgage.
2. What is the *simple interest rate?* This is the quoted rate of the loan. If a mortgage is negotiated for 15 years at 8 percent with a 3-point origination fee, the simple interest rate is still 8 percent.
3. What is the *effective interest rate?* This is different from the simple rate in that it is the actual cost of borrowing after considering origination fees. In the preceding example the effective interest rate would be 8.2 percent.
4. What is the PITI? PITI is the total monthly payment of *principal, interest, taxes,* and *insurance* that is so important to know when a family budgets for the purchase of a home.
5. Will I have to pay PMI? PMI stands for *Private Mortgage Insurance.* If your down payment is less than 20 percent, PMI may be added to the amount of your monthly mortgage payment, which may run up to $50 for every $100,000 of home debt.
6. How long can I take out an *interest only loan?* With this type of loan, you only pay the interest charges, not the principal, up to the first 10 years of your mortgage. But watch out! When the period of interest-free borrowing is up, you may have only 20 years left of a 30-year mortgage to pay for the entire mortgage. This monthly increase in mortgage payment could force you into foreclosure if you cannot meet the new, higher payments.

What Types of Mortgages Are Offered?

Most mortgages provide for repayment over a 10- to 30-year period in equal monthly payment amounts based on a fixed rate of interest. Each payment includes both repayment of principal and payment of interest, with early payments representing mainly interest and later payments representing mainly principal. This is known as the *fixed-rate mortgage payment*.

However, rising home prices have spurred a 40-year mortgage now being offered. The selling point is the lowering of monthly payments, but you would only save about $80 a month as compared with a 30-year, $300,000 mortgage, and it would take much longer to build any equity (value) in the home.

The volatile economic climate of the late 1970s—in particular, soaring interest rates—led to the increased use of another type of mortgage, the *adjustable-rate mortgage* (*ARM*). This type of mortgage is usually a long-term loan, providing for repayment in 20 to 30 years. It differs from the traditional fixed-rate mortgage in that the interest rate on the loan changes at stated intervals. Thus, as interest rates rise, the amount you must pay the bank each month rises too; as interest rates fall, so do your monthly payments.

How Does the ARM Work?

The amount you must pay each month on an adjustable-rate mortgage loan depends on three factors:

1. *Interval.* The period of time between adjustments of the interest rate. Typical intervals are six months and one year.

2. *Index.* A guideline used in determining the current interest rate on the mortgage. The index will be clearly defined at the time the mortgage is made. Any of a number of widely accepted financial guidelines may be used as an index; one typical index is the current interest rate on U.S. Treasury bills. As the index goes up or down, so does the interest rate on your mortgage, and along with it, your monthly payment.

3. *Cap:* A predetermined figure limiting the movement of the interest rate on your mortgage in any single interval. If an adjustable-rate mortgage includes a cap, and not all do, the interest rate may not change by an amount greater than the cap, even though the variation in the index might call for a greater change.

As you can see, an adjustable-rate mortgage has one major disadvantage for the borrower: it's impossible to know beforehand how large your monthly payments will be in the future. Thus much of the security of the traditional fixed-rate mortgage is forfeited.

Adjustable-rate mortgages have earned their place in the mortgage market. They have great appeal because they usually offer lower initial interest rates than comparable fixed-rate mortgages. The trade-off, however, is that you won't know how long this advantage will last. The year 2007 is a good example of higher-changing interest rates on ARMs. In my opinion, it's better for most home buyers to choose fixed-rate mortgages, especially for those planning to "stay put" for a while. In volatile economic times, fixed rates offer peace of mind—you always know exactly how much you will owe.

What Are the Basic Requirements for a Mortgage?

Lenders usually require that your housing costs do not exceed 28 percent of your family gross income. When you add to the 28 percent your fixed payments for auto, credit cards, loans, and the like, your total fixed debt should not be more than 36 percent of your gross monthly income. Also, do not attempt to secure a mortgage whose cost will be more than 2.5 times your annual income. A $100,000 annual family income is just enough to purchase a home with a mortgage of $250,000.

How Does Refinancing a Mortgage Work in Today's Market?

When possible, it may be advantageous for you to switch mortgage methods by refinancing if interest rates go way down as they did in 2003–2005. But it is not always true that a lower interest rate alone means that refinancing is the way to go. For example, it could take many years to recoup the cost of the up-front fees, which could include lawyer's fees, title search and insurance, recording taxes, and, possibly, bank origination fees. In comparing figures, you must also consider the tax consequences before any refinancing decision can take place. Remember, by reducing your mortgage payment (which includes tax-deductible interest), you reduce the only tax deduction for interest which is left for the middle-income investor. This then raises your taxable income. So think carefully and weigh all the factors necessary to make an intelligent choice. Home-financing experts suggest this rule of thumb: do not refinance your existing mortgage unless you can benefit by at least 2 percentage points off the old mortgage rate.

Table 19.1 gives the monthly mortgage payments under a fixed-rate mortgage. For example, a $200,000 mortgage at 7 percent for 20 years would be calculated as follows:

1. Look down the "Interest Rate" column to find the 7.00 percent row.
2. Go across the 7.00 percent row to where it intersects with the "20" year column. The amount is $7.76.
3. Multiply the $7.76 by 200 (represents $200,000).
4. The result is a $1,552 monthly payment.

A further consideration, however, is pretax versus after-tax money. Assume that you have a 30-year, 10 percent, $100,000 mortgage that you will refinance

Table 19.1 Monthly Mortgage Payments for Each $1,000 Owed

Interest Rate %	Years				
	10	15	20	25	30
6.00	$11.11	$8.44	$7.17	$6.45	$6.00
6.25	11.23	8.58	7.31	6.60	6.16
6.50	11.36	8.72	7.46	6.76	6.33
6.75	11.49	8.85	7.61	6.91	6.49
7.00	11.62	8.99	7.76	7.07	6.63
7.25	11.75	9.13	7.91	7.23	6.83
7.50	11.88	9.28	8.06	7.39	7.00
7.75	12.01	9.42	8.21	7.56	7.17
8.00	12.14	9.56	8.37	7.72	7.34
8.25	12.27	9.71	8.53	7.89	7.52
8.50	12.40	9.85	8.68	8.06	7.69
8.75	12.54	10.00	8.84	8.23	7.87
9.00	12.62	10.15	9.00	8.40	8.05
9.50	12.94	10.45	9.33	8.74	8.41
10.00	13.22	10.75	9.66	9.09	8.78
10.50	13.50	11.06	9.99	9.45	9.14
11.00	13.78	11.37	10.33	9.81	9.51
11.50	14.06	11.69	10.67	10.17	9.90
12.00	14.35	12.01	11.02	10.54	10.28

at 7.5 percent. According to Table 19.1, your present monthly mortgage payment would be $878 (10 percent), whereas your new refinanced monthly payment would be only $700 (7.5 percent). You would consider that it would be a monthly savings of $178 ($878 – 700), but that is based upon pretax money. In order for you to get your after-tax savings, you must multiply your tax bracket rate (e.g., 28 percent) by the pretax savings ($178) and then subtract:

$178	Pretax savings
– 50	($178 × .28 rounded off)
$128	After-tax savings

No matter which type of mortgage you obtain, you'll receive significant tax benefits during the repayment period. These benefits arise from the fact that interest payments on the original purchase of a home, up to $1 million, are deductible from your taxable income for federal income tax purposes. For most homeowners, that's a substantial amount.

How Do Closing Costs and Fees Affect My Mortgage?

If you're currently shopping for a home (and a mortgage), you should be aware of two other factors that will affect the cost of home buying: closing costs and points.

Closing costs are one-time expenses that include the cost of a title search, title insurance, surveying fees, attorney's fees, mortgage recording tax, and many other smaller fees that can total as much as 5 percent of the value of the home you're buying. Before purchase, you should receive from the lending institution a good-faith estimate of what your closing costs will be.

Points are one-time lump-sum charges levied by the bank at the time you buy your home. A point is 1 percent of the total amount of the loan; the bank may charge from 2 to 4 points. For example, if you take out a $150,000 mortgage from a bank that charges 4 points for the loan, you will have to pay the bank a $6,000 fee at the time of purchase. To receive the most for your money, you should estimate how long you intend to own the home. Then decide on the best combination of interest rate and points. Because points are an up-front fee, whether you sell your house and pay off the loan after only 15 years or to a maturity of 30 years, remember that the longer you hold the loan, the smaller the impact the points will have on the effective rate of mortgage.

For example, if you have a 15-year mortgage at 8 percent and are charged 3 points, your effective rate is 8.2 percent. Simply divide the 3 points by 15 years, and add the result to the interest charged to find your effective yield:

$$3 \div 15 = .002 \text{ or } .2\%$$
$$8\% + .2\% = 8.2\%$$

Here is another way to compare mortgage loans. Assume you are offered this choice: a 30-year, $100,000 mortgage with 3 points (costing you $3,000 up front) at 7.5 percent ($700 monthly) versus a 30-year no-point 8 percent ($734 monthly) mortgage. Which would be more advantageous to you? The difference in your monthly payments would be $34 ($734 − $700). If you took the 7.5 percent loan, the $34 monthly savings would go toward your getting back your $3,000 (3 points), and you would break even in less than 8 years. This means that every month after the eighth year, you would be ahead by $34 a month. Over the 30-year mortgage, you could save close to $9,000.

Any Other Pointers on Points?

Points paid in connection with a loan taken to purchase real estate are tax deductible as interest in the year the loan is closed. Points paid in connection with a refinance must be amortized over the life of the loan. For example, if a borrower pays 3 points to refinance a $100,000 loan to be paid over 30 years, a total of $3,000 will be paid in points. The deductible interest for the points will be $100 per year ($3,000 ÷ 30 years).

Usually, the more points a borrower pays, the lower the interest rate on the loan. Generally, every one-half point change in points is accompanied by a one-eighth point change in the interest rate in the opposite direction. So an 8.75 percent mortgage with 2 points would become an 8.5 percent mortgage with 3 points.

Here's the bottom line on points. A buyer who plans to keep property for a short time should shop for a loan with a higher interest rate but lower points, whereas a buyer who intends to keep property long term should look for a lower interest rate and be willing to pay more points up front.

What Is a Home Equity Loan?

Up to this point, we've been concentrating on the most common type of mortgage loan—the "first mortgage"—normally taken out to make home purchase possible. However, many homeowners who already have mortgages are taking advantage of the equity they have built up in their homes by borrowing against that equity. These loans are called *home equity loans* and are a convenient source of needed cash. Many banks will lend up to 80 percent of the equity of your home—that is, the value of your home less the unpaid balance of your mortgage—without requiring lengthy loan applications or long waits for approval. However, do not fall into the trap of thinking that the net value of your home (after mortgage liability is considered) always becomes the amount you will be able to borrow on a home equity loan.

Consider this scenario: You have a $200,000 home with a $75,000 mortgage remaining. The bank states that its limit for a home equity loan is 80 percent of the appraised value. Therefore, you assume that the loan amount will be:

$200,000	Value of home
− 75,000	Mortgage remaining
$125,000	Equity in home
× 80%	Bank's appraisal limit rate
$100,000	Line of credit for home equity loan

Not necessarily correct, as some lenders have become very conservative in their method of computation. In the above example, even if you have $125,000 of equity in your home, you may not be able to receive 80 percent of it. Rather, the lender could compute your line of credit in the following manner:

$200,000	Value of home
× 80%	Bank's appraisal limit rate
$160,000	Bank's appraisal limit
− 75,000	Mortgage remaining
$ 85,000	Line of credit for home equity loan

Also remember that after you take out a home equity loan, you will have to make two monthly loan payments (one for the original mortgage and one for the second mortgage) to retain your ownership of a single piece of property.

What Are the Basic Types of Home Equity Loans?

Home equity loans come in two basic flavors: revolving line of credit and fixed rate. A *revolving line of credit account* is much like a standard credit card account—with the advantage of potential tax deductions. Customers can borrow as much as they like, up to a predetermined credit limit. For the first five to ten years they can make interest payments only, giving them the power to manage their cash flow. After the interest-only period, they pay off the balance in monthly installments at a variable rate of interest. Variable rates make the most sense for investors who know they are going to sell the property they are paying off in five to ten years.

With a *fixed-rate home equity loan*, the borrower pays off the loan with regular monthly payments at a constant rate of interest. Fixed rates are usually best for long-term borrowers looking to lock in a favorable interest rate, such as those in 2003–2005. Although the points are deductible for refinancing on home equity loans, as stated before, they cannot be deducted all at once but must be gradually written off over the years that you remain in the house. On the original purchase of a home, however, you can deduct the cost of the points at one time.

What Tax Ramifications Are There with Home Equity Refinancing?

Immediately after the 1986 Tax Reform Act, U.S. taxpayers found that they had lost most of their interest deductions on personal debt. But by taking out a home equity loan, they were still able to deduct the interest charge regardless of the purpose the funds were used for. The laws have changes slightly, but within the limits of sensible debt management, it is still advantageous to secure a home equity loan when you need money.

A home equity loan can turn some impossible dreams into reality. For example, such a loan is ideal for financing a child's education. It is often less expensive than a normal personal loan, the interest you are charged is usually tax deductible, and the payback period can be spread over 20 years. Or you may use the funds for that dream "retreat" that you were never able to afford. In today's economy, financing for vacation homes is not always readily available; and when it is, it is usually encumbered with stringent restrictions. Now, through home equity loans, these impossible dreams can become a reality.

A word of advice: Do not change your mortgage to fit the home you want. Better to change your home to fit the type of mortgage you can afford.

And on the topic of mortgages, it is amazing that yesterday's nest egg can't buy today's birdhouse.

It's a Wrap

- Mortgages come in two basic types: fixed rate and adjustable rate.
- If adjustable-rate mortgages appeal to you, be sure to evaluate how often the rate will be adjusted, what index governs the change, and whether the rate is "capped" at a stated maximum.
- Generally you will qualify financially for a mortgage if your housing costs don't exceed 28 percent of the family's monthly gross income. Another benchmark is that your total fixed debt (including car payments and the like) shouldn't exceed 36 percent of your gross monthly income.
- It may pay to refinance your mortgage if the new rate is at least 2 percentage points below the old one.
- Closing costs and points (one-time banking charges) affect the true rate of any mortgage or refinancing.
- Once you've paid off a fair percentage of your mortgage, home equity loans can be an excellent source of credit.

"The squeaky wheel may get the oil, but it is also the first one to be replaced."

CHAPTER 20

Mortgages—In Reverse

"A conventional mortgage will turn your income into equity, while a reverse mortgage will turn your equity into income."

Do I Need to Read This Chapter?

- Am I house-rich but cash-poor?

- Do I need income during retirement?

- Am I aware of the advantages and drawbacks of reverse mortgages?

- Do I realize that such mortgages offer a variety of payment plans?

In the previous chapter, we discussed the conventional mortgage. Let's reverse the topic and take a regular mortgage and stand it on its head. In other words, rather than borrowing a lump sum of money and paying it back monthly, let's get the entire loan in a lump sum or in monthly payments sent to us; and then we'll pay it back only if we sell the house or, better still, have our heirs pay for it at the time of our demise. In other words, you can live in your house for the rest of your life, receive monthly income or get payments anytime you want, and have your estate pay for all this after your death. It costs you nothing! The growth of RMs has been phenomenal. In 2001, only 8,000 were accepted, in 2005 over 48,000, and in 2006, 86,000 RMs were transacted.

How Can Reverse Mortgages Make Retirement Easier?

The beauty of reverse mortgages will be appreciated by the millions of retirees who have found it difficult, in today's economy, to make ends meet. It is true that most retirees own their own home, with a great deal of equity in it, but they do not have sufficient income to live their remaining years in the lifestyle that they have dreamed about. Most of these people are house rich and cash poor. Certainly they can sell their home for additional cash, but then where would they live? They can borrow through home equity loans (only if they qualify and have sufficient current income, which most do not), but they must still pay back a portion of the debt each month.

What to do? The answer is the reverse mortgage (RM)! Bear in mind that the topic of reverse mortgages can be a lengthy and complicated one. I will attempt, in the next few pages, to give you a clear, concise overview of what this program is all about, but more research on your part is needed.

What Is a Reverse Mortgage?

The *reverse mortgage* is a home loan that is treated in the opposite fashion of a *standard mortgage,* because the money goes from the lender (a bank, for example) to you, the homeowner. In other words, instead of your borrowing a large amount of money and making small monthly repayments to the lender, you borrow small amounts over a period of years, even for the rest of your life.

You do not give up any ownership when you take out an RM. All privileges of ownership stay with you as well as all responsibilities (taxes, insurance, maintenance, etc.). If you sell your home, the money that is owed becomes due and will come from the proceeds of the sale of the home. If you die before any sale is made, your estate will pay the amount that is owed.

Who Is Eligible for a Reverse Mortgage?

To be eligible for an RM (lenders have different requirements) you must own your home (single family, condo, co-op, townhouse, or a two-to-four unit dwelling), and you must be at least 62 years age. You do not want to be too young (in your early sixties) to take out an RM since your monthly income will be much less than if you were 10 years older. The reason that older people get a higher monthly income is that they have fewer years left to live, the value of their home will have increased, and the possibility of one of the spouses becoming widowed is greater.

 As for payout methods, many possibilities are available to you:

1. Single lump-sum payment
2. Lifetime monthly advances (most popular)
3. Monthly advances for a specific period of time
4. A line of credit (my choice)
5. Any combination of these payment methods

Monthly payments, credit line withdrawals, and lump-sum payments to homeowners are not to be considered as income for tax purposes. The income also does not affect social security and Medicare benefits.

What Is the Structure of the Reverse Mortgage?

All reverse mortgages are known as "rising-debt" loans because the amount you owe grows larger over a period of time. After you receive your first monthly advance, that is the amount that you will owe. But the next month you will receive more money, and that is added to what you already owe from the month before. The pattern goes on for each month that you live. You own the home during your lifetime, and the title rests with you. However, after your demise, if your heirs fail to repay the loan, the lender has the right to foreclose the property. Most RMs allow you to repay the loan at any time.

Medicare and social security eligibility are not based on either your assets or your income. Therefore, whatever advances you receive from the RM will not affect any benefits you receive from public programs. If you receive SSI, RM monthly advances will not affect your benefits as long as you spend the money within the month you receive it.

Bear in mind, and this is most important, that all income you receive from the RM (whether monthly or in a lump sum) is nontaxable. That means that you get to keep every penny you receive.

What Are the Drawbacks?

Of course, certain disadvantages are attached to the RM. The costs attributed to reverse mortgages (closing fees, points, etc.) are usually higher than the costs of other loans, and the interest rates charged by the lender are on a compounding basis. Because these fees can be high, you should plan to take out the RM only if you intend to live in the house for a long period of time. Also, this type of mortgage will give your heirs less equity in the home you leave them.

And another point to ponder: if RMs are as good as they appear to be for older homeowners, why have so few seniors made use of them? The reason lies in the fact that the terms of such agreements are harder to understand than those of other types of loans, going beyond the comprehension of most retirees. Another question to raise is that if reverse mortgages do represent a very lucrative market for lenders, why have most of the financial institutions ignored them? The answer is that an insured RM is neither a simple loan agreement backed by real estate nor a simple life insurance or annuity policy funded with cash. In other words, both banks and insurance companies must stretch their expertise way beyond their normal boundaries in order to design and market this product, which is both risky and expensive. Because of the complexity of the reverse mortgage, you must meet with a counselor (who will examine the reverse mortgage with you) before your application can be accepted. After the meeting, closure could take about two to three months for completion.

How Is the Amount of Payment to You Determined?

The amount of money you receive from your lender will depend upon three factors:

1. *Age.* How old you are at the closing of the mortgage will determine, in part, the amount of your income. Naturally the older you are, the more money you will receive, since you have fewer years left to receive this income. If you are

married, some lenders will use the age of the younger spouse; others will average the two life ages together in order to determine their payment to you.

2. *Equity.* The value of your home will determine the monthly income you will receive. Some lenders may have minimums or maximums on the value of your home. For example, at today's current rates, a person age 70 with a $200,000 house could receive $700 monthly for life or $113,000 in a credit line.

3. *Costs.* The costs of closing fees, insurance, and interest will determine the net amount of your monthly receipt. There is now a method for homeowners to determine the potential cost of a loan. It is known as *total annual loan cost (TALC)*, which is a disclosure form that all lenders must provide to anyone interested in securing a reverse mortgage. This program will inform the borrower of the approximate total annual cost of the loan expressed as an interest rate. It gives the homeowner the real cost of the loan by showing the total annual percentage rate (*a*) after two years, (*b*) at life expectancy of the homeowner, and (*c*) at some point beyond life expectancy. Because the effective cost of an RM decreases the longer it is held, the form reflects different costs for different time periods. TALC rates make it possible for homeowners to compare the actual cost of reverse mortgage programs with very different types of itemized costs.

Let me clarify the major difference between a standard (also known as *forward*) mortgage and a reverse mortgage. In a standard mortgage, your monthly payments to the lender become equity for you in the future, whereas in a reverse mortgage you turn your present equity into monthly income (as a debt). In other words, a standard mortgage builds up your equity with each payment you make, while a reverse mortgage spends down your equity with each payment you receive. Remember, you can never fall behind or even have late payments since there are never any payments due on your part.

What Types of Plans Are Offered?

You'll want to select the method of income payment that suits your lifestyle and situation. Generally, lenders offer three plans:

1. The *tenure plan* provides monthly repayments to you for as long as you live in your home. These payments will continue until you die, sell, or move away.

2. The *term plan* provides a monthly advance for a specific number of months that you select (higher income each month than the tenure plan). When the time period runs out and the lender's repayments to you cease, you are not required to make payments back to the lender as long as you live in the house.

3. The *line of credit* lets you decide when you would like additional cash. If you combine the tenure or term plan with the line-of-credit plan, you will have not just income each month but also the option of meeting any unexpected expenses (having to leave your home for health reasons, for example) that may occur in the future. Remember that your concern is in the future, because that is where you will be spending the rest of your life.

What Other Information Should You Know about the Reverse Mortgage?

1. Watch out for the "default" clause that appears in some contracts. This acceleration means that certain conditions could force you to sell your home before you die. These may include an extended stay at a nursing care facility, failure to pay property tax, failure to maintain and insure the property, personal bankruptcy, fraud, and condemnation proceedings.

2. Look to see if there is an "appreciation sharing" clause that permits the lending institution to share in any appreciation or increase in value of the home upon its ultimate sale.

3. Remember that an RM is a loan only against your home equity; thus you can never owe more that the value of your home at any time. This limited liability is known as the nonrecourse limit, stopping the lender from seeking more money from your other assets or from your heirs. In other words, if you should live many years more than was initially anticipated (thus receiving more income than your house is worth), the lender cannot go after your estate to make up the difference.

4. Look at the RM in the same manner as a single-premium annuity policy. Under the annuity concept, you receive a monthly income for the rest of your life by taking money out of your capital and paying one lump-sum payment in advance. The reverse mortgage works in a similar fashion, but instead of giving the lender a large amount of money, you merely put up your house as the collateral for the funds. The big difference is that you still have your capital.

5. The lending institution that holds your reverse mortgage will get the money it paid to you (principal, interest, and costs) when the home is sold. *Let me emphasize how crucial it is to examine these costs carefully.* Although the interest rate that is charged to you is the one that is most visible, expenses can vary considerably and may include origination and insurance fees, interest on loan advances, and, of course, closing costs. The best method to treat all the various charges involved in the process is to insist that all loan costs be combined into one single rate. This is known as the *total annual percentage rate (TAPR)*, which will show all costs that will become due at the loan's maturity.

6. The lender must send you monthly advances until you sell, give away your home, or die. At that time, under any of these conditions, the money owed is paid back to the lender. However, the vast majority of homeowners will never themselves actually pay back the money that has been advanced to them. Rather, the amount owed will be paid after their death by their estate, normally from the sale of the house. What you are actually doing, then, is using and enjoying the money "while you are living." After your demise, your heirs will meet your obligations and retain whatever is left for themselves. Remember that you are not taking any money out of your children's pockets, as they are not paying anything that you owe from their personal assets. What you are doing instead is leaving them a little less. However, you should inform them of the RM because they will have to pay off the RM debt if they decide to keep the house in the family. In other words, you are spending part of your children's inheritance.

And on the topic of children, when you teach your child, you teach your child's child.

It's a Wrap

- Reverse mortgages may be an ideal solution for those who own their home "free and clear" but have little monthly income.
- You do not give up any of the benefits or responsibilities of homeownership by holding a reverse mortgage.
- You do not repay a reverse mortgage unless you sell, move, or die (in which case, the estate is responsible).
- Reverse mortgages allow you to draw down the equity in your home through a lump-sum payment, monthly advances, or a line of credit.

- Payments enjoyed through reverse mortgages are not considered as income for purposes of tax, social security, or Medicare.
- Reverse mortgage lenders may be hard to find. If you do locate one, you may pay high closing costs to secure your loan.
- You can repay a reverse mortgage at any time.
- If you owe money on your reverse mortgage when you die, your heirs must pay the balance (normally from the sale of the house).

"Aspire to inspire before you expire."

CHAPTER 21

Planning Your Retirement—An Overview

<hr>

"Retirement takes all the fun out of Sundays."

Do I Need to Read This Chapter?

- Am I thinking about the financial and emotional implications of retirement?

- Do I know at what age I want to retire?

- Do I understand how pension payouts work?

- Am I clear on IRA rollover rules?

I have read of five emotional stages that people will go through before and during retirement:

1. *Imagination.* About 10 years before retirement, you begin to dream about that period of leisure life.

2. *Anticipation.* A few years before retirement, you begin to realize what a different lifestyle you will be entering into. This is a period of both excitement and worry.

3. *Liberation.* The first year of the period of retirement allows you the free time to read, travel, reconnect, and plan.

4. *Reorientation.* The honeymoon year is over, and it's time to settle in and realize the vast amount of time you have on your hands and how costly retirement can be.

5. *Reconciliation.* Now is the time to reflect and learn what you can and cannot do, both physically and financially.

In the following chapters, various retirement plans are discussed. Whether you are employed by a corporation or a government agency, are self-employed, or are working part time, some of the options explained will affect your future financial plans.

About 38 percent of all workers had traditional pension plans 25 years ago. Today, that number is less than 20 percent and shrinking, as employers continue to reduce their fringe benefits (medical, pensions).

How Does Early Retirement Play a Role in the Various Retirement Plans?

There is a story of a beautiful bird that was powerful and free. It had magnificent, colorful plumage, of which it was very proud. One day the bird decided to pluck its feathers, one by one, in order to make a nest in which it could rest in comfort and security. Now it cannot fly.

Don't consider retiring until you are both financially and emotionally ready. Why? Because people have not been properly prepared for retirement in America. We spend a third of our lifetime preparing for a career but almost no time in preparing for the period afterward.

Why Should You Plan Ahead for Retirement?

Because of the medical breakthroughs that have allowed us to live longer, retirement can be as long as 20 to 30 years. Your income from social security and pension may not be enough to cover your lifestyle during your retirement. Yet people are not saving enough to bridge the gap. Add taxes and inflation to this picture, and you understand why planning ahead is so important. Remember, Fix a roof before it rains.

 Are you puzzled at this point? Are you thinking that there are thousands of books and magazines on retirement? Of course there are. But few of them cover the key point: the feeling of being retired. Today's unanswered question seems to be not so much what happens physically to people when they retire as what happens to them emotionally. The American public, the government, and the medical profession put more effort into helping folks reach old age than in helping them enjoy it. Can you imagine filling 10 hours a day (3,650 hours a year) in leisure? That huge amount of time hangs over every retired person like unspent capital. I have met many retired women who complain about having their husbands always around. One told me, "I married him for better or worse, but not for lunch."

How Long Will Your Money Last?

"Longevity risk" is the concept of the possibility of outliving your money. Lots of decisions, not all of them voluntary, help to determine when you will retire. If you have any say in the matter, I advise your being very careful about what age you will leave the workforce. The decision to retire should be based on your financial status, and careful planning is mandatory. For example, people who are nearing retirement or have begun retirement with a fixed-asset base may be concerned whether their money will last as long as it will be needed. If you are forced to dip into your principal in order to make ends meet, Table 21.1 may be of great help to you. It shows how long your money will last if you must draw from it at a rate faster than it is growing. As an illustration, suppose your assets are earning an 8 percent annual return and you must withdraw 15 percent of your principal each year in order to live comfortably in retirement. As shown in the table, your money should last approximately 10 years. Some advisors state that you will need about 80 percent of preretirement income to keep your current standard of living after you retire. They base this percentage on the fact that you will no longer have work-related expenses. I do not believe this. Most retirees will need their full 100 percent as they now can take longer vacations, develop hobbies, and partake in a vast amount of costly entertainment. Your spending during retirement can even be higher

Table 21.1 Earnings and Withdrawals

If Principal Is Earning at This Rate	And You Are Withdrawing at This Rate										
	16%	15%	14%	13%	12%	11%	10%	9%	8%	7%	6%
12%	12	14	17	23			Here's how many years				
11	11	13	15	18	24		your principal will last				
10	10	12	13	15	19	25					
9	10	11	12	14	16	20	27				
8	9	10	11	12	14	17	21	28			
7	9	9	10	11	13	15	18	22	31		
6	8	9	10	11	12	13	16	19	24	33	
5	8	8	9	10	11	12	14	17	20	26	37

than that during your working period with the high cost of medical care and former employers' cuts in their health plans. You must realize that you can save for a limited period in your life, but your spending is for all your life. Thus you must have sufficient assets during your working years in order to balance your retirement period.

How Do Lump-Sum Distributions Work?

Every day, for various reasons, people receive large lump-sum distributions representing the accumulated value of their pension plans. This may occur when you retire, or it may occur sooner if you become disabled, if you leave your present employer, or if the company decides to terminate your pension plan. In any case, when you receive such a lump-sum distribution, you face a problem: How do you minimize the taxes on this often sizable payment?

What Is an IRA Rollover?

A method to reduce the taxes on your lump-sum distribution is to roll it over—that is, reinvest it—in an IRA. This must be done within 60 days of receiving the distribution, or you will lose the tax-shelter status otherwise conferred by the IRA. You don't have to pay any current income taxes on the distribution amount if you deposit it in an IRA, nor will you owe taxes on the income that accumulates in the account. The IRA funds become taxable only upon withdrawal, which may begin after you reach age 59½ and must begin by age 70½. See the next chapter (Chapter 22) for specific rulings on IRAs.

And on the topic of retirement, before you decide to retire, take a week off and watch daytime TV.

It's a Wrap

- Retirement is a major life change, financially and emotionally.
- In cashing out a pension, look to minimize taxes.

"The 'Haves' and 'Have Nots' can be traced back to the 'Dids' and 'Did Nots.'"

The IRA

◆◆

"You can plan for tomorrow today, but you can't plan for today tomorrow."

Do I Need to Read This Chapter?

- Am I eligible for an IRA?

- Am I aware of the recent changes in IRA rules?

- Do I know that, under certain conditions, I can withdraw from my IRA before age 59½ without penalty?

- Am I clear on the rules for mandatory IRA withdrawals after age 70½?

- Have I investigated various investment options for my IRA?

- Do I understand the difference between transfers and rollovers?

The *individual retirement account (IRA)* is a method of investment originally designed to help individuals not covered by company pension plans save for their retirement. On January 1, 1982, the law governing IRAs was changed to make them available to anyone with earned income (wages, fees) whether or not the individual was covered by a company pension plan.

How Does the IRA Work?

First, some basic ground rules. Your IRA is a savings account containing funds that can be invested in any of a number of different financial instruments. (I'll offer some guidelines on your options in a moment.) By law, you may contribute to your IRA up to 100 percent of the first $4,000 that you earn each year ($5,000 if you are over age 50). If a husband and wife are both working, they can establish an IRA and contribute up to $4,000 per year to each account, for a family total of $8,000. In 2008, that limit goes to $5,000 single and $10,000 jointly. Add an extra $1,000 per person if you will be over age 50.

By establishing the spousal IRA, the government finally recognized the value of the work that women do in their households. More important, the spousal IRA recognizes that women who don't work outside the house still need to think about saving for retirement. Women fail to save enough for their own retirement because they tend, during their lifetime, to move in and out of the workforce, causing their savings to be sporadic. Also, they live longer than men, thus requiring their savings to be stretched further. And, of course, women still earn less than men, which compounds the reasons just mentioned.

Previously, a nonworking spouse and a working spouse could invest together into an IRA a combined total of $2,250. A change was made that now permits stay-at-home spouses and their employed mates a total contribution of up to $8,000, which puts them on par with families in which both spouses work.

How Will My IRA Grow?

Many advertisers are touting the fact that a $4,000 annual deposit into an IRA (at 8 percent) by a 25-year-old would be worth over $1 million when the person reached age 65. Table 22.1 shows the value for different years and rate yields for a constant $4,000 annual contribution. The figures are very impressive.

Don't Forget
January may not be your favorite month weatherwise, but if you're investing in an IRA, you should learn to love it. It is very important that you make your IRA contribution in the beginning of the year. Over the long run, the tax deferral you get from the compounding of your earnings on that money can actually be more valuable than your IRA contribution. If you earn 8 percent on your $4,000 annual contribution, the $320 interest on the money you earn each year is compounded from the beginning of the year. If you wait until the end of the year, you will lose a whole year's compounded interest.

Table 22.1 Value of Principal for a $4,000 Yearly IRA Contribution

Year	Interest Rate		
	6%	**8%**	**10%**
1	$4,240	$4,320	$4,400
5	$23,902	$25,344	$26,862
10	$55,886	$62,582	$70,124
15	$98,690	$117,298	$139,800
20	$155,970	$197,692	$252,010
25	$232,626	$315,818	$432,728
30	$328,206	$489,384	$723,774
35	$472,484	$744,408	$1,192,508
40	$656,190	$1,199,124	$1,947,408

What Are the Tax Consequences of the IRA?

The money you contribute to your IRA is deducted from your income for tax purposes, providing immediate tax benefits, and is called a *deductible contribution.*

If you earn too much income, or already participate in a 401(k) or similar retirement plan, your tax-deductible contributions to a regular IRA are gradually phased out. This means that some of your contributions to a regular IRA cannot be deducted from your income. The contributions that are not tax deductible are called *nondeductible* contributions. Here are the income limits at which your tax-deductible contributions phase out:

- *Single filers that participate in a plan.* If your modified adjusted gross income (MAGI) is more than $50,000 and less than $60,000, some of your contribution is nondeductible. Above $60,000, your entire contribution is nondeductible.

- *Married persons filing joint return and you (but not your spouse) participate in a plan.* If your modified adjusted gross income is more than $75,000 and less than $85,000, some of your contribution is nondeductible. Above $85,000, your entire contribution is nondeductible.

In 1998, a new form of IRA was initiated—the Roth IRA. Although the contributions you make from income from working up to $4,000 ($5,000 if you are over age 50) are not tax deductible, the investment earnings are eliminated while the traditional IRA simply defers them. The longer you have until you retire, the more earnings will be and the more you will have saved by avoiding taxes on those gains. Only joint filers with adjusted gross income of $150,000 or less and single filers with less than $110,000 of income can set up the Roth IRA.

1. Investment gains can be withdrawn tax free as long as you have held the account for at least five years.
2. Your after-tax contribution can be withdrawn without penalty or tax at any time.
3. There are no required minimum distributions, which gives you more flexibility in planning your estate. If you wish, you can leave the entire amount of a Roth IRA to your beneficiaries.

Also, you can benefit from a Roth IRA if you:

1. Don't qualify for the deduction through the traditional IRA.
2. Want to continue the tax-sheltered investments.
3. Are in the same or a higher tax bracket at retirement.

What Are the Rules for IRA Distributions?

Since the IRA was created specifically to make it easier for working people to save for their retirement, there are built-in restrictions on your access to IRA funds:

1. You can begin withdrawing your IRA money without penalty after reaching age 59½.
2. If you must withdraw money from your IRA before that time, you must pay an extra 10 percent penalty tax on the amount you withdraw, unless you are disabled.
3. You must start withdrawing from your IRA at age 70½.

How Bad Are the IRA Penalties?

The penalty for early withdrawal deters many young people from opening IRAs. When you're 25 years old, 59½ may seem an eternity away, and more than 30 years may seem like an impossibly long time to tie up your money. However, the effects of the penalty aren't nearly as severe as you might think. Because of the tax benefits derived both at the time of the contribution and during the accumulation of tax-free interest, IRA accounts become profitable fairly quickly even when the penalty for early withdrawal is taken into account. With five or six years of compounding, your income will compensate for the withdrawal penalty. After that time, even if you incur the 10 percent penalty, you will have increased your money faster than otherwise possible because of the tax benefits.

Therefore, don't let the early withdrawal penalty discourage you unduly. An IRA is still a highly beneficial investment.

I'm Turning 70½. What Now?

When you reach age 70½, you must begin to take money out of your IRA. The first year, however, the government gives you a grace period until April 1 of the following year. After that first year, your withdrawal must be made by December 31. Be aware that if you take advantage of the delay in the first year, you will have to take two years' worth of withdrawals, which could push you into a higher tax bracket and make your social security benefits more exposed to tax.

The minimum amount of withdrawal each year is based on your life expectancy, or if a beneficiary is named, on the joint life expectancy of both. To compute the withdrawal, you divide the amount in the IRA by the appropriate life-expectancy figure. At age 70, a life expectancy of 15 years would mean $\frac{1}{15}$ of your total IRA balance. In years to follow, you can reduce the original expectancy by 1 year ($\frac{1}{14}$, $\frac{1}{13}$, $\frac{1}{12}$, etc.). This is known as *term certain*. Another method available is to recalculate (*annual recalculation method*) the number of years of life expectancy each year. Once you choose a method, though, you must stay with it.

Comparison of the Traditional and the Roth IRA

	Traditional	Roth
To be eligible:	Under age 70½ with compensation Single filers' income up to $60,000 Joint filers' income up to $85,000	Any age with compensation (subject to income limits); also nonworking spouses Single filers' income up to $110,000 (for full contribution) Joint filers' income up to $160,000 (for full contribution) See partial contribution limits
Per year maximum contribution	$4,000 or 100% compensation. Individuals age 50 or older (in the calendar year for which they make the contribution) can additional "catch-up" contribution of $1,000	$4,000 or 100% compensation. Individuals age 50 or older (in the calendar year for which they make the contribution) can contribute an additional "catch-up" contribution of $1,000
Contribution tax status	Contributions may be tax deductible	Contributions are *not* tax deductible
Federal tax	Federal tax-deferred growth	Federal tax-free growth
Withdrawals	May withdraw after age 59½ without penalty	Can withdraw contributions anytime without penalty or tax

If one spouse dies, only the survivor's life expectancy can be used. When both parties die, the entire balance of the IRA must be paid out within one year to whoever is designated. That lump sum could produce a major tax bill for your beneficiary. By using the term-certain method, the beneficiary gets the money in small amounts annually, just as the maker of the IRA would have received.

No matter which method is chosen, you must make a definite decision. If you do not, for example, let the government know whether you wish your IRA money paid out over individual or joint life expectancies by the year you reach 70½, the IRS will make that choice for you through the individual life-expectancy method. Also, you will lose your choice again if your IRA does not specify "term-certain." The IRS will make the distribution using the annual recalculation method.

A change in the law allows you to extend your IRA withdrawal period to cover the combined life expectancy of you and your spouse. This figure will usually be higher than the life expectancy of either husband or wife. For example, as an assumption, a 70-year-old man is expected to live 12 years;

a 70-year-old woman, 15 years. However, one or the other might be expected to survive for 18 years. Therefore, the 70-year-old couple can use the 18-year life-expectancy figure as the basis of their withdrawals if they wish—and they can recalculate their combined life expectancy each year as well.

What Happens If You Die Before You Become Eligible to Use Your IRA Funds?

Whenever you open an IRA, you must designate a beneficiary. Then, in the event of your untimely death, that person must make some key decisions. If your beneficiary is your spouse, he or she may choose any of the following options:

- The spouse an withdraw IRA funds as a lump sum, which would be taxable during that year.
- The spouse can take yearly distributions based on his or her life expectancy.
- The spouse can use a portion of the money for current needs and roll over the balance.
- The spouse can convert the IRA into his or her own account. The new owner will have all the rights and obligations of the former owner.

Most spouses choose to roll over the money left to them into their own IRA. However, if the beneficiary is not a spouse, he or she has only five years to take all the money out of the account and cannot roll over the funds into an IRA. Also, if you name as beneficiary your estate, the money in the IRA will be taxed as ordinary income as of the date of your demise.

How Do IRAs Relate to Revocable Living Trusts?

In the view of most experts, it is not a good idea to make a revocable living trust the beneficiary of an IRA if the owner is over 70 years of age. People use a revocable trust because they may not want a beneficiary to have access to all the money at one time, or they fear the long and costly probate procedures. Some investors want their retirement funds managed by professionals after they die, and the revocable trust affords them this feature.

However, the problem arises when the IRA owner (who is over 70½ and has been recalculating the minimum payout each year) dies. Since the revocable trust has no life expectancy, all the money in the IRA is paid into the trust and becomes immediately subject to income tax. If the deceased had named a beneficiary, the beneficiary could withdraw the money based on his or her own life expectancy.

What Investment Options Are Available for an IRA?

When you invest in an IRA, the law requires that a trustee be named to administer the account. The trustee must file reports with you and the federal government. Typical IRA trustees include commercial and savings banks, savings and loan institutions, brokerage houses, insurance companies, and other types of investment firms.

As for the type of investment, any of a wide range of choices may be suitable for your IRA, depending on your age and financial status and the degree of risk you wish to take. The only restrictions on IRA investments are these:

You may not invest your IRA funds in collectibles, such as postage stamps, coins (except certain U.S. gold and silver coins), antiques, or art.

You may not invest your IRA funds in life insurance contracts.

You may not make an investment in which you have a direct interest, as, for example, if you were to buy a home with IRA funds and then rent it from the IRA account.

Here are some of the most popular investment choices for IRA accounts:

1. *Certificates of deposit.* An IRA bank account usually takes the form of a certificate of deposit. Rates may be fixed in advance or variable. If the rate is variable, find out just how it is set and how often it is adjusted—weekly, monthly, or whatever. In general, the most conservative investment strategy is to invest for the shortest available term.

2. *Stocks and bonds.* If you wish, you can deposit your IRA money with a stockbroker, who will act as your trustee. However, you direct the account yourself: you make your own investment decisions, and you can buy and sell

stocks and bonds, moving your funds from one investment to another, without incurring any taxes on the money.

3. *Mutual funds.* You can deposit your IRA money in a mutual fund and so invest, not in a few self-selected stocks, but in a managed portfolio of many issues put together by a brokerage firm. You may wish to choose a broker who offers a "family of funds" of different types among which you are free to switch your investment from time to time without charge or penalty. Also, remember that there's no need to invest in any of the special tax-exempt mutual funds; your IRA investment is already sheltered from all levels of taxation. Stick to funds that are normally taxable; these usually offer a higher rate of return. Also, look into zero coupon bonds (see Chapter 10) for funding your IRA.

How Should You Choose among These Investment Options?

One prime consideration should be how well you have otherwise provided for your retirement. If your IRA is your sole retirement plan, you should invest conservatively; if you have a substantial savings outside of the IRA—income that you expect to continue after retirement, or a secure company pension plan—you can afford a bit more risk. Your age is another important factor. Here are some guidelines to use depending on your present age:

Ages 20 to 40. When you are young, growth should be a primary goal; a relatively high degree of risk is tolerable. *Suggestion*: Invest your IRA in a diversified portfolio of common stocks or in a mutual fund managed for growth of assets, not income.

Ages 40 to 50. Stocks are still an attractive choice; however, if you expect to begin withdrawing your IRA funds when you reach age 59½, redirect some of your funds from growth stocks into current income-generating investments.

Ages 50 to 60. At this point, growth is less important, and risk less acceptable. Move some, up to half, of your investments out of stocks and into bonds, in order to minimize risk and increase your current flow of income.

Age 60 and over. By now, most of your IRA funds should be in income-producing investments with maturities of five years and less. This will provide safety and maximum current interest.

What about Rollover Distributions to IRAs?

All eligible rollover distributions are subject to a mandatory 20 percent withholding tax. Although this 20 percent withholding would still be considered part of the distribution, which is subject to income tax, you can claim a federal tax refund if the 20 percent withholding results in overwitholding for the year. There are two ways to avoid current taxation on this mandatory 20 percent withholding.

1. You elect to do a *direct rollover*. This means that your distribution is moved directly to another retirement plan or IRA rather than distributed to you. In the case of a direct rollover, the 20 percent withholding would not apply. Under this method, you would need to have your employer or plan coordinator write a check payable to the trustee of your new plan, putting on the memo line of the check the words "Direct Rollover." Once this transfer is made into your IRA, you can take the money out the very next day without the 20 percent withholding. However, you may do so only once a year. If you are under the age of 59½, the entire balance must be put back into an IRA within 60 days, or a 10 percent penalty is imposed.

2. You may add your own after-tax funds, up to the amount withheld, to the amount that you actually received in order to roll over an amount equal to your entire taxable distribution. Sounds complicated? Use this as an example: Assume Marc Weintraub elects to receive a lump-sum distribution of $100,000 from his retirement account. Because of the 20 percent withholding rule, he would receive only $80,000. However, since he is entitled to roll over the entire $100,000, $20,000 of personal funds could be added to bring the total amount of the rollover up to $100,000. The 20 percent withheld at the time of distribution would be refunded when he files his tax return. If Marc does not choose to add the additional $20,000 personally but instead rolls over only $80,000 of the $100,000 received from the original trustee, he must include the $20,000 as taxable income for that year.

If there is a waiting period for you to get into your new employer's plan and you do not want to follow step 1 or 2, you can get the plan coordinator to transfer your funds to a "conduit" IRA. This type of IRA is used as a temporary account for rollovers in order to keep them separate from other IRA funds since no comingling of funds is acceptable for rollovers. This conduit IRA must be set up at a place where no other IRA of yours exists.

Keep the following points in mind when reviewing the 20 percent withholding:

1. The 20 percent withholding applies only to lump-sum withdrawals and not to periodic withdrawals such as those taken by retirees who are taking a monthly payout.
2. Two types of distributions are not eligible for rollovers and thus are not subject to the 20 percent withholding:
   - Required minimum distribution received after age 70½
   - Payments received in 10 or more annual installments or in a series of equal installments extending over the participant's lifetime
3. It is the participant's responsibility to inform his or her employer or plan sponsor of a desire to transfer.

What Are the Basic Differences between the Transfer and the Rollover?

Both transfers and rollovers are ways to move retirement funds from one custodian to another. It is the way in which the funds are moved that differs:

A *transfer* means moving IRA funds from one account directly to another, with no distribution of funds to the account owner. Typically, you would make a transfer if you wanted to consolidate several IRAs, if you were to move and wanted your funds managed by an institution close by, or if you weren't happy with your current trustee's service or account management. The IRA places no limits on the number of transfers you make. And because you never actually receive the funds, you are not required to report these transactions at tax time. You can transfer all or only part of an account, and no tax is withheld from the amounts you transfer.

A *rollover* involves a distribution of retirement funds to the owner, after which the funds are put into another account. Rollovers can be made between IRAs or from a qualified employer retirement plan to an IRA. If you plan to participate in a company retirement plan—for example, a profit-sharing or

401(k) program—you will usually receive all funds in which you are vested if you leave the company for any reason or if the plan is terminated. Depending on your length of service with your employer, this distribution could be sizable. If you choose to keep it, you will pay tax on the distribution, which means that a significant portion—depending on your tax situation—will go to the government. But if you roll it over into an IRA, you defer taxation and keep your retirement funds growing until you really need them later, after retirement.

As noted earlier, you can also withdraw funds from one IRA and roll them over into another IRA. And, finally, you can roll over inherited funds from your spouse's IRA or qualified retirement plan.

Whatever the distribution's source, you may roll over all or any portion of the distribution, but the IRS requires that you deposit rollover funds no later than the sixtieth day after you receive them. Any amount you fail to roll over within this period will be taxable as ordinary income (unless, in an IRA-to-IRA rollover, it represents a return of nondeductible IRA contributions). You may also have to pay a 10 percent penalty for taking a premature distribution.

> **&Don't Forget**
>
> This important rule governs IRA-to-IRA rollovers: you are permitted to make only one rollover from a given plan in any 12-month period. That is, if you take a distribution from IRA 1 and roll over the funds to IRA 2, you must wait 12 months from the date of the distribution before you can make another rollover from IRA 1. If you make more than one rollover from the same plan within a 12-month period, you may have to pay a 10 percent premature distribution penalty.

Neither a transfer nor a rollover affects the amount of the deductibility of your annual contributions to your IRA. They are separate transactions, involving only funds that were previously saved for your retirement.

The IRA is certainly a plan to look into for your retirement since it can become an excellent vehicle for future income.

And on the topic of retirement plans, remember to plan for the future now because that is where you will be spending the rest of your life.

It's a Wrap

- Individual retirement accounts are like long-term savings accounts with tax-deferred benefits.

- Stay-at-home spouses and their employed mates can contribute a combined total of up to $8,000 in IRAs if they qualify.

- You can make tax-deductible contributions to an IRA if you earn up to $50,000 individually or $80,000 jointly.

- Making IRA contributions at the start of the year greatly improves your long-term yield.

- You can begin withdrawing from your IRA at age 59$\frac{1}{2}$; you must begin doing so at age 70$\frac{1}{2}$, which is based on life expectancy.

- IRA investors must name a beneficiary, who will have several withdrawal options in the event of the original investor's untimely death.

- IRAs are generally invested in CDs, stocks, bonds, and/or mutual funds.

- Rollover distributions to IRAs are subject to 20 percent withholding tax, but there are ways to avoid this tax.

"Every exit is an entrance somewhere else."

CHAPTER 23

The 401(k), the SEP, and the Keogh Plan

◆◆◆◆◆◆◆◆◆◆◆◆◆◆◆◆◆◆◆◆◆◆◆◆◆◆◆◆◆◆◆◆◆◆◆◆

"In two days, tomorrow will be yesterday."

Do I Need to Read This Chapter?

- Am I clear on the different retirement savings options that may be available to me?

- If my employer offers a 401(k), am I making the most of it?

- If I'm self-employed, have I investigated the benefits of SEPs and Keoghs?

An increasingly popular way of saving for retirement is the *401(k) plan,* named after the tax law provision that makes it possible. The 401(k) is known as the *deferred salary reduction plan* and allows an employee to set aside part of his or her salary into a tax-sheltered account that grows tax free until after retirement. Don't confuse the 401(k) with a 403(b). A 403(b) is a retirement plan designed for employees of nonprofit organizations (schools, hospitals, etc.), whereas the 401(k) is for employees of private, for-profit businesses. Salary deductions for a 403(b) are treated in the same manner as the funds in the 401(k) account, which is excluded from taxable income, while the interest earned compounds tax deferred until you withdraw the funds.

Many employers offering 401(k) plans will match contributions. An employer may add an amount for each dollar you contribute, up to a certain percentage of your salary or add a fixed sum. It is an automatic return on your investment and boosts your total retirement amount over a plan. Remember, though, that your employer's matching funds are treated as a pretax contribution, and you will have to pay taxes when you withdraw those funds.

Also, a 401(k) plan can provide a great deal of flexibility, offering a wide range of investment options. The choice becomes yours, letting you be as aggressive or conservative as you wish.

How Does the 401(k) Differ from an Ordinary IRA?

Since you don't have to pay current income tax on the money you deposit in your 401(k) account, the plan is something like an individual retirement account. However, unlike an IRA, a 401(k) plan must be set up by your employer.

 To qualify for a 401(k), you must meet all these requirements. You must:
Be full-time employee
Be over the age of 21
Have worked for the company at least one year
Be willing to contribute (in 2007) 20 percent of your gross income or $15,500 ($20,500 if over age 50), whichever is less

What about Withdrawal from a 401(k)?

If you leave the company, you can withdraw your 401(k) savings and keep the money if you wish. However, the amount becomes subject to income tax during that year. You can avoid taxation by rolling the money over into an IRA. To do so, you must transfer the money directly from your trustee to the IRA's trustee, making certain that you never take possession of the funds. In this trustee-to-trustee relationship, you will avoid the 20 percent withholding tax. If you consider that the average employee will change jobs six times during his or her career, this is certainly a major advantage. You are also eligible to withdraw your 401(k) money at any time without having to pay a penalty if you suffer a financial hardship.

Once you reach the age of 59½, the money in your 401(k) funds is yours to do with as you please. Of course, it is taxable when you withdraw it. However, your income will probably be lower after you retire, and so might your tax bracket. And the 401(k) account has another major advantage over the IRA when withdrawal time comes. If you withdraw your IRA funds in a lump sum, you must suffer a big tax bite during that year.

If the owner of the 401(k) dies before withdrawal, the amount of money in the plan is distributed to his or her beneficiaries, and the money is taxed as ordinary income to the beneficiaries. However, if the money is left to a surviving spouse, that spouse may transfer the funds to his or her IRA account.

How about 401(k) Investments in My Ex-Employer's Stock?

If some of your money is invested in your employer's company stock, rolling over your 401(k) when you leave the firm may not be the best idea. It could be better if you take the shares rather than roll them into an IRA. The reasons for this procedure are these:

1. You will owe tax only on the value of your shares at the time they were put into your 401(k) because the transactions will be based on a lower cost basis. For example, suppose the value per share of stock at the time it went into your 401(k) was $10 per share, but now, when you are ready to leave, its value jumped to $35 per share. By taking the stock and not rolling it over, you will owe taxes on the $10 figure (your cost basis), not the $35 market value.

2. When you sell the stock, you will pay capital gains rather than your ordinary tax rate.

3. Your heirs could receive the gains on these shares tax free. Because you held these shares and have not placed them in an IRA, your heirs' cost basis would be the market value of $35, which would mean they would owe no taxes on your gains. Rolling into an IRA would then have the effect of having your heirs owe ordinary income tax on the value of the shares you left them.

4. If your company goes out of business or fails financially, your 401(k) plan is protected by the Employee Retirement Income Security Act. Because the

401(k) is not considered an asset of your employer, it is held in trust in a separate account for you.

5. With the collapse of Enron, thousands of employees' retirement savings were wiped out. Thus, in 2007, a new law required that all 401(k) statememts be sent to contributors quarterly and must include advice concerning the benefits of diversification.

Also the law allowed a son or daughter, domestic partner, or parent to roll over money from a 401(k) from a deceased person without paying taxes on it immediately. Prior to 2007, only a spouse could do this. In order to achieve this new status, a nonspouse beneficiary must set up an Inherited IRA account in the name of the deceased through a trustee-to-trustee transfer. That beneficiary must then send a letter to the former employee of the deceased stating that the check that is issued should be in the name of the institution that will be the new trustee of the account.

What Is a Roth 401(k)?

In 2006, the government established the Roth 401(k). Unlike the traditional 401(k), where contributions are made on pretax earnings (which reduce your taxable income) but become taxable upon retirement, an employee's Roth 401(k) contribution is made in after-tax money, with withdrawals being tax free.

This will benefit those who may be paying taxes at a higher rate during their retirement years than they are now paying due to other income from investments, and it will also benefit those planning to work during retirement.

1. You can invest in a traditional 401(k) and a Roth 401(k) as long as you do not exceed the contribution maximum in total.
2. You can invest in a Roth 401(k) and a Roth IRA (see Chapter 22) as long as you meet the income limits for a Roth IRA. There are no limits for a Roth 401(k) plan.

As you can see, the 401(k) plan is a very attractive investment option for you as an employee, especially since the usual employer matching-contribution program in effect doubles your annual savings at no cost to you. And if you can afford to contribute to both a 401(k) account and an IRA, do that, too. You'll benefit right now as well as when you retire.

Comparing Retirement Plans

	Roth IRA	Regular 401(k)	Roth 401(k)
Earnings not to exceed	$160,000	No limit	No limit
Maximum contribution	$4,000 ($5,000 over age 50)	$15,500 ($20,500 over age 50)	$15,500 ($20,500 over age 50)
Up-front tax break	No	Yes	No
Taxable withdrawals	No	Yes	No
Partial withdrawal	No	Yes (age 70½)	Yes (age 70½)

How Does the SEP Work?

For a small business (proprietorship, partnership, corporation) of less than 100 employees, a *simplified employee pension*, or *SEP*, is an excellent pension-planning tool since it can help business owners, including those self-employed, to achieve financial security for their retirement. It was authorized in 1978 by Congress to give small businesses (even self-employed workers without employees) a program of current tax deduction and future pension benefits.

The business sets up an IRA for each employee and contributes, each year, as much as $44,000 or 25 percent of earnings. These contributions are tax deductible to the company. Employees may decide how to contribute the funds to their IRAs and can take the IRAs with them when they leave the firm. There is no complex administration, and the start-up and maintenance costs are slight.

 For small businesses and their employees, as well as self-employed individuals who work alone, SEPs are attractive retirement vehicles. SEP investors enjoy tax benefits in the present, as well. Before investing, here is what you should know:

1. Employer contributions to the SEP are tax deductible to the company and are not considered taxable income of the employee. These monies accumulate in the employee's SEP/IRA on a tax-deferred basis.
2. No start-up or annual filing costs are required to be sent to the U.S. Department of Labor. As its name implies, it is a simple plan to administer. The paperwork usually amounts to no more than a one-time completion of a model plan. Unless changes are made in the plan, you do not have to file annually, as you do with a Keogh.

Continued

3. All amounts from the SEP are considered ordinary income, with distribution of monies beginning no later than age 70½. Any withdrawal prior to age 59½ may be subject to a 10 percent penalty.
4. All eligible employees over age 21 must be included in the plan.
5. The same percentage that the employer receives must be applied to each employee, including yourself.
6. Lump-sum distributions from the SEP do not qualify for special income averaging, as they do for Keogh plans.
7. Unlike conventional company pension plans, in which employees usually have to wait a number of years before gaining access to their contributions, the SEP allows employees the right to any contributions the employer makes for their benefit.

There is also a plan known as *SIMPLE* (*savings incentive match plan for employees*) in which an employee can contribute up to $10,000 ($12,500 if over age 50) annually with a mandatory employer contribution (up to 3 percent of salary) added to it. This plan was purposely devised to be extremely simple for the employer to set up and for the employee to contribute to. Two conditions apply: organizations offering the plan cannot have more than 100 employees, and SIMPLE must be the only qualified retirement plan offered.

SIMPLE lives up to its name. It doesn't demand the complicated nondiscrimination test required by other plans, and the IRS paperwork isn't as complex.

Are you a deadline kind of person? One of the major features of the SEP is the extra time allowed to initiate it. Many people look for last-minute tax deductions before the April 15 deadline. You can set up a SEP a few months into the next year, as compared with the Keogh plan, which requires completion by the last day of the year.

How Does the Keogh Plan Work?

The Keogh plan is a pension plan designed for the self-employed individual, whether the work is full or part time. In other words, you can work for an employer full time, but if you have any income from self-employment, part of that self-employment can be contributed to your own Keogh plan.

A Keogh plan account is similar to an IRA in several ways. Your annual contribution to a Keogh account reduces your taxable income, and the sums in your account grow tax free until you withdraw your investment after reaching the age of 59½; the upper limit on withdrawal is age 70½. At that time, the sums you withdraw are treated as ordinary taxable income. However, your income will probably be lower after retirement, so that the size of your tax bite will be smaller. Early withdrawals prior to age 59½ carry a 10 percent penalty. Therefore, as with an IRA, you should invest in a Keogh account only sums you don't expect to need until retirement. Liquidity is not one of the characteristics of a Keogh account.

What Are the Differences between the Keogh and the IRA?

As you will see subsequently, not everyone is eligible for a Keogh account. While the maximum amount you may contribute to an IRA in any year is $4,000 ($5,000 if over age 50), you may invest up to a maximum of $44,000 or 25 percent of your earned income, whichever is less, in a Keogh account. Withdrawals from IRAs and Keoghs are also handled differently. With both, you can withdraw the money either in a lump sum upon retirement or in installments.

1. A *money-purchase* Keogh requires a *fixed* percentage of your income each year.
2. The other type of Keogh is a *profit-sharing* plan. These allow *variable* contributions each year.

How Do You Qualify for a Keogh Plan?

To qualify for a Keogh account, you must be self-employed as the sole proprietor of a business, an unincorporated professional, or a partner in any unincorporated partnership. In addition, if your business has any employees, you are required to include in the plan all those who have worked for you longer than three years. You must contribute to their retirement funds the same percentage of their salary that you are contributing to your own. (Naturally, the employer's share of the Keogh investment for employees is treated as a deductible business expense.) The Keogh funds may be invested in almost any kind of instrument favored by the employer, including a certificate of deposit, stocks and bonds, a money market fund, or an insurance account. Collectibles are virtually the only common type of investment not allowed. The employer may choose to manage the Keogh personally or may invest the money in an annuity contract purchased from an insurance company or a mutual fund managed by a broker.

Ever since their introduction, Keoghs have been among the most popular pension plans. If you are eligible for a Keogh plan account, you should certainly give it serious consideration as an investment option. It is a kind of super IRA that allows the self-employed professional or business proprietor to reduce his or her current taxable income while saving a substantial sum toward retirement. *Remember*: Judge each day not by the harvest you reap, but by the seeds you plant.

Employees should ask their human resources managers for more information on these plans, while small employers can get full information on the plans from their business advisors.

And on the topic of advice, never say *never* and always avoid *always*.

It's a Wrap

- Many employers offer the retirement savings plan known as a 401(k) and may even provide matching funds. 401(k)s are available to full-time employees who meet certain basic conditions.

- Those with 401(k) money invested in their employer's stock should be aware of tax restrictions that will come into play if they leave the company.

- Small businesses and self-employed individuals can benefit from simplified employee pension plans (called SEPs) and Keoghs, which allow investors to reduce current taxable income while saving for retirement.

"If quitters never win and winners never quit, what happened to quit while you're ahead?"

CHAPTER 24
Social Security

◆▸▸◆◆◆◆◆◆◆◆◆◆◆◆◆◆◆◆◆◆◆◆◆◆◆◆◆◆◆◆◆◆◆◆◆◆◆◆◆◆◀◆

"I don't mind being a senior citizen; I just don't look forward to graduation."

Do I Need to Read This Chapter?

- Do I know how social security works?

- Am I trying to decide whether to collect social security at age 62 or collect it later?

- Am I a woman who is counting on social security? Am I alert to all my options?

- Am I, or any family members, eligible for nonretirement social security benefits such as Medicare, disability income, or survivor's benefits?

Some people overlook their social security benefits when calculating their projected retirement income. Other people may count too much on these benefits. Financial planning is a system that must encompass all phases of investments; so know the rules of social security—because for many of us, it has become our most common investment.

How Does the System Work?

Both you and your employer contribute a percentage of your wages to social security, up to a designated maximum each year, as well as a percentage to Medicare with no limit. These contributions by both employees and employers are broken down into three separate trust funds:

OASI—old age and survivor insurance. This is a self-contained account separate from other U.S. Treasury revenue which will fully take care of benefit payments to retirees and their survivors. These funds may not be spent for any other purpose.

DI—disability insurance. The same rules apply here as to OASI except that benefit payments go for the disabled.

HI— health insurance. Known also as Medicare, the fund pays all costs of hospital (Part A) but only 20 percent of doctors' fees and other charges (Part B). The balance is funded from general Treasury revenues.

How Are Retirement Benefits Calculated?

Social security benefits are based on earnings averaged over most of a worker's lifetime. Your actual earnings are first adjusted, or "indexed," to account for changes in average wages since the year the earnings were received. Your benefit is then calculated on your average monthly indexed earnings during the 35 years in which you earned the most. The government applies a formula to these earnings and arrives at your basic benefit, or *primary insurance amount (PIA).* This is the amount you would receive at your full retirement age, for most people, age 65. However, beginning with people born in 1938 or later, that age will gradually increase until it reaches 67 for people born after 1959.

As you can see from the above, the benefit computation is complex, and there are no simple tables that I can present that will tell you how much you will receive. However, there are several ways you can determine an estimate of your retirement benefits:

1. Request a social security statement. Make your request over the Internet, and the government will mail you a detailed report of your lifetime earnings and an estimate of retirement, disability, and dependent benefits.

2. Compute your own benefit estimate using a program that you can download for your PC. A version for the Mac is also available.

3. Use the government's online calculator.

4. Read the government's publication *Your Retirement Benefit: How It Is Figured.*

 The monthly benefit may be increased annually by the cost of living adjustment based on the consumer price index.

What Happens If You Want to Retire before Age 65?

Many individuals have asked me what I think about retiring before age 65. I have always felt that *it is better to retire too early than too late*. However, you have to understand the social security payout implications.

Consider retirement as the goal not of reaching retirement age, but of entering a retirement zone. At the center of this zone is the standard retirement age, which is 65 if you were born before 1938 and 65-plus (up to a maximum of 67) if you were born after 1959. At that center point you will be entitled to receive 100 percent of your primary insurance amount as it is computed from your record earnings. On the low side of the retirement zone is age 62, which will provide you with early retirement benefits between 70 and 80 percent of your PIA. It is 80 percent if your full retirement age is 65 and 70 if your full retirement age is 67.

If you decide to collect benefits as early as age 62, monthly benefits may be reduced by up to 25 percent. Consider this option if you must retire early or if you decide that enough is enough — and also if you feel you may not live to full life expectancy.

If you decide to collect benefits at full retirement age, 65–67, you will receive 100 percent of the benefits accrued to you. Consider this option if you are still working, as there is no penalty for your employment. Also, if you expect to live till your life expectancy and can rely on other investments until you reach full benefit age, this is the best method.

If you decide to collect benefits at a later date by deferring benefits payments to you till you are age 70, for every year that payments are deferred, the increase could be as much as 5 to 8 percent. Consider this option if you have other means of income or expect to live beyond your life-expectancy age.

What is the best course of action? Of course, each of us is different, and various factors such as health, age, and finances will enter into the decision, but here is an example using approximate amounts of benefits:

At age 62, the average benefit is about $1,450.

At age 65, the average benefit is about $1,800.

At age 70, the average benefit is about $2,150.

Thus, there is an approximate difference of $700 per month between retiring at age 62 and retiring at age 70. However, if you did choose to receive social security benefits at age 62, you would have received about $140,000 by the time you turn 70 years of age, and the person who will first start at age 70 to receive social security will have had nothing. Still, the person who retires at 70 will get about $700 more per month for the rest of his or her life.

When Are You Eligible for Full Social Security Benefits?

Year You Were Born	Your Full Retirement Age
1937 or earlier	65
1938	65 and 2 months
1939	65 and 4 months
1940	65 and 6 months
1941	65 and 8 months
1942	65 and 10 months
1943–1954	66
1955	66 and 2 months
1956	66 and 4 months
1957	66 and 6 months
1958	66 and 8 months
1959	66 and 10 months
1960 and later	67

Source: Social Security Administration.

What Is "Unretirement"?

Take note of this important point. It can make a big difference in your retirement; yet many people aren't aware of it. If you take retirement at age 62, it does not mean that you will be locked into 80 percent of your social security benefits for the rest of your life. You are allowed to stop your social security benefits and begin them again years later, thus giving you a higher monthly check. This can occur, for example, if during your retirement you take a job that pushes your earnings above the limit, which in turn results in a cut in your benefits.

One method to "unretire" is to call the Social Security Administration (SSA) and report that you are "unretiring" yourself. In order to do this, you will have to furnish the SSA with an estimate of what you will be earning. You will still remain on the benefit roll, but you will not receive a monthly check. At the point you decide to reenter the retirement world, you simply notify the SSA of your intentions. When you again begin to receive your monthly check, you may notice a change in the amount you received upon your initial retirement. For each month that you receive social security benefits before the age of 65, the SSA will reduce your payments by ⅚ of 1 percent, but the months or years you had suspended your benefit check do not count. Your new check, now that you are retired again, would be larger because it would reflect a reduction by only the number of months you actually received your benefit check before "unretiring."

For example, if you retire at 62 and take benefits for one year before you rejoin the workforce, when you retire again, your new benefits will be calculated as though you retired only one year early (age 64), which would give you a 6.5 percent (approximate) reduction, instead of a 20 percent reduction, for the rest of your life. Also, any benefits would include an annual cost-of-living adjustment that was made during your suspended time.

What Happens If You Want to Retire after Age 65?

If you decide to work past age 65, you move to the other side of the zone, known as the *high end*. At this point you will receive a higher monthly social security benefit (more than 100 percent) when you do finally retire. The amount will range from a 3.5 percent increase to an 8 percent increase depending on your date of birth. At age 70, you will have reached the highest end of the retirement zone and will not receive any further increase in benefits. However, you do not have to retire to collect your full social security check because you are entitled to full benefits after reaching age 65 no matter how much you earn.

Also, as far as social security benefits are concerned, it makes no difference what time of the year you retire. Most people, in fact, retire toward the end of a calendar year simply as a matter of convenience and personal preference. However, the social security law permits you to retire at any time during the year without forfeiting any benefits; payments start any month you choose, provided you meet all the conditions of eligibility.

Have you set your retirement date? I recommend applying for social security benefits about three months earlier. This leaves plenty of time to process your claim and handle any questions or problems that may arise.

How Do You Know You Are Getting Accurate Social Security Benefits?

It would be unthinkable for a person to let years go by without balancing a checkbook; yet that same individual will usually wait until age 65 before making certain that his or her social security account had been accurately credited. By then, if there are errors, it may be too late.

However, there is a way to remedy this situation while you are currently employed. Contact your social security office and ask for the free "Request for Earnings and Benefit Estimate" statement, which will verify your earnings record to date. Merely save your W-2s (or tax forms if you are self-employed) and compare the figures. Forty quarters of coverage will entitle you to receive full social security benefits at retirement. By periodically examining your social security account (every three to five years), you will be assured that the income paid from your account will represent all that you have earned.

Are There Special Rules for Widows and Widowers on Social Security?

When a person who has worked and paid social security taxes dies, the widow or widower may be eligible for survivor's benefits. Up to 10 years of work is needed to be eligible for benefits, depending on the person's age at the time of death.

Social security survivor's benefits can be paid to:

- A widow or widower. Full benefits at full retirement age or reduced benefits as early as age 60.
- A disabled widow or widower. As early as age 50.

- A widow or widower at any age if he or she takes care of the deceased's child who is under age 16 or is disabled and is receiving social security benefits.

If your divorced spouse dies, you can receive benefits if the marriage lasted 10 years or longer and you are age 60 or older (or age 50 if you are disabled.) Benefits paid to a surviving divorced spouse who is 60 or older (age 50 if disabled) will not affect the benefit rates for other survivors.

In general, you cannot receive survivor's benefits if you remarry before the age of 60 unless the latter marriage ends, whether by death, divorce, or annulment. If you remarry after age 60 (50 if disabled), you can still collect benefits on your former spouse's record. When you reach age 62 or older, you may get retirement benefits on the record of your new spouse if they are higher.

Your remarriage would have no effect on the benefits being paid to your children.

If you are collecting survivor's benefits, you can switch to your own retirement benefits (assuming you are eligible and your retirement rate is higher than the widow's or widower's rate) as early as age 62.

In many cases, you can begin receiving retirement benefits on either your own or your spouse's record at age 62 and then switch to the other benefit when you reach full retirement age, if that amount is higher.

What Are the Family Benefits of a Social Security Plan?

The social security tax that you and your employer pay places you and your family in line for collecting more than just retirement benefits. You may also collect Medicare and disability income. If you become disabled, you get benefits at any age (assuming you have enough quarters of coverage). In order to qualify for disability benefit, you must have earned 20 credits of coverage during the 10-year period ending with the calendar quarter in which you became disabled. However, if your disability is blindness or if you become disabled before reaching age 31, more lenient rules apply.

A child (either natural or adopted) may be entitled to benefits upon the death of a parent. To qualify, the child must have been a dependent and (1) be unmarried and be either under age 18 or, if a full-time high school student, under age 19 or (2) regardless of age, be disabled before age 22. The child then would receive a monthly benefit equal to 50 percent of the amount the parent would have gotten at age 65.

Keep in mind that there is a maximum on family benefits. The benefit percentages for family members are the maximum each relative can collect. When more than one family member is collecting benefits based on the insured's earnings record, the actual size of the benefits checks is likely to be smaller. Why? The social security law places a dollar cap on the total monthly benefits paid to a family based on the earnings of one family member.

Thus, you can see that in order to plan for retirement, all areas of income, whether actual or potential, must be considered.

And on the topic of planning for retirement, remember that it wasn't raining when Noah built the ark.

It's a Wrap

- Social security is a costly investment—and an involuntary one at that—so it pays to know how it works.
- The social security insurance program includes old age and survivor's insurance, disability insurance, and health insurance known as Medicare.
- You can qualify for SSI in either of two ways: by working and earning a minimal amount for at least 40 quarters or by being the nonworking spouse married to a retired or disabled worker.
- If you retire at age 62, begin collecting social security and then decide to "unretire," you can avoid being locked into the 80 percent benefit level for the rest of your life.
- By waiting until age 65 or older to collect SSI, you will receive higher benefits, no matter how much you may earn.
- At age 70 you are entitled to full SSI benefits, plus additional increments.

- It's advisable to check the accuracy of your social security records every three to five years.

- Women can collect SSI based on their own work record, their spouse's work record, or several other options if divorced or widowed.

- Children may be entitled to SSI benefits upon a parent's death, subject to certain family maximums.

"If you worry about what people will think about you, it is because you have more confidence in their opinions than you have in your own."

CHAPTER 25

Will It?

"The only real thing of value we can give our children is what we are, not what we have."

Do I Need to Read This Chapter?

- Have I been putting off the making of my will?

- Am I aware that more than 6 out of 10 Americans will die without a will?

- Am I confused by all the legalese surrounding wills?

- Have I been named an executor of a will? Am I clear on my duties?

- Have I taken those duties into account when naming my own executor?

This chapter is essential, because out of all the possible threats to your family's assets (inflation, downturn in the market, etc.), only one is definite—and that is your death. I have discussed, in previous chapters, topics ranging from financial planning for young children through financial planning for retirement. Now this chapter completes the life cycle.

By law you have the right to own property, to use it as you wish during your lifetime, and to determine who shall receive it after you die. Everyone makes use of the first two rights, but many give up their third property right by failing to write a will. Did you know that more than 6 out of 10 Americans die without a will? This is a shame, because without one you lose control of your estate. This loss affects not only the disposition of your property, but also the people who should receive your property after you die. Writing a will is a way of taking care of the people you love in a time when you will not be there.

What Is a Will?

A *will* is simply a set of written instructions that specify what should be done with your property after you die. The *testator* (the person whose will it is) and the lawyer will both make important decisions today that will take place in the future and affect other people's lives. A will names those people who will receive your property in the amounts that you decide. It also assigns specific shares of your property to each one and describes any particular conditions under which the distribution should occur. Remember, this must be in writing and witnessed.

If you fail to prepare a properly executed will, several unpleasant consequences may follow: your property may not be distributed as you had hoped it would be, your heirs may suffer a greater tax burden and higher administrative costs, and your family and friends may be subject to needless worry and squabbling. Preparing a will is an essential part of meeting your financial responsibilities. An improperly drawn-up or executed will can be rejected by the courts. The decision can render the document invalid, leaving your estate without a will (intestate)—a topic covered at the end of this chapter.

 Be aware that your spoken wishes and instructions don't carry any legal weight. In other words, don't expect to be on your deathbed and issue your will verbally. To have a legal basis, you must put your will in writing.

How Do You Begin to Draw Up a Will?

Let me start by urging that you stay away from prewritten wills or "how-to" books encouraging you to draw up your own will. Use an attorney. Your will and your estate are too important to fall into the do-it-yourself category.

Before you consider who should receive your possessions at death, you must have some idea of what you own. Start by listing all your assets with their real or estimated value. The total is your gross estate. Because state and federal estate taxes can cut into your gross estate, it's important to know the exact value of your assets. If your taxable estate (equal to your gross estate less debts and expenses) exceeds $2,000,000 through the year 2008, your survivors will face federal estate taxes, which can be steep. In the year 2009, the exemption increases to $3,500,000.

It should also be noted that no federal estate tax is due on assets left to your spouse or to a charity. The law, however, varies from state to state on the treatment of estate tax.

Because personal and family circumstances change, you should review your will at least once every five years to make certain that it still reflects your current wishes and needs. If only minor changes are needed from time to time, these can be made by means of a written statement (called a *codicil*) attached to the original document. The help of a lawyer is needed for amending a will.

&Don't Forget A will doesn't have to be "forever." That is, you can change it. And you should if one or more of the following events occur:

1. You marry, separate, or divorce.
2. Your beneficiary or executor dies.
3. You move to another state.
4. Federal, state, or estate laws change.
5. Family circumstances change.
6. Financial matters change.
7. You change your mind.

As the years go by, we all accumulate assets that are impossible to list in the will. You cannot keep amending the document every time you purchase something of value. Thus you will need a provision in your will, known as a *residuary clause,* which describes how the remainder of your assets not listed in the will should be distributed.

Who Carries Out the Instructions in a Will?

The instructions you leave in your will are to be carried out by a person you designate as the *executor*. If no one is named in the will as executor (or *personal representative,* as it is called in Florida and some other states), the court will appoint an administrator.

As you see, it's necessary to choose wisely when naming an executor, so make certain that the person you have in mind is willing to undertake the job and understands what it entails. When naming an executor, keep in mind the job requires attention to detail. It can even be burdensome. So select accordingly. I have always recommended that a spouse or adult child, a close friend, or a relative be chosen over a lawyer. The major reason is, of course, cost.

$ Getting $ Started An executor must fulfill this entire list of duties:

1. The executor must obtain the original copy of the will and submit it to probate—that is, request court approval of its validity.
2. The executor may be required to publish a notice of death for a specified period of time.
3. The executor must inventory, appraise, and safeguard all assets of the estate.
4. The executor must open a checking account on behalf of the estate and maintain complete records of all transactions.
5. The executor must apply for all appropriate death benefits, including those available through social security, pension plans, the Veterans Administration, labor unions, and fraternal organizations.
6. The executor must pay all outstanding debts of the deceased.
7. The executor must file and pay local, state, and federal income and estate taxes.
8. The executor must distribute all remaining assets according to the terms of the will.
9. The executor may be required to submit a final accounting to the court.

Do Spouses Need Separate Wills?

It is just as important for a wife to have a will as for her husband. A married couple often has interlocking or reciprocal wills prepared at the same time. These are separate documents that are carefully interrelated and designed to meet the mutual objectives of both parties. For example his-and-her wills should specify how the children are to be cared for in the event both parents die at the same time.

And on the topic of marriage, how you own your money is just as important as knowing what you own. Transferring assets from one spouse to another might in some cases be your best financial move. For instance, a joint savings or checking account could be convenient today, but the surviving spouse might need those funds if the account is "frozen" when one of the account holders dies. Also, the law will protect the rights of spouses to receive a minimum share of an estate. In other words, in most states spouses cannot be completely written out of the will unless a prenuptial agreement states so. (See Chapter 28.)

Also, a child who is not mentioned in the will may be entitled to a portion of his or her legal share as if no will were available. However, this does not preclude a parent from excluding a child if specific mention is made in the will.

How Can You Be Certain That the Distribution of the Estate Will Be without Problems?

You can make probate (the settling of the will) easier by following these simple procedures:

1. If you have made previous wills, tell your lawyer to destroy all earlier ones.

2. Choose a successor executor if your original choice cannot serve. Also, list contingent beneficiaries in the event your first choice may die before you or decline the inheritance.

3. In the event you have young children, pick a guardian in case they should become orphans.

4. Devise an order of payment if your estate becomes too small to pay all legacies.

5. Decide in advance whether the executor is to receive the standard compensation or a bequest from you.

6. Keep your will in a safe place (your lawyer's office and a copy at home) but preferably not in a safe deposit box; if the box is sealed upon your death, getting into it may be time consuming and difficult. If you insist on the safe deposit box, open two of them and put your will in your spouse's safe deposit box and vice versa.

7. When making any bequest, leave a percentage of your estate rather than a fixed dollar amount, because your assets may either grow or shrink over the years. Remember the decrease in value in 2001–2003 for stocks owned? For example, it is better to say that "I leave 10 percent of my estate to XYZ Charity" than to give a specified amount—$50,000, for example. If your estate

should be reduced in value for whatever reason by the time you pass on, the $50,000 could be excessive in relation to the needs of those to whom you are leaving the balance of the money. Just remember that you will not be able to bequeath any property you own that is jointly held.

8. Make certain that your will is properly drafted, or it may be interpreted in a manner that you did not wish. For example, if you want to disinherit a child, be sure to specify in your will that you are doing it. If not, the child might later claim to have been overlooked by mistake. Don't use your will to throw your final insult at any individual; find some other means to get even.

9. If a beneficiary in your will (including your spouse) must enter a nursing facility, remove his or her name from the will. If you don't do this, the bequest may be seized as payment when you die and the will is probated.

10. In certain situations, it's better to leave property in trusts rather than in out-right bequests. A trust is simply an arrangement for transferring the title to your property (your ownership) to another person or company to hold in trust for you or anyone you designate. Trusts set up under a will are called *testamentary trusts* and become effective upon the death of the person who drew up the will. The trustee holds the property you otherwise would have bequeathed outright, and invests and administers it for the benefit of your stated beneficiaries. Trusts are frequently written into wills to ease the impact of estate taxes (particularly of minors until they have matured). There are countless ways of setting up trusts, and so great care must be exercised to obtain the best possible legal tax advantages. (See Chapter 26.)

Is My Will Likely to Be Contested?

Do not concern yourself about having your will contested, because more than 99 percent of all will contests are unsuccessful. Remember that very few people are legally able to mount a contest, only those who would have a claim on the estate should the will be overturned. A will can be contested only because of how it was completed, not on the basis of *what it contains*.

The most common claims are based on the incompetence of the testator (the one who made the will), fraud or undue influence, or the suspicion that the will was not properly signed. If you want to assure no future challenges, use the "no-contest" clause (interrorem clause). It will make any heir a bit hesitant to mount a contest. This clause provides that if any heir should challenge a will, he or she would forfeit all inheritance under the will's conditions.

Will All My Property Be Passed On through My Will?

Bear in mind that not all property goes through the courts (probate). Any asset that has a designated beneficiary would pass outside the will. In fact, a large portion of your estate is likely to pass outside probate court without any effort on your part.

For example, the balance of your employee retirement plan, your IRA or Keogh account, and your bank account with a "paid-on-death" (POD) clause, as well as the proceeds of your life insurance policy, will go directly to your designated beneficiaries. Also, any property you own jointly with rights of survivorship will automatically go to the co-owner upon your death.

If you live in one of the community property states (Arizona, California, Idaho, Louisiana, Nevada, Texas, Washington, and Wisconsin), half of all the assets that you acquired during your marriage (except gifts or inheritance) belong to your spouse, with the other half passing under your will.

What Happens If You Die without a Will?

If there is no will whatsoever, severe problems can arise. Without a will (*intestate*) you, in essence, have condemned your estate to an unnecessarily prolonged and expensive wait. What happens is that your local court appoints an individual who will administer the distribution of your property in accordance with the laws of your state. However, with a will, it becomes your decision—not that of an outside administrator—as to what happens to your estate. And what about minor children? If you and your spouse do not have a will and you both should die at the same time (an auto accident is a common occurrence), a court will render a decision about who will raise your children. Is that what you want to happen? By drawing up a will, you name a guardian and a trustee to work with your finances for the children's benefit.

States vary in the handling of after-death distributions of property intestate. In some states, the surviving spouse will receive the property if there are no descendants. In other states, parents may be involved in the distribution. In some states, if there are descendants, the spouse will receive one-third of the property, and the children will get equal shares of the balance. If there is only one child, the spouse will receive half. If there are children of a deceased child, they will share in the same manner of their deceased parent. If there is no spouse or child, the mother and father of the deceased will each get one-half of the estate. If there is only one parent, the survivor will get all. If both parents are deceased, their siblings will share equally; and if they are dead, their children will receive the parents' share. If no brothers or sisters exist, the estate will be distributed to more distant relatives in patterns that vary from state to state. If there are no surviving relatives, the estate will go to the state by *escheat*.

It may be just as important for you to bequeath your values as it is your valuables. While a traditional will tells your loved ones what you want them to have, an ethical will tells them what you want them to know. In an ethical will, you can share with your family and friends your personal values and beliefs.

What might you write about? Ask yourself the following questions:

1. What would you like your family to know?
2. What was your biggest regret and your proudest moment?
3. What role had religion played in your life?
4. What do you want your family to do when you have passed on?

Remember that planning and then making a will is one of the wisest investments that you can make in your life—and after.

And on the thought of planning, it is not what happens to you that counts. It is what you do with what happens to you that is important.

It's a Wrap

- Financial planning is not complete without making a will, in writing and properly witnessed.
- Consult an attorney to prepare a will; don't "do it yourself."

- Your survivors must pay federal estate taxes if your taxable estate (equal to your gross estate, minus debts and expenses) exceeds $2 million (2007–2008). However, federal tax is not levied on assets left to a spouse or charity.

- The person who carries out the instructions in your will is the executor.

- Spouses should have interlocking or reciprocal wills drawn at the same time.

- Allot your estate by percentages, rather than by fixed-dollar figures, because your assets may increase or decrease dramatically before you die.

- If a beneficiary in your will (including your spouse) enters a nursing home, have your attorney remove his or her name from the will at once. Otherwise, your assets may be seized as payment immediately upon your death.

- Assets with a designated beneficiary, such as retirement plans and insurance policies, will pass directly to that person upon your death.

- Dying without a will (intestate) causes enormous complications that vary by state. Yet over 60 percent of Americans will die without one.

- An ethical will informs your family of your values, not your valuables.

"Death is more universal than life. Everyone dies, but not everyone lives."

CHAPTER 26

Trust Me

◆◆◆◆◆◆◆◆◆◆◆◆◆◆◆◆◆◆◆◆◆◆◆◆◆◆◆◆◆◆◆◆

"Money never changes, only pockets."

Do I Need to Read This Chapter?

- Do I know that trusts can help avoid probate and transfer my assets immediately to my heirs?

- Am I aware that trusts are an excellent way to protect my wishes in complicated estates involving second marriages and blended families?

- Do I own real estate in more than one state? If so, do I realize that I should have a living trust to cover it?

- If I'm interested in trusts, have I also considered their drawbacks?

- Have I considered other vehicles for estate planning?

- If I'm trying to shelter assets from nursing home seizure, am I aware of the role (both good and bad) of irrevocable trusts?

- Am I clear on the changes in Medicaid rules?

Are There Alternatives to Having a Will?

A will and a trust are both legal documents that transfer your assets to your designated heirs upon your death. For each, a person is appointed to distribute your assets. The person who distributes your assets in a will is the executor, and in a trust it is the trustee. But that's where the similarity ends.

One of the major drawbacks of a will is the cost and time to probate it. The process, at a minimum, can take four to eight months; and if you have property in another state, or if any disgruntled relatives contest the will, your heirs might have to wait for years for the settlement. Also, administrative and legal costs during the probate process could run 10 percent or more of the estate. The easiest way to avoid probate and have your assets transferred immediately is to set up a *revocable* or living trust (*intervivos trust*), which transfers your assets to the trust while you are alive.

Since the use of trusts in financial planning is extremely complex, a full discussion of trusts is not the purpose of this chapter. Rather, I shall provide a brief description of the many uses of trusts and their impact on financial planning. It is my intent to encourage you to continue to explore with your attorney, and any other person involved in finance, the many aspects of trusts that may meet your specific needs.

How Do You Create a Revocable Living Trust?

In every trust document, there are three principals:

1. The *trustor*, or grantor, is the person or persons who created the trust and transferred the assets into it.
2. The *trustee* is the person or persons charged with the task of managing the assets in the trust. He or she makes all the financial and business decisions concerning the trust assets. Trustees have the right to buy, sell, trade, exchange, mortgage, and encumber. In fact, trustees can do virtually anything with trust assets except use them for their own benefit.
3. The *beneficiary* is the person whose only role is to enjoy the assets.

A living trust is created to be effective during the lifetime of the one who creates the trust. It is revocable if the creator states in the trust agreement that he or she has the right during his or her lifetime to terminate (revoke) or change the conditions of the trust at any time and without the permission of anyone else. A living trust may be irrevocable if the creator does not reserve the right to revoke the trust.

When creating the living trust, you must realize that you are required to switch the titles of everything you are placing in the trust from your name to the name of the trust.

When you create your trust, you can lawfully become (in most states) all three parties: the trustor, the trustee, and the beneficiary. Under this arrangement, you can act as your own trustee, giving yourself control over your estate while you are alive. You then can appoint a successor trustee if you should become incapacitated or should die. Because the trust is revocable, it can be changed at any time you wish.

What Are the Major Advantages of the Revocable Living Trust?

In addition to avoiding the costs of probate, a living trust affords many advantages to both the trustor and his or her heirs:

1. A revocable trust can be changed or terminated at any time before the trustor dies.

2. Because the trustor retains the right to get back all property transferred to a revocable trust, those assets are not considered gifts for estate, gift, or income tax purposes. Any income that comes from the assets in the trust will remain taxable to the trustor during his or her lifetime.

3. Unlike a will, a living trust can (in many states) attempt to shield the estate from creditors. With a will, the executor is required to notify the creditors of the death of the maker of the will—by mail or newspaper advertisement— so that they can submit any claims against the estate. No such publicity would take place in a living trust since no public notification would be needed.

4. The trust avoids the courts and the general public. For example, when an estate goes through probate, the court freezes its assets for several months and makes notice that interested parties can come forward if they wish to contest the will. However, the assets of the trust are not frozen, and in many cases the trust is dissolved and assets distributed to the beneficiaries long before the disgruntled heir has a chance to act. He or she would then have to sue each beneficiary separately.

5. A living trust provides for the designation of future heirs. For example, if you decide to leave all your worth to your son, Tom, and years after your death your son should get divorced (or die), Tom's wife will wind up with most, if not all, of your assets. If she should remarry and begin a new family, your son's children (your grandchildren) could wind up receiving little or

none of the inheritance that you left their father, Tom—funds you had assumed would be later used for their benefit. A living trust could keep your assets intact so that they would not be distributed to your son upon your death. This method can be used to ensure your grandchildren the rightful access to your funds regardless of what happens to your son or to his marriage.

The procedure is simple. You name Tom your successor trustee and set up the trust so that he will be able to draw income and a small portion of the principal while he lives. At his death or divorce, or at a certain period of time you designate (when the children reach age 21, 30, 40, or whatever you determine), the trust would be terminated and the assets given to Tom's children (your grandchildren). The wife would have no control in this situation.

Here is another example. Suppose this is your second marriage, and a good one, but you want to leave your assets to your children from your previous marriage. You may think that your wishes would be followed in a will, but that may not be the case. In many states, the law says that you cannot disinherit a spouse. Thus, even though you decided to leave all your property to your children, there could develop a successful challenge in the courts, resulting in the possible loss of a portion of your estate against your wishes. With a living trust (in some states), the property in the trust that passes to the children at your death cannot be challenged by a surviving spouse.

6. Although not generally known, anyone owning real estate in more than one state should have a living trust. This is so because the trust will avoid "ancillary probate," a costly, time-consuming judicial process that develops when death occurs to the owner of the real estate property in a state other than the one in which the deceased owner lived.

7. Last, but not least, a living trust can be a source of comfort if you should become incapacitated. If a successor trustee is appointed, a debilitating illness will not cause financial hardship since your trustee has the authority to pay your bills and handle your investments in a prudent manner. It thus avoids the possibility of having guardianship proceedings, which are costly and difficult to administer. Another simple method to accomplish the same objective is to designate a *durable power of attorney* to someone to make financial and living decisions on your behalf in the event you should become incapacitated.

&Don't Forget Another good vehicle for complicated second-marriage and blended family situations is a *Q-TIP trust*. (No, it has nothing to do with the little cotton-tipped sticks you keep in your medicine cabinet). Under this trust, your spouse, upon your death, will receive income from your estate for as long as he or she lives. Upon the spouse's demise, the principal of the estate passes to the beneficiary you choose, *not* to the beneficiary of your spouse. Thus you can protect your assets in a second marriage for your children, but still leave income to your beloved new spouse.

What Are the Disadvantages of the Living Trust?

Although you do not have to go through the costly process of probate, the living trust is not without disadvantages, which include the following:

1. By creating it, you have to place everything you own into the trust, known as "funding the trust." Any property you own or acquire later must have new deeds drawn up on them. If you hold any assets outside the trust, you may have to go through probate anyway. You can remedy this drawback by placing any "outside assets" into joint ownership with right of survivorship. Bear in mind that jointly held property can duplicate much of the same benefits as a living trust since the property will pass outside the courts (probate) and will go directly to the surviving joint owner.

2. It will almost always cost more to establish a living trust than to write a will. Legal fees can be higher, and assets must actually be transferred to the trust, which can add additional costs. Also, if you appoint another person as trustee, you will have to pay a fee in accordance with state law (unless the trustee waives the fee).

3. The right to choose your own fiscal year to defer taxes will be lost.

4. The funds in the trust must be used up before the trustor can get special social service benefits (Medicaid, for example).

5. No tax advantage regarding estate taxes is gained by the revocable trust. Nor is there any income tax savings since all income from the trust passes through to the individual's personal income tax return.

6. You may need to have a simple will regardless of the living trust because you cannot use a trust to name a guardian for your minor children.

7. You will need a will with a "pour-over" clause stating that any property that you forgot to put into your living trust should go there after your death. Those assets will then be subject to probate, but it will not be a lengthy or costly process if your estate is small and if the majority of your assets lie within the confines of the living trust. This extra process may take only a few days to complete. Yet it is crucial to have such a pour-over clause since there most certainly could be assets that you have overlooked while making the living trust.

8. Certain types of assets, such as jewelry and automobiles, are difficult to place in a trust because insurance companies are often reluctant to write a policy for a trust. Also, some assets need not be placed in a trust because they already pass (upon death) to the named beneficiary outside the probate court. These assets could include IRAs, retirement benefits, life insurance proceeds, and annuities.

9. Even if you try to cover every eventuality, there are certain circumstances under which a living trust could be rendered inoperative and probate would be required. This situation might arise when:

   - Assets are currently subject to litigation (in the event of a lawsuit).
   - A tax audit is in progress.

What Other Vehicles Are Available for Estate Planning?

If you were to die tomorrow, the odds are that your heirs would be able to settle your estate without paying an inheritance tax because of changes in federal and state tax codes in the past two decades. The federal exemption was only $60,000 in 1976, but is $2,000,000 currently (2007–2008) and will be $3,500,000 in 2009. The federal tax is based on your taxable estate and the taxable portion of any gifts you made during your life. Adding taxable gifts to an estate is a way for the government to discourage people from dodging the federal estate tax by giving away all their property before they die.

&Don't Forget

What makes a cash gift taxable or not? Here are the magic numbers. You can give up to $12,000 each year to as many people as you wish tax free; and if your spouse joins in making the gift, $24,000 per recipient tax free is permitted. Any amount over this annual exclusion is taxable.

If you give more than $12,000 to a couple, you can avoid any IRS hassle if you make out two separate checks. For example, a $24,000 gift to your son and his wife should be written in two checks of $12,000 each, one to your son and one to his wife. If you wish to give a sizable amount at one time, you can do so through *self-cancellation installment notes (SCIN),* which will cancel out over a period of years. For example, you loan $60,000 to your son, accepting five annual notes of $12,000 each. As agreed, one note is to be paid back to you each year. But at the anniversary of each note, you forgive its payment, thus meeting the requirement of the $12,000 gift limit. However, if you should die during the period that the notes are still outstanding, the value of the notes will remain in your estate and will be considered for estate tax purposes.

Any Special Guidance for Large Estates?

For those of you who have sizable estates, there is a method of leaving large funds without heavy federal taxation. By bequeathing the estate to your spouse, no tax is incurred. When the surviving spouse dies, tax is then applied to the beneficiaries of the estate over $2 million. However, by creating a bypass trust, you are able to have sizable estates (up to $4 million) pass onto your children tax free. Here's how it works. In your will you place up to $2 million in a bypass trust and leave the rest to your spouse. In this way, the $2 million exemption and the unlimited marital deduction that is allowed shield the estate from federal estate taxes. The bypass trust pays income to your spouse and names the children as beneficiaries when the spouse dies. No control can be exercised by the spouse over the bypass trust. When the spouse does pass on, the amount of the trust is not part of his or her estate and so can be passed along (coupled with the spouse's estate) up to $4 million tax free. Since no one can predict who will die first, both spouses should provide for this trust. In 2009, you can shield up to $7 million.

How Does an Irrevocable Trust Work?

Robert Browning wrote, "Grow old along with me, the best is yet to be." That statement may not be true for seniors since the best years may have already passed. No matter what any poet, orator, or sage may say, old age is still old age. Someone once said that you know you are growing older when everything hurts and what doesn't hurt doesn't work. Older people are of interest to doctors and hospitals, real estate brokers, and travel agents, not always as people, but as sources of income. As your ability to earn money decreases, so too does your stature as a person. Therefore, keep that money for yourself, having the knowledge that you are financially independent.

The word *irrevocable* has been bantered around as a way of sheltering assets from nursing home seizure. All too often I encounter situations in which older people (especially widows) are so concerned about the high cost of nursing facilities that they contemplate placing their assets, through an irrevocable trust, into the hands of their children.

The looming prospect of nursing homes and Medicaid payments only serves to complicate this already thorny matter. You probably know that certain laws have governed Medicaid since 1993. "Medicaid planning," as some call it, is a set of loopholes that allow older people the means to avoid the cost of nursing homes. Through various methods, these people give most of their assets to their heirs, thus making themselves eligible for government assistance. A 2006 ruling states that these gifts (set up as irrevocable trusts) must be given away at least 60 months (if assets are transferred to a trust rather than to a person) before Medicaid takes effect. This time period is known as the "look-back period", and if not properly executed, could yield severe penalties.

Aside from the Medicaid situation, the irrevocable trust does serve a purpose in financial planning for a large estate. This type of trust cannot be changed once it is written—thus the name *irrevocable*. As you are aware, estates over $2 million are levied with estate taxes when the assets of the deceased are distributed to the heirs. These taxes must be paid within nine months after death. However, the taxes can be reduced by the irrevocable trust if the maker is willing to give away certain assets before he or she dies.

It is obvious that any trust should be set up by an estate attorney or one who specializes in elder care law that is sensitive to your needs. Interview several, and inform them about your estate. You may lack the legal knowledge, but certainly you can evaluate how comfortable you feel discussing family and financial matters with each lawyer.

And on the topic of the law, we have about 35 million laws and regulations to enforce the few lines of guidance contained in the Ten Commandments.

It's a Wrap

- Trusts can help you transfer your assets immediately to your heirs by avoiding probate.

- Trusts are especially worth investigating if you want to make sure your estate goes directly to *your* heirs, not those of in-laws or blended families.

- Revocable or living trusts are advisable for people who own real estate in more than one state.

- Trusts may be a good means of sheltering assets from nursing home seizure, but consult an attorney specializing in family law or elder law before taking this step.

- Irrevocable trusts are most suited to financial planning for a large estate.

"The word listen *contains the same letters as the word* silent.*"*

CHAPTER 27

For Women Only—
An Introduction

◆◆◆◆◆◆◆◆◆◆◆◆◆◆◆◆◆◆◆◆◆◆◆◆◆◆◆◆◆◆◆◆◆◆◆

"You will be a financial success if you spend what you have left after savings, instead of saving what you have left after spending."

Do I Need to Read This Chapter?

- Am I a woman who understands the need to manage my own finances?

- Married or single, do I want to make sure I have all my financial bases covered?

- How do I choose a financial planner if one is needed?

- What emotional factors enter into money matters?

How Does Financial Planning Differ for Women?

Here are statistics that may surprise you. Approximately one-half of all marriages will end in divorce. Nearly 80 percent of married women (that's 8 out of 10) will become widows and remain widows for about 12 years. If the husband is under 40 years of age, he is three times more likely to be disabled than to die;

and after age 55, the chances are he can be disabled for a year or more. Also, on average, a female retiring at age 60 can expect to live another 21 years.

Ready for more grim facts? Today, women constitute 75 percent of the elderly with incomes below poverty levels—yet a great percentage of widows in poverty were not poor before their husbands died. Some of the reasons are not hard to pinpoint. For one thing, with all their progress in the workplace, women still generally earn 20–30 percent less than men. Less income means less money available for saving. Also, because women tend to change jobs more frequently, they miss out on pension benefits since many employers require at least five years of service before benefits are vested.

At the same time, because of their role as primary caretaker of children and elderly parents, women are out of the workforce an average of 11½ years over a lifetime compared with 16 months for men. This not only results in lower income, but limits chances for promotions that boost salary. And salary is the basis for determining the level of employer and social security retirement benefits.

But if you decide to work longer, there could be a major difference in benefits from social security. Are you aware that social security benefits are based on the 35 years of your highest earnings? When children become part of the family, females leave the workforce for several years to care for them. Thus, the years in which you had low earnings can still be included to reach the 35 years. If, however, you work just a few more years, that extra work time will allow you to replace those low-earning years with higher-compensation years, giving you larger benefits.

I don't mean to depress you, but I want you to know the facts. About 30 percent of divorcing women are now entitled to financial support from their ex-spouses (that figure includes child support). Of these women, a third of them may never see the money that is due them. Because of this, the average woman's standard of living may drop 40 percent in the first year after divorce, while a man's may rise 15 percent. About 50 percent of men over the age of 65 receive a pension. The comparable figure for women is less than 30 percent.

The implication is simple and stark: the chances are excellent that at some time in a woman's life, she will be alone and forced to manage her own finances. If you're presently single, you already understand this. If you're married, take heed.

Please don't misunderstand the following recommendation. I strongly believe it is essential for a married woman to consider herself financially separate from her husband—all the more so if he supplies most of the family's income and handles most of the financial decisions. You must make a financial plan of your own to provide for the likelihood that eventually you'll be managing your money independently.

Where to Begin?

To establish your own financial identity, the absolute minimum is to open personal checking and savings accounts and to obtain one or more credit cards in your name only. Why is this necessary? Because a woman whose assets are entirely tied up in joint accounts with her husband, and whose credit cards are all in her husband's name, may face severe financial problems in the future. If you become divorced or widowed, your credit history will be based entirely on your husband's finances, not your own. You may learn, to your dismay, that you lack the financial standing to qualify for your own line of credit. When financial need strikes, this can be a devastating handicap.

Furthermore, any money held in a joint account with your husband may be frozen by the bank or financial institution upon his death, leaving you with no access to funds until after your husband's estate is settled. And in the event of divorce, you may find that all jointly held funds are divided equally, even though you may have contributed more to some accounts.

Next, you should begin to develop an independent retirement plan, one not based on assumptions about your husband's contributions. This may be an uphill struggle. The U.S. retirement system depends largely on social security and private pension plans, both of which are directly tied to the number of years an individual has spent in the workplace. However, the career patterns of women differ greatly from those of men, largely because of the time most women devote to raising their children, but also because of other factors, such as willingness to relocate—and sacrificing their own seniority as employees—when their husbands' careers demand it. As a result of these "liabilities," working women often fail to remain on the job long enough to qualify for their own pension plan.

Do You Keep Copies of the Documents That Define the Provisions of Your Pension Plan?

In addition to asking questions of company or pension plan officials, you should keep copies of the summary plan description (SPD) and any amendments. The SPD is a document that pension plan administrators are required to prepare, and it outlines your benefits and how they are calculated. The SPD also spells out the financial consequences—usually a reduction in benefits—if you decide to retire early (earlier than age 65 in many plans). You probably received a copy of the SPD when you joined the pension or savings plan, but you may request another one from your employer or plan administrator. Also remember to keep pension-related records from all jobs. They provide valuable information about your benefit rights, even when you no longer work for a company.

What Happens to Your Pension If You Change Jobs?

You may lose the pension benefits you have earned if you leave your job before you are vested. However, once vested, you have the right to receive benefits even when you leave your job. In such cases, the company may allow you to, or in certain cases may insist that you, take your pension money in a lump sum when you leave. However, other companies may not permit you to receive your pension money until retirement. The rules for your plan are spelled out in the SPD.

A word of caution: if you receive your pension in a lump sum, you will owe additional income taxes, and may owe a penalty tax. A better way is to reinvest your savings in another qualified pension plan or an individual retirement account (IRA) within 60 days. You avoid tax penalties, and you keep your long-term retirement goals on track.

If you do want to reinvest the money, it is important that you do not directly receive it. If you receive the money directly, you will have to pay 20 percent withholding tax on the amount you receive and then file for a refund in the next year, providing proof that you have transferred the funds to an IRA. Instead, instruct the pension plan administrator to transfer your pension money directly to an IRA you have established or to another qualified pension plan. This is easy to do using simple forms supplied by the new plan. If you want help with the forms, representatives of the plan are generally available to assist you.

Are You Entitled to a Portion of Your Spouse's Pension Plan Benefit If a Divorce Occurs?

As part of a divorce or legal separation, you may be able to obtain rights to a portion of your spouse's pension benefit (or he may be able to obtain a portion of yours). Retirement plans are considered marital property. In most private-sector pension plans, this is done using a qualified domestic relations order (QDRO) issued by the court. You or your attorney should consult your spouse's pension plan administrator to determine what requirements the QDRO must meet.

The point, then, is that married women, whether working outside the home or not, must plan for retirement independently of their husbands. You should develop your own savings and investment plan with a definite goal to be attained by retirement age. And you should become as fully informed about your family's finances as your husband.

Because women tend to have less money to invest, they're often more fearful of taking losses. But they live longer than men, which means women have longer retirements—and riskier investments typically return more over the long term. Remember, you have about 20 years in retirement, and so some part of your portfolio should be in stocks.

How Do You Choose a Financial Planner?

Once you have developed an overall plan, you may want to "go it on your own." Or you may use a financial professional, one who shares your sense of values and objectives. Financial planners are paid for their work in one of three ways: commission only, fee only, or fee plus commission. Under a commission-based compensation, financial advisors receive compensation from trades that they do for you, whether or not they are profitable. For fee-based accounts, there is an all-inclusive annual fee for financial recommendations and portfolio construction advice. This fee is a percentage based on the assets the client has in the portfolio. Therefore the fee-based advisor does not have any incentive to trade a specific investment but rather to make certain the client's assets grow. When considering an individual as your financial professional, make certain to inquire about his or her education, degrees, and certificates. The most creditable credentials are the certified financial planner (CFP) and the charted financial consultant (ChFC), each requiring difficult education training, courses, and testing.

 Today, more than half of all American women work outside the home, at least part time. They're savvier about finances than their grandmothers and even their mothers were. I applaud this transformation in women's outlooks, and I encourage even more self-education through the following steps:

1. Find a qualified, licensed professional advisor who can help you draw up a financial plan. With your advisor's assistance, develop a written statement of your personal investment policy, outlining your goals and risk tolerance. Why written? In times of high market volatility, it's tempting to make major changes based on an emotional response to peaks and troughs. Looking back to your own statement of purpose will help you stay on course.

2. When you have decided on the type of financial professional you want, visit a few. Ask them for information on how other clients' investments have performed under their guidance. And carefully try to assess how well the planners have been able to achieve for their clients the objectives you are seeking. But most important is to ask yourself if you are comfortable with this person handling your financial affairs.

3. Develop a long-term, systematic investment philosophy and a well-allocated portfolio. (*Portfolio* or *asset allocation* refers to the mix of investment classes you utilize, including stocks, bonds, CDs, cash, etc.) With guidance from your chosen professional, set realistic expectations for performance, and commit to an *investment discipline* that meets your comfort level. By this I mean monthly investments that you can live with.

Continued

4. Make regular, periodic investments in order to take advantage of *dollar cost averaging.* (See Chapter 6) Remember the adage: "Buy low, sell high." No one (not even a professional) can accurately and consistently predict market behavior. Since the market naturally rises and falls over time, investing at predetermined points throughout the year means that sometimes you will be buying when investment prices are lower, sometimes higher. Over the lifetime of your investment plan, you will average out these cycles for maximum efficiency of your investment dollar.

Should Women Have Their Own Wills?

Every woman should have her own will and keep it up to date. It could even be argued that a wife's will is more essential than her husband's since, in most cases, she will outlive him and thus be responsible for not one but two estates—his and hers. This is so even when a wife has few assets of her own. Consider this scenario: A husband dies, leaving all his property to his wife. Shortly afterward, she dies intestate, that is, without a will. All the family's assets would be disposed of according to the laws of intestacy applicable in her state. The result may or may not be in accordance with her wishes.

What Are the Financial Ramifications of Remarriage?

Second marriages usually bring great happiness. Often, they also bring financial complications, especially for women. As always, it pays to be prepared. Consider these possibilities to protect yourself financially:

1. A prenuptial agreement (see Chapter 28) can help you by allowing you to keep any assets out of the hands of your new spouse if something should happen to the new marriage (death, divorce, etc.). Newly married couples may feel that this written agreement shows a lack of trust, but in truth it actually helps keep family harmony. I have seen adult children's concern (the new husband may get all their mother's money) put aside by the use of the prenuptial agreement. To play it safe, hire a different lawyer than the one your new partner uses so that each is represented in drafting this agreement.

2. Consider the consequences of remarrying and its effect on social security benefits. If you are a widow who is not a senior citizen and you are collecting social security benefits based upon your late husband's social security account, remarriage will stop your benefits. However, if you wait until that golden age, you will then be able to draw on your new mate's social security account or your late spouse's account, whichever is greater.

3. You are entitled to a one-time capital gains exclusion (up to $250,000 single, $500,000 for a couple) on the sale of your main home providing you have lived in that home for at least two out of the last five years. Married couples can take advantage only once even if each owns a home. Therefore, before remarrying, you should consider selling your home and your intended's home so that you will get two exclusions instead of one.

How Can Assets Be Owned?

In order to plan financially, you must understand the concept of ownership. Joint ownership is the most common method by which married couples take title to their house and other assets. It may also be used by others who wish to share the control of some property. Let's examine the three basic types of joint ownership, each of which has certain special legal and financial characteristics you should know about:

1. *Joint tenancy.* With this type of ownership, both owners have a complete and undivided interest in the property. Neither owner can sell or transfer his or her interest in the property without the consent of the other owner. When one owner dies, the property immediately passes to the surviving owner without having to go to probate (the acceptance of the will of the deceased by an appropriate court). For joint tenancy to be in effect, the names of both owners must appear on the deed or other ownership documents. Both married couples and single people use joint tenancy as a method of guaranteeing ease of transfer of property upon the death of one of the owners.

2. *Tenancy in common.* With this type of ownership, each owner has title to half the property. If one owner dies, his or her share does not automatically pass to the survivor. Instead, it is disposed of in accordance with the will of the deceased. This method is used by friends or relatives who wish to form a joint ownership and share its benefits while they are alive but want to retain the right to decide individually what happens to their share of the property when they die.

3. *Community property*. In certain states, husband and wife share equally in any property either one accumulates while they are living together. This is so, regardless of whose name appears on the deed or ownership papers. Such jointly owned property is called *community property*, and the states where this is a matter of law are called *community-property states* (Arizona, California, Idaho, Louisiana, Nevada, New Mexico, Texas, Washington, and Wisconsin).

There are exceptions under the law to community property: (1) property obtained by either spouse prior to the marriage; (2) property acquired after the marriage by gift or inheritance, and (3) property acquired in non-community-property states. Note that the fact that you have moved from a community-property state to a non-community-property state does not automatically exempt you and your spouse from the community-property law. You are still subject to the law for property you obtained while married and a resident of the community-property state.

What of the Emotional Stress That Women Face?

In researching this chapter, I came across some wonderful statements by Judith Stern Peck regarding financial planning for women. Her thoughts and practices provide rich food for thought: She states:

> As I embarked on my own development and moved toward empowerment, I identified a process of seven stages that I call "the seven A's": *awakening, anger, autonomy, anxiety, analysis, acquisition of knowledge*, and *application*.

> My *awakening* occurred as I was contemplating my divorce. I suddenly became aware that I would be called upon to negotiate a "business deal," for which I was ill-equipped. I had spent most of my adult years raising my family and pursuing a career in the mental health field. I was ill-informed about money matters.

> As the extent of my dependency dawned on me, I could feel the *anger* take over. I was angry at all the men in my life—my then-husband, my father, and all those who had perpetuated this myth that men attended to money matters and that they would take care of me. I was angry that such an aura of mystery had been created for me around money, and that there was such a gap in my financial education. I called upon female friends/lawyers to help me. I asked which questions to ask and attempted my own "speed" course in finance. My reaction to the anger was my determination never to depend on the men in my life so completely for money matters.

My anger propelled me to the next stage—*autonomy*. I knew that I had to gain a sense of independence and control over my life. I realized that I was fighting my own inner contradictions; that is, the desire to have personal power was fighting the desire to be taken care of. I faced this contradiction many times—with lawyers, accountants, and financial advisors.

The fourth stage, *anxiety*, is one that surfaces after the fight for autonomy is won but the feeling of autonomy has not been integrated. This occurs over and over again with women who are experiencing divorce or some other crisis in their lives. Anxiety usually surfaces from the contradictions that revolve around the need to take care of oneself, the desire to be taken care of, and the discomfort due to the lack of skills needed to take care of money matters.

The last two stages of the empowering process are the *acquisition* of knowledge and expertise, and the *application* thereof. These two stages can be experienced through a variety of avenues. The bookstores are filled with self-help books relating to money matters while the newsstands offer a variety of magazines on the subject. Also, there are various courses that are offered in seminar format to enhance knowledge around financial issues. The learning curve becomes increasingly challenged daily, as long as the anxiety is never too overwhelming.

The process of the seven A's is a painful but rewarding one. It requires differentiating the emotional contradictions that we have learned through our family and societal contexts from the practical, rational information and understanding of issues that we can acquire. This process, which enhanced my development and self-definition, has motivated me to help others empower themselves.

1. *Start now.* The earlier you start, the more that tax deferral and compounding of interest can work for you and the greater the chance that your variable investments can grow.
2. *Save regularly.* The old adage "Pay yourself first" applies here. As a rule of thumb, you'll need to save at least 10 percent of your income each year—above what you expect to receive from social security and your employer's basic retirement plan—to have enough funds for retirement.
3. *Don't touch your retirement savings.* Whatever the temptation, don't cash in your retirement accumulations if you change jobs. Even if you put the money back later, it will be very hard—if not impossible—to match what you could have accumulated had you left your funds intact.
4. *Invest—don't just save—for retirement.* "Safe" savings products, such as money market accounts, may preserve your principal and provide some interest, but their returns have historically barely kept up with inflation. To amass sufficient funds for retirement, you'll need to invest at least some of your accumulations in equities. Although past performance does not guarantee future results, over time equities have historically produced rates of return

Continued

way above inflation and have outperformed interest-earning securities, such as bonds.

5. *Educate yourself in financial matters.* For general financial information, there's a host of newspapers, magazines, newsletters, and books (this book is my suggestion) that can help you in your planning. And talk to relatives and friends about their financial plans and experiences.

6. *Be a role model for your children and grandchildren.* Show them you are an equal partner in managing your family's finances. Take them to your bank and open a savings account for them. Encourage schools to teach economic fundamentals to students of all ages.

How Can You Ensure a Secure Future?

We all want assurance that our future will be financially secure. Because women usually live longer and earn less than men, their concerns are even more urgent. But regardless of your current situation or age, it's never too early—or too late—to plan for the future.

If you follow your own way and invest for the future, no matter how hard it is for you today, you will gain a sense of security knowing that, maybe for the first time in your life, you have done something for yourself.

And on the topic of doing for yourself, since you have to do the things you have to do, be wise enough to do some of the things you want to do.

It's a Wrap

- Despite great financial gains made by women in recent decades, they still tend to earn less and suffer greater poverty in old age than men do.

- All women, whether they live alone or in a relationship, should plan and be prepared to manage their own finances.

- Every woman should have her own will and keep it up to date.

- Women who are remarrying should consider a prenuptial agreement (this subject is detailed in the next chapter).

- There are three different types of joint ownership: joint tenancy, tenancy in common, and community property. It pays to examine them all before taking title jointly to any home or asset.

"The tragedy in life is not that it ends so soon, but that we wait so long to begin it."

CHAPTER 28

Prenuptials and the Marriage Vow

"Courtship is the feast. Marriage is doing the dishes."

Do I Need to Read This Chapter?

- Am I about to marry, especially not for the first time?

- Do I have preexisting, separate property to protect? Does my future spouse?

- Does the subject of premarital agreements somehow make me uneasy?

- Have I thought about all the factors such an agreement should address?

Prenuptial agreements, like estate planning, are no longer exclusively for the rich and famous. The likelihood is great that people marrying today will have preexisting separate property to protect. There is no better method to protect a party's rights, assets, and those financially dependent on each of the parties than by a legally binding contract called a *prenuptial agreement*. The terms *prenuptial, premarital,* and *ante nuptial* are virtually synonymous.

What Is a Prenuptial Agreement?

In addition to being a contract, a prenuptial agreement is a plan to achieve protection of assets. Those assets acquired prior to the marriage are known as *nonmarital property*, and assets acquired during the marriage are known as *marital property*. The use and ultimate distribution of assets involves arm's-length negotiations between the soon-to-be spouses. While this notion may dampen the fires of love ("Love means never having to say 'sign here.'"), it is imperative that the parties act openly and in good faith and that they take the time to develop a plan in order to satisfy each other's wishes.

The nature of a prenuptial agreement and its inherent legal requirements and characteristics provides each party the freedom to protect his or her non-marital property from each other. Provisions affecting marital property and other issues arising from the marriage are subject only to notions of fairness and equitable constraints. It cannot be overemphasized that any financial plan should take advantage of the protection available from prenuptial agreements.

 Don't Forget — A wise person once quipped that a prenuptial agreement is like putting an asterisk next to the vow "I do." That is a true statement—and a smart practice.

What Elements Make Up a Prenuptial Agreement?

Like any other legal contract, a prenuptial agreement must satisfy basic legal requirements. The agreement must be in writing and must be executed by the parties whose signatures are witnessed or notarized, and there must be consideration, which is the marriage itself. Indeed, while prenuptial agreements are entered into prior to marriage, the terms and conditions are effective *only* upon marriage. The marriage may be a civil or religious ceremony, so long as it is a valid, recognized ritual affecting a legal union.

All 50 states recognize prenuptial agreements, although the laws of each state are not uniform. There is a Uniform Prenuptial Agreement Act, but not every state has adopted its provisions, and some of those states that did have made modifications.

In addition to being in writing, executed, and witnessed, a prenuptial agreement must possess characteristics common to all contracts and essentially required in some form by every state law. It is important to appreciate, however, that in determining the validity of a prenuptial agreement for whichever reason, generally only the facts and circumstances existing *at the time the agreement was made* are considered by the court.

What Are the Categories to Be Addressed in a Prenuptial Agreement?

 Each party must enter into the prenuptial agreement freely and voluntarily. Courts are sensitive to the personal relationship of the parties, with its attendant frailties and emotional influence. Consequently, courts will not enforce agreements where the circumstances indicate that one party took unfair advantage of the other. The terms of the prenuptial agreements must be fair.

The parties should include any topic important to each of them in their prenuptial agreement. There are available preexisting forms that contain standard language of a prenuptial agreement, but these standard forms are run-of-the-mill and probably will not deal with specific topics or situations unique to each party.

The prenuptial agreement should contain a blueprint of which assets and income of each spouse are to be used during the marriage and for what purposes. The prenuptial agreement can act like a business plan in this regard. The agreement can also state how joint assets are to be distributed after the marriage, whether it ends by reason of death of one spouse or divorce. A discussion of important provisions follows.

Separate Property and Separate Income

Simply identifying each party's separate property is not sufficient. Since one of the major purposes of a prenuptial agreement is to preserve the nonmarital assets of each spouse for the children of the first marriage or other family members of each spouse, the prenuptial agreement should be specific in describing each spouse's desires in this regard. Therefore, the prenuptial agreement should state under what circumstances or to what extent, if any, one party has any rights or interest in the nonmarital property of the other.

The prenuptial agreement should state clearly when and how much of, if at all, nonmarital property and income from this property is to be used in the marriage and for what purpose. Very often, nonmarital property or income of one spouse, even though it is identified as nonmarital income, is used to satisfy debts incurred after the marriage by the other spouse. Generally, the debts incurred by one spouse (the "debtor spouse") can be collected from the other spouse unless the vendor or creditor is notified that one spouse is not responsible for debts of the other. This is true even though the spouse paying the debts does not use or have enjoyments from the items purchased by the debtor spouse.

For example, if one spouse charged purchases on a joint credit card and cannot pay the balances, the nondebtor spouse can be forced, legally, to pay for those purchases using his or her separate property. Worse yet, suppose one spouse makes a large purchase on credit, like a boat, and puts it in joint name, but the other spouse is not happy with the purchase. If payments are not made and the value of the boat becomes less than the debt on it, the other spouse may have to use his or her own income or separate property to pay the balance.

Thus, the prenuptial agreement should clearly state how major purchases and joint debt are to be paid. Spouses who must use separate, nonmarital property to satisfy joint debts or debt of the other spouse should be reimbursed. This can be accomplished in a well-thought-out prenuptial agreement. Also, the identification of joint funds (wages or other earnings while married) and the use of such funds should be specified.

Income Tax Returns

A joint debt that always occurs after the marriage is income tax owed on a joint return filed by the married couple, whether federal or state. The total amount of income tax owed on a joint return can be collected from either spouse without regard to which spouse's income or losses produced the amount of tax owed.

As a rule, it is very difficult for a spouse to be relieved of paying joint income taxes, even where the total tax was caused by the other spouse. But there are limited circumstances in which a spouse may not be held responsible by the tax authorities for paying joint income taxes. This occurs where a spouse did not know or did not have reason to know that income or losses were omitted or not reported properly on the joint return and where under the circumstances, because of the spouse's ignorance in preparing the joint tax return, it would be unfair to hold that spouse responsible for the total tax.

If a spouse truly does not know about the other's financial affairs, for example, because the other spouse has concealed the information, or the business and financial affairs are too complex for any reasonable person to understand, then the law says it is unfair to hold the unsuspecting spouse responsible for all or a portion of the joint income taxes. The key point is that an "innocent spouse" has to prove his or her status as "innocent" in order to obtain relief from payment.

Nonetheless, a so-called innocent spouse who signs a joint income tax return cannot simply turn his or her back on the obvious realities of the couple's financial circumstance. What a spouse knows or should have known about the information reported on the tax return is judged by whatever a reasonable person standing in the shoes of the spouse would know or understand.

Pensions and IRAs

As stated earlier, people use the prenuptial agreement to preserve separate assets for the children of their first marriage or other separate commitments. Pension funds are a classic type of separate asset that a party may want to keep separate from the new spouse. To accomplish and maintain separate asset status for pension funds, prenuptial agreements generally provide that the new spouse waive his or her rights to receive the pension funds of the other spouse. This waiver is necessary because the law mandates that "spouses" be named the primary beneficiary of pension funds. If a spouse is not named a recipient of pension money, the spouse must consent in writing to giving up his or her rights to such money.

A person is considered a spouse only if he or she is legally married to the other person and the marriage has not been formally ended by a decree of divorce. A legally valid divorce, then, terminates the spouse status. A separation agreement alone may not be sufficient.

If you're about to be divorced, take note. To ensure that your soon-to-be ex-spouse has no claim to your pension fund, your separation agreement should contain an explicit clause waiving pension funds until the final divorce.

Prenuptial agreements pose a problem involving the waiver of pension rights because persons entering a prenuptial agreement are *not* spouses on the day they sign the agreement. Remember, a prenuptial occurs *before* the marriage even though its terms become effective after the marriage. Since persons signing prenuptial agreements are not married on the day they sign, they are not spouses. The result is that any waiver of rights to pension funds is not made by a spouse. As a consequence, any waiver of rights to pension funds contained in a prenuptial agreement is likely not to be valid because it was not signed by a spouse. The fact that the people signing the prenuptial will become a spouse a short time later does not make the waiver valid. In order to validate the waiver right to pension funds that may appear in a prenuptial agreement, it will be necessary for the parties to re-sign the waivers when they become spouses.

Other Categories

- A prenuptial agreement can provide for alimony and other maintenance and support, as well as the division of joint or marital property, in the event the marriage fails. The prenuptial agreement, however, cannot deal with child custody issues since this is against public policy.

- The prenuptial agreement cannot eliminate spousal support by one or both parties during the marriage. Similarly, a person cannot be relieved of the obligation to support his or her children. A provision in the prenuptial agreement eliminating or limiting child support is likely not to be enforceable.

- While the prenuptial agreement does not include the parties' wills, it should contain an outline of each party's general intentions of how marital and nonmarital property would be distributed upon death.

The discussion contained in this chapter is only the tip of the iceberg in dealing with prenuptial agreements. Remember that an attorney should be consulted before drawing up any agreement and that the attorney should be separate from the other spouse's.

And on the subject of marriage, marriage is the only union that cannot be organized, because both sides think they are management.

It's a Wrap

- Premarital legal agreements are not just for the rich and famous; they are for everyone who has preexisting, separate property to protect.

- While premarital agreements seem cold and calculating to some, these agreements usually provide long-term fairness and peace of mind.

- Any premarital agreement must meet the conditions of a basic legal contract. That's why it's advisable to draw up such agreements under a lawyer's guidance, rather than trying to do it on your own.

- Premarital contracts should address the issues of separate property, separate income, tax returns, pensions, IRAs, alimony, and the division of joint or marital property in case the new marriage should fail.

- Child custody issues are beyond the scope of premarital contracts.

"Accept the fact that some days you are the pigeon and some days you are the statue."

CHAPTER 29

Unpleasant But Necessary—Health Care Issues for Seniors

◆◆◆◆◆◆◆◆◆◆◆◆◆◆◆◆◆◆◆◆◆◆◆◆◆◆◆◆◆◆◆◆◆◆◆◆◆

"Get everything done before you are."

Do I Need to Read This Chapter?

- Have I thought about what will happen to me if I become disabled

- Do I need to provide for my own long-term care?

- Am I clear on how to qualify for Medicaid in the event that I lack long-term care insurance?

- Have I considered a prepaid funeral?

- Do I understand the life insurance provision known as the accelerated death benefit?

- In the event of total incapacity, do I want my life to be artificially prolonged?

- Have I drawn up a living will?

Although we do not like to discuss death and disability, at some time these areas must be covered. Especially as a woman, the odds are that you will be alone if a severe disability hits you. Just walk through any nursing home and see the imbalance in numbers between women and men.

Is Long-Term Care Insurance Important?

All of us who own a house have homeowner's insurance to protect us from the possibility of a fire. Yet, if you are over the age of 65, you have about 10 times the chance of going into a nursing home as you do of having your house burn down. We do not, for most of us, think of long-term care insurance (LTCI) to protect us from the possibility of the tremendous costs of a nursing home stay.

What choice do you have if nursing home care is required? Of course, you could pay for it out of your own pocket, or you could deplete your assets down to a level of meeting state requirements of Medicaid. But that would mean that you would have to give your assets away to meet the 60-month waiting period. Long-term care insurance is an answer to keeping you independent while protecting the assets you worked your entire life to acquire.

What Should I Look For in a Long-Term Care Policy?

Recognizing the market for long-term care, many insurance companies are offering some protection, usually pertaining to convalescence in nursing homes or similar health care facilities. Before purchasing such a policy, acquaint yourself with the many terms and concepts they entail:

1. Type of care.
   - *Skilled care.* A 24-hour-a-day-care program.
   - *Intermediate care.* Occasional nursing assistance and rehabilitative care.
   - *Custodial care.* Helping with normal needs (bathing, eating, etc.). Medicare does not cover this.
2. *Elimination period.* In order to reduce the high cost to you, an elimination period is imposed. This elimination period (from 21 to 365 days) places the cost of daily maintenance on the covered individual for the number of days you choose before the insurance begins to pay. Naturally, the longer the elimination period, the lower the insurance premium. Consider a longer elimination period if you have other assets available to get you through this initial period. Also, make certain that your daily reimbursable rate, once the elimination period is over, is at least two-thirds of the total daily cost of your care.

3. *Guaranteed renewability.* The policy you choose should have no termination date but should be renewable for life.

4. *Prehospitalization requirement.* Make certain that the policy does not require that you be hospitalized before being admitted into a nursing home.

5. *Alzheimer's and other disease coverage.* Certain conditions may not be covered under the policy such as Alzheimer's, which in insurance language is known as an "organically based medical condition."

6. *Inflation adjustment.* This is a provision that will provide for automatic benefit adjustments to cover any inflationary increases in long-term cost care.

7. *Medical history.* Be certain you understand about any "preexisting" medical clauses in the policy.

8. *Facility approval.* Find out, before you sign up, if the facility you choose is approved by Medicaid so that you can qualify for future benefits.

9. *Tax deduction.* Just as a sidelight, a portion of the premiums for LTCI is tax deductible if you itemize your tax return. What you do is to add your premium costs to other medical expenses (not reimbursed), and if the total amount exceeds 7.5 percent of your adjusted gross income, you have a deduction.

Will Medicaid Cover My Long-Term Care Needs?

People who do not purchase long-term care insurance may eventually qualify for Medicaid, by transferring their funds to other parties. Although I am not in favor of this method of protection, let me explain the procedures. Before August 1993, people who transferred funds to other parties could be ineligible for Medicaid coverage if their transfer took place less than 30 months prior to entering a nursing home. Then the law increased the time (known as the ineligible, or look-back, period) to 36 months and added a penalty clause if the transfer was made before the ineligible period was up and the individual filed for Medicaid coverage. In 2006 the look-back period was further increased to 60 months with new penalties added. Here is some good news for married couples. Although it is true that you must get rid of most of your assets to qualify for Medicaid, you do not have to go broke entirely. An at-home spouse can keep up to half of all financial assets with a maximum reaching a bit over $70,000 (varies depending upon your state). You may, in addition, also keep the house, the car, and personal and household effects not included in the maximum figure.

Also, if you want to avoid giving everything away in order to apply for Medicaid, grant a Power of Attorney to your children, with instructions for them to enforce the power by paying for your stay out of your funds if you should enter a nursing home, keeping the balance only after you have rightfully qualified for Medicaid.

Bear in mind (depending on the state in which you live) that there could be a significant difference in the type of care facility and neighborhood you will experience under private pay versus Medicaid. That one factor alone should make you give a second thought to transferring your assets to your children and living under "artificial poverty" for an event that may never materialize.

What about Prepaid Funerals?

As I have stated before, a female will usually outlive her mate. Thus you will probably make the funeral arrangements for him; but when you die, who will do this for you?

With today's high cost of funerals, leaving decisions to your grieving family does not make much sense. You could arrange with a funeral home for a prepaid plan where you would specify the type of casket and services you would want and then pay for it in installments or one lump sum. This type of plan is designed for those individuals who do not want to burden their family with high funeral costs or who have no family and no one to make necessary arrangements. There are, however, disadvantages to this arrangement. You may change your mind, you may move, the funeral home may go out of business, or any number of other possibilities.

Prepaid funeral programs are not considered assets for Medicaid eligibility, and so the state cannot make you use the money in the contract to pay for nursing home care. Bear in mind that the average funeral cost is about $7,000.

The best method is to plan and pay for your funeral without involving a funeral director or giving up control of your money. Simply write down what you want done, and give copies of these instructions to your family or to whomever you may appoint to enforce your power of attorney.

Yet the most sensible method to set aside money for a funeral is to open a *Totten trust.* In this type of trust, you state that upon your demise, the funds should go to the person designated, who is responsible for your funeral. No lawyer is needed to establish this trust. Because the trust is revocable, you can add or take out money anytime (you may decide that a wooden deck is preferred to a wooden casket), but taxes must be paid on any income from the trust. Although the proceeds will be included in your estate, this trust is not subject to probate, and so the money can immediately be spent. Any investment vehicle can be used. A simple bank account with a paid-on-death (POD) beneficiary may be all that is needed.

What Is the Accelerated Death Benefit?

The *accelerated death benefit,* also known as ADB (see Chapter 16), is a provision in a life insurance policy that allows a living person (the insured) to collect tax free a partial value of the death benefit of the policy while he or she is still alive. This situation can occur if the insured is terminally ill and needs money immediately. For the first time in life insurance history, a person does not have to die to make the death benefit available. What a wonderful idea to be able to have some of that money now so that the insured could close his or her life accomplishing some long-held dreams (vacations, gifts, debts paid, etc.) that he or she would never have been able to do were it not for this clause in the policy.

However, ADB defeats the major purpose of life insurance, which is to provide for the surviving beneficiary, who must live after the insured passes away. An alternative to the accelerated policy is to borrow against the policy's cash surrender value, if only because that income is not taxable.

Do You Need a Living Will?

A living will takes care of you as you die, not afterward. And that is so important to understand.

I believe that a living will should be drawn up by an attorney. Prepared forms can be obtained from various organizations and may be acceptable, but since the area of living wills is so debatable, I would choose the attorney route for the small additional cost involved. After the will has been completed, I urge you to discuss its contents with your family so that they will understand in absolute terms that it is your intent to have your instructions carried out regardless of how they may feel.

A living will should state that you do not wish to have any medical procedure done for you that would artificially prolong your life. "No extraordinary measures" is a phrase commonly used. A while back I came across a letter describing the feelings of an individual regarding "right of choice," and thought it appropriate in this chapter.

> To my family and/or caregivers:
>
> Realizing that death is a certainty and as much a part of life as being born, if the time comes when I can no longer take part in decisions for my own future, I wish this statement to stand as an expression of my wishes while still of sound mind. I fear the indignities of deterioration, dependence and hopeless pain more than death itself. I therefore ask that medication be mercifully administered to help relieve my suffering. And if there is no reasonable expectation of my recovery, I request that I be allowed to die with dignity and not be kept alive by artificial means or heroic measures.

What to Think About

In effect, a living will expresses your wishes and enforces your decisions when you are no longer able to do so for yourself. Far from a token gesture, it is a document to be taken seriously and administered with the utmost care. As you contemplate the creation of your living will, take these issues into account:

1. Different states have different requirements for completing and signing a living will.
2. The necessary number of witnesses may vary.
3. Some states specify that witnesses may not be related to you.
4. A notary public may need to attest to the signing of your living will.
5. In some states, living wills are valid for limited periods of time and thus must be updated regularly.
6. Do you live in different states at various times of the year? If so, you must create separate living wills and medical proxy documents (health care proxies) for each state where you reside—not just the one you claim as your primary residence. This is the only way to be sure your wishes will be honored, regardless of quirks in laws from state to state.

&Don't Forget A *health care proxy* is a written document granting an individual (agent), designated by you, to make decisions (if you are not able to do so) for you in all medical situations based upon your predetermined wishes and beliefs.

Will My Living Will Affect My Insurance Policies?

I have been questioned about insurance coverage and the living will. Public policy and state statutes explain that living wills cannot affect an individual's insurance contract. A person's personal decision to have life-support systems withheld or withdrawn is not to be considered suicide and thus in no way can invalidate any life insurance policy. But there is much more to say about feelings of choice. I firmly believe that it is each patient's right to decide on his or her life and death. With a person's expectations for life, a person's feelings of pain, and a person's expenditure of money, that person is the one who will ultimately pay the price. Therefore, to that person belongs the right to call the tune. But it doesn't always happen that way.

Many adult children or even spouses will not permit the disconnection of a feeding or breathing machine regardless of the wishes of the patient, because most of us do not wish to let go. "Perhaps later," we may say, "after a forthcoming rite of passage (anniversary, graduation, wedding, birth of a grandchild, etc.), but not now." We therefore attempt to extend the time by machines and tubes and insane efforts to keep the patient breathing a few more days or weeks. A desperate need born of guilt. All of us must learn to close and say good-bye. Closing does not mean shutting the door and turning away. Closing is the realization that there is our own life after the death of a loved one. It is in the form of memory, and becomes our responsibility to carry that memory while living life to the fullest. Every family member must understand this.

And on the topic of life and death, there is nothing that nature has made necessary which is more easy than death; we are longer coming into the world than going out of it. There is not any minute of our lives wherein we may not reasonably expect death. The more complete one's life is, the less one fears death. People are not afraid of death, per se, but of the incompleteness of their lives.

It's a Wrap

- Long-term care insurance can protect your estate from being depleted by long stays in a nursing home or similar facility.

- Study the provisions of any long-term-care policy very carefully, using the guidelines in this chapter as a starting point.

- Medicaid, a type of government health insurance, will pay for long-term care under certain conditions, but be aware of the stringent requirements.

- Each state, through its office of aging, has a public official who can help guide individuals and families through the maze of long-term complexities.

- The most sensible way to set aside money for your funeral is through a simple and revocable vehicle known as a Totten trust.

- Certain life insurance policies offer an accelerated death benefit, allowing you to collect on your policy while you are still alive.

- By creating a living will, you can gain control over medical procedures that would artificially prolong your life.

"The fear of death keeps us from living, not from dying."

Epilogue

I hope that your reading of the material in this book has given you insight into the financial world and has taken the "utterly confused" status of investing into a more comprehensible realm. Bear in mind:

To look is one thing.

To see what you look at is another.

To understand what you see is a third.

To learn from what you understand is something else.

But to act on what you learn is all that really matters.

And that is the point. You must act now so that you can build a firm financial future for you and your family. Remember that the flowers of all tomorrows are in the seeds of today.

Glossary

Adjustable-rate mortgage: A type of mortgage in which the interest rate charged may be changed at fixed intervals, usually in response to changes in some predetermined financial index.

Amortize: To spread the cost over a period of time.

Annuity: A form of insurance in which the policyholder, called the *annuitant*, pays a specified sum of money and in return receives regular payments for the rest of his or her life.

Appreciation: An increase in the value of any property; used especially in reference to an increase in the value of a stock, bond, or other security.

Assay: To analyze gold or silver bullion and so determine the proportion of precious metal it contains.

Back-end load: A sales fee or commission charged by the management of a mutual fund at the time the shares in the fund are sold. (See also *Front-end load*.)

Balloon mortgage: A type of mortgage in which the entire principal comes due within two to five years, at which time the loan must be repaid or refinanced at current interest rates.

Beneficiary: The person who receives financial benefit as a result of a will, an insurance policy, or a trust fund.

Bond: An IOU issued by a corporation or government agency promising to pay a specified amount of interest for a specified period of time in exchange for an amount of money being lent to the corporation or agency.

Broker: A person or firm engaged in buying or selling stocks, bonds, real estate, or other investment instrument on behalf of another person or firm. Brokers are normally licensed by one or more government agencies that monitor and regulate their activities.

Bullion: Gold or silver of a specified purity, in the form of coins or, more commonly, bars and ingots.

Bypass trust: A trust allowing the surviving spouse of the trustor to receive income from the property during the spouse's lifetime, after which the property passes to the designated heirs.

Callable bond: A bond that may be redeemed at the option of the issuing corporation or government agency before its maturity date.

Capital: The total assets of a firm, including cash, land, buildings, equipment, investments, and accounts receivable.

Cash value: See *Surrender value.*

Certificate of deposit: A certificate representing an investment of a specified sum of money in a bank at a specified interest rate guaranteed for a particular period of time.

Closing costs: Costs paid by the buyer of a home at the time of purchase. Closing costs include such charges as appraisal and surveying fees, title search costs, and lawyers' fees, and may range from 2 to 10 percent of the purchase price of the home.

COBRA: A federal law that requires corporations to continue to offer health coverage for 18 months after coverage terminates. The employee is responsible for full payment of coverage.

Collateral: Property whose value is offered as a guarantee of repayment of a loan. If the loan is not repaid, the creditor is entitled to ownership of the collateral.

Common stock: A security that represents partial ownership in the issuing corporation. The holder of a share of common stock has the right to receive part of the company's earnings and to vote on certain policy decisions facing the company. (See also *Preferred stock.*)

Compound interest: Interest computed by applying the percentage rate not only to the principal but also to previously earned interest. The more frequently interest is compounded, the greater the effective yield of an investment.

Condominium: A form of real estate ownership in which the owner holds the title to his or her own dwelling unit as well as a share in common properties such as lobbies, parking areas, and recreational facilities.

Consumer price index (CPI): An index that measures monthly price changes for the cost of living, including food, clothing, and shelter.

Convertible bond: A corporate bond that may be exchanged at the option of the bondholder for shares of common stock in the same corporation.

Cooperative: A form of real estate in which the owner buys one or more shares in a corporation that owns and manages land and buildings. Each share in the corporation entitles its owner to occupy part of the property, such as an apartment.

Coupon bond: A bond with interest coupons attached that are clipped by the holder and redeemed at specified intervals for interest payments.

Credit union: A savings institution that is owned by its depositors, who are technically considered shareholders. Like a savings bank, a credit union accepts deposits and makes loans, often at lower interest rates than those offered by banks.

Creditor: A person or institution to which a debt is owed. The holder of a bond issued by a corporation, for example, is a creditor of the corporation.

Custodial account: A savings or investment account, often in the name of a child, with another person, such as a parent, listed as custodian. The custodian manages the account, but the income belongs to the owner of the account and may normally be used only for his or her benefit.

Debenture: A corporate bond whose value is not guaranteed by a pledge of collateral.

Depreciation: A decline in the value of a piece of property over time. The depreciation of income-producing property is treated as a loss and so is deductible from income for income tax purposes; the amount of the tax deduction is computed by formulas that vary according to the nature of the property.

Diversification: Investment of funds in a variety of instruments having differing yields, maturities, and degrees of risk. Diversification is generally considered a beneficial investment strategy.

Dividend: A portion of a company's profits distributed to the stockholders. In a given year, a company's board of directors may or may not pay a dividend, depending on the company's financial status and anticipated future needs.

Dividend reinvestment plan (DRIP): The automatic reinvestment back into the company of dividends earned on corporate securities for future earnings to the investor. Usually there is no commission charge for this service.

Dow Jones Industrial Average (DJIA): The most common quoted stock market index, composed of traded American company stocks.

Down payment: A partial payment for a piece of property, such as a home, made at the time of purchase, with the understanding that the balance will be paid later.

Equity: The value of a piece of property to its owner and above any portion of that value that has been offered as collateral for a loan. For example, the owner of a house worth $350,000 on which a $90,000 mortgage has been taken has $260,000 in equity.

Estate planning: Planning how and where your assets will be distributed.

Executor: A person named in a will to manage the settlement of the estate according to the instructions given in the will.

401(k): A retirement plan known as the deferred salary reduction plan. It allows an employee to set aside part of his or her salary into a tax-sheltered account that grows tax free until withdrawal. A 403(b) is similar but only for employees of nonprofit organizations.

Face value: The value of a stock, bond, or insurance policy, usually printed on the front (or "face") of the document. The face value of a security usually differs from its selling price.

Federal Reserve: The central monetary authority of the United States. The Federal Reserve issues currency, sells U.S. government securities, and extends credit to member banks.

Foreclosure: The process whereby the holder of a mortgage receives ownership of a property after the owner has failed to repay the loan.

Front-end load: A sales fee or commission charged by the management of a mutual fund at the time the shares in the fund are purchased. (See also *Back-end load*.)

Health care proxy: A form that gives the person you choose to act as your agent to make all health care decisions for you, except to the extent you say otherwise in this form.

Income averaging: A method of computing income tax liability by which an unusually large amount of income received in a single year is spread out over several years, thus reducing the rate of taxation.

Individual retirement account (IRA): A savings or investment plan that allows an individual to accumulate funds toward retirement while deferring income taxes on both the amount invested and the interest earned up to $4,000 per year ($5,000 if age 50 or over).

Inflation: An increase in the general level of prices for goods and services in an economy. This usually occurs when too much money is chasing too few goods and services.

Insurance: A contract in which one party—usually a company organized for the purpose—promises to pay a specified sum of money in the event that the second party suffers a financial loss through death, accident, injury, or some other misfortune.

***Inter vivos* trust**: A Latin term meaning "during the life of." This is another term for the revocable living trust because it becomes effective while the maker is living.

Intestate: The condition of dying without having made a valid will. When a person dies intestate, his or her estate is usually distributed in accordance with state laws.

Junk bond: A corporate bond rated BB or lower by Standard & Poor's rating service or Ba or lower by Moody's rating service. Junk bonds carry a relatively high degree of risk but generally pay a high rate of return.

Keogh plan: A savings or investment plan for self-employed people, the purpose and benefits of which resemble those of the IRA. However, the Keogh plan allows a larger amount of money (25 percent of income) to be sheltered from income taxes each year. (See also *Individual retirement account*.)

Liquidity: The ease with which invested funds can be sold or otherwise converted to cash.

Living trust: A trust that takes effect during the lifetime of the person who establishes it. At the death of the maker of the trust, probate is avoided, and the assets can be immediately transferred to the beneficiary.

Living will: A signed, witnessed statement of the wishes that no medication, artificial means, or "heroic measures" be used to prolong life.

Load: The commission charged by the firm that manages a mutual fund; normally it is a percentage of the amount invested.

Margin: Cash or credit advanced by a broker to allow the purchase of stocks or bonds for only a fraction of the full price. Making such a purchase is known as *buying on margin*.

Maturity: (1) The date on which a loan must be paid. (2) The period during which the loan may remain outstanding.

Money market: The market in which various kinds of high-yielding, short-term securities are bought and sold. Interest rates on the money market respond quickly to changes in financial and economic conditions.

Money market deposit account: A bank account whose funds are invested in money market securities.

Money market fund: A mutual fund that invests in money market securities.

Mortgage: A loan made with the ownership of personal property, such as a house, given as collateral. If the loan is not repaid, the holder of the mortgage has the right to ownership of the property.

Municipal bond: A bond issued by a state or local government or one of its agencies. Interest earned on municipal bonds is normally exempt from federal income tax, and sometimes from state and local income tax as well.

Mutual fund: An investment company that pools the funds of many individuals and invests them in stocks, bonds, or other securities. Those who invest through a mutual fund are called *shareholders* and receive dividends whose size depends on the performance of the fund's investments.

No-load fund: A mutual fund that does not charge a commission on investments.

Option: A contract giving the right to buy or sell a specified quantity of stock at a specified price within a specified period of time.

Par value: The value printed on the face of a stock or bond; often the same as the initial selling price. The resale price of a stock or bond usually *differs* from the par value.

Pension: An arrangement in which regular payments are made to a retired employee by his or her former employer or by a government agency.

Points: An interest charge levied by a mortgage lender at the time a house is sold. For each point charged, the buyer must pay the lending institution 1 percent of the mortgage amount. On some mortgages, no points are charged; on others, 3 points or more.

Portfolio: The complete array of investment holdings belonging to an individual or an institution.

Power of attorney: A document that gives another person power to work on your behalf under certain conditions.

Preferred stock: A security representing partial ownership in the issuing corporation. Holders of preferred stock have a prior claim to the earnings and assets of the company over holders of common stock. Preferred stock usually carries no stockholder voting privileges and usually pays a fixed annual dividend. (See also *Common stock*.)

Premium: (1) The amount of money paid to purchase a life insurance policy or an annuity. (2) The amount by which the selling price of a stock or bond exceeds its face value or par value.

Principal: An amount of money lent or invested.

Probate: A process of carrying out the instructions of a will within the court system.

Prospectus: A formal document prepared by a corporation issuing stocks, bonds, or other securities that is made available to all prospective buyers of the securities. It includes the names of the corporation's officers, as well as the corporation's financial condition and its recent record of profits and losses.

Redemption: The repurchase of a bond or other form of indebtedness by the issuing corporation or government agency.

Registered bond: A bond registered in its owner's name. Interest is paid at regular intervals to the registered owner; the bond may be transferred only by changing the registration.

Reinvestment: (1) The practice of returning all or some of a company's profits to the business for use in financing growth, plant, or equipment purchases. (2) An arrangement whereby dividends or interest earned by shares in a mutual fund is automatically used to purchase additional shares in the fund.

Return on investment: The amount of profit received on an investment as a percentage of the amount of capital invested. Also called *yield*.

Reverse mortgage: A home loan that is treated in the opposite fashion of a standard mortgage because the money goes from the lender (bank) to the homeowner.

Revocable living trust: A trust established during the grantor's lifetime in which a change or revocation can take place at any time.

Savings and loan association: A financial institution, technically owned by depositors, that invests primarily in home mortgages.

Savings bank: A state-charted financial institution that accepts deposits and offers loans at regulated interest rates.

Securities and Exchange Commission (SEC): The U.S. federal regulatory agency charged with controlling the issuing, buying, and selling of stocks, bonds, and other securities. The SEC supervises the operation of securities exchanges, registers brokers, and enforces laws governing the issuance of securities.

Security: A written instrument that either certifies partial ownership of a business or promises repayment of a debt by a business or government agency.

Series EE U.S. savings bond: An appreciation-type savings security between the owner and the United States. The owner lends money to the United States, and the United States must repay that money with interest when the bond is redeemed. (You can cash Series EE bonds anytime after 12 months.) Interest stops accruing 30 years after issue.

Series I U.S. savings bond: Basically the same contract as that of series EE, but interest accumulates monthly (with semiannual compounding) and is paid when the bond is redeemed. Interest earnings are inflation indexed. The I bond earnings rate is a combination of two separate rates: a fixed rate of return (set by the Treasury Department) and a variable semiannual inflation rate (based on changes in the CPI).

Shareholder: The owner of one or more shares of stock in a corporation or mutual fund.

Stock: A share in the ownership of a corporation.

Surrender value: The amount of money for which a life insurance policy may be redeemed prior to the death of the policyholder. In most cases, the surrender value of a policy increases annually during the life of the policy. Also called *cash value*.

Tax bracket: The level at which an individual's income is taxed, normally determined by the size of his or her taxable income. The higher the taxable income, the higher the tax bracket and the higher the rate of taxation.

Tax deferred: Not subject to income tax until a later date.

Tax exempt: Not subject to income tax.

Tax shelter: Any device or strategy by which a taxpayer can avoid paying income taxes on a portion of his or her income. Examples include individual retirement accounts, Keogh plan accounts, and 401(k) accounts.

Term: The period of time during which an investment or an insurance policy is in effect.

Term insurance: A form of life insurance in which the benefit is payable only if the insured person dies during a specified period.

Treasury bill: A short-term obligation of the federal government, sold at a discount from its face value; the discount represents prepayment of the interest on the loan. At maturity, the bill is redeemed for its full face value.

Treasury bond: A long-term obligation of the federal government, sold in minimum amounts of $1,000, with a maturity period of 10 to 30 years. Treasury bonds are sold both by the federal government and in the secondary market, where the prices fluctuate in accordance with changes in interest rates.

Treasury note: An intermediate-term obligation of the federal government, sold in minimum amounts of $1,000. Like Treasury bonds, Treasury notes are available on the secondary market at varying prices.

Trust: An arrangement whereby property is transferred from one party, called the *trustor*, to a second party, called the *trustee*, for the benefit of a third party, called the *beneficiary*. Trusts are usually established in order to reduce tax liability, streamline the transfer of assets after death, and/or maintain some control over the use of assets after they have been transferred.

Unit trust: An investment plan in which an investor buys a share in a portfolio of corporate or municipal bonds. The investor receives a specified rate of interest on his or her investment payable over a specified period of time, depending on the maturity dates of the bonds in the portfolio.

Universal life insurance: A type of life insurance policy in which part of the premium payment is used to provide life insurance protection and the remainder is invested in any of a variety of high-yielding instruments.

Volume: (1) The number of shares of a particular stock that are bought or sold on a given day. (2) The total number of shares of stock that are bought or sold on an organized exchange on a given day.

Whole life insurance: A type of life insurance policy in which premium payments are continued at the same level throughout the life of the policyholder, with death benefits payable whenever the policyholder dies.

Will: A written document prepared according to legal specifications which provides for distribution of the writer's assets after his or her death.

Yield: See *Return on investment*.

Zero coupon bond: A corporate, municipal, or Treasury bond sold at a discount from its face value. Upon maturity, the zero coupon bond is redeemed for the full value, with the discount representing the interest earned on the investment.

Index

About the Author

Joel Lerner is a retired professor and former chairman of the Business Division at Sullivan County Community College, a part of SUNY, where he taught for over 35 years. He is also a member of the board of trustees at that school. In addition to authoring numerous books that have sold close to two million copies, Lerner has produced his own TV and radio series and continues to address thousands of people every year on the topic of financial management.